american defense policy since 1945

A PRELIMINARY BIBLIOGRAPHY

compiled by
John Greenwood

with the advisement of
Robin Higham

edited by
Geoffrey Kemp, Clark Murdock, Frank L. Simonie

American Defense Policy
since 1945

NATIONAL SECURITY STUDIES SERIES

Sponsored by the National Security Education Program
of New York University, in cooperation
with the National Strategy Information Center

Editorial Board

AMERICAN DEFENSE POLICY SINCE 1945

A PRELIMINARY BIBLIOGRAPHY

compiled by
John Greenwood

with the advisement of
Robin Higham

edited by
**Geoffrey Kemp, Clark Murdock,
Frank L. Simonie**

PUBLISHED FOR THE NATIONAL SECURITY EDUCATION PROGRAM
BY THE UNIVERSITY PRESS OF KANSAS
Lawrence/Manhattan/Wichita

KANSAS STATE UNIVERSITY LIBRARY BIBLIOGRAPHY SERIES
NUMBER 11

Foreword

During the academic year 1969-1970, the National
Security Program of New York University, in cooperation with the National Strategy Information Center of
New York City, sponsored a series of conferences for
college and university faculty members interested in
the teaching of national security, defense policy,
civil-military relations, defense economics, and related areas. Out of these conferences grew a number
of projects designed to extend and improve academic
education and scholarly research in the national security field.

Prominent among these projects was a publication
series under the general editorship of Professor Frank
N. Trager of New York University. This is the second
item in the series to appear. The first is a book of
readings titled *National Security and American Society: Theory, Process, and Change*, edited by Frank N.
Trager and Philip S. Kronenberg. Subsequent publications in the near future will include books and monographs on various aspects of national security education. Their working titles are:

1. *Nuclear Proliferation: Phase II*, edited by
Robert Lawrence and Joel Larus.

2. *Modular Syllabus for Courses in National Security*, edited by T. Alden Williams and David Tarr.

3. *The Statistics of the U.S.-Soviet Military Balance, 1945-1972* by Geoffrey Kemp and Clark Murdock.

4. *Congressional Hearings on American Defense Policy, 1947-1971: An Annotated Bibliography*, compiled
by Richard Burt; edited by Richard Burt and Geoffrey
Kemp.

This bibliography is an attempt to update selectively previous bibliographies in American defense policy. It is hoped it will be of use to students, teachers, and other researchers trying to cope with the mass of material available in the field. The framework selected allows for updating of the bibliography from time to time and its integration with other publications in the series.

Contents

Introduction   *xiii*

I. BIBLIOGRAPHY OF BIBLIOGRAPHIES   *1*

  A. General Literature   *2*

  B. Military Policy, Doctrine, and Strategy   *4*
    1. General, Nuclear, and Conventional
      Warfare *4*
    2. Guerrilla Warfare *7*
    3. Arms Control and Disarmament *9*

  C. Defense Policy Making and Administration   *11*

  D. U.S. Armed Forces   *13*

  E. Weapons and Weapon Systems   *15*

  F. Support Elements   *17*
    1. Science, Technology, Research, Devel-
      opment *17*
    2. Logistics, Supply, Manpower, the
      Draft *20*
    3. Civil Defense *20*

  G. Space Programs   *22*

  H. Military History; Korean War; Vietnam
    War   *23*

    I. Political, Social, and Economic Impact
       of Defense Policies   *25*

    J. Defense Policy in the U.S.S.R. and China   *26*

    K. Regional U.S. Defense Policies   *28*

    L. Institutional Publications and Indices
       to Periodicals   *29*

  II. THE FACTUAL CONTEXT: DATA AND DESCRIPTIVE
     MATERIAL   *31*

 III. STRATEGIC THOUGHT AND MILITARY DOCTRINE IN
     THE NUCLEAR AGE   *43*

    A. General Strategic Thought   *44*
      1. Strategic Theory Applicable to All
        Types of Warfare *44*
      2. Land Power *57*
      3. Air Power *58*
      4. Sea Power *60*

    B. Nuclear Weapons, Deterrence, and General
      War   *62*

    C. Limited War, Including Guerrilla Warfare
      and Counterinsurgency   *77*

  IV. THE DEFENSE POLICY MAKING PROCESS   *89*

    A. General Literature, Including Civil-
      Military Relations   *90*

    B. The Department of Defense   *101*
      1. The Pentagon and Office of the Sec-
        retary of Defense *101*
      2. Inter-service Relations and the
        Joint Chiefs of Staff *108*
      3. The Military Departments *113*
          General Literature on the Armed
          Forces, *113*; U.S. Army, *118*; U.S.

Navy, *121*; U.S. Air Force, *124*;
U.S. Marine Corps, *128*; Reserve
and National Guard Forces, *129*
   4. Budgeting, Planning, Systems Analysis, Operations Research *131*

C. The President and Other Executive Agencies   *142*
   1. The Presidential Office *142*
   2. National Security Council *144*

D. Congress and Executive-Legislative Relations   *146*

E. Non-Governmental Inputs into Policy
Making   *150*
   1. Defense Industries, the "Military-
Industrial Complex" *150*
   2. Private Interest Groups, Public
Opinion, Defense Research Organizations *156*

V. DEFENSE POLICY OUTPUT, WEAPONS SYSTEMS,
AND MILITARY PROGRAMS   *159*

A. General Literature   *161*

B. Offensive Strategic Nuclear Forces   *166*
   1. General Issues *166*
   2. Land Based Missile Systems *171*
   3. Sea Based Missile Systems *172*
   4. Manned Aircraft *173*
   5. Communications and Command and Control *176*
   6. Basing Requirements and Deployment
176

C. Defensive Strategic Forces   *177*
   1. General Issues *177*
   2. Continental Defense against Air Attack *177*
   3. Ballistic Missile Defense *178*

General Issues, *178*; Specific
Programs, *183*
4. Civil Defense *184*

D. General Purpose Forces: Non-Nuclear   *188*
1. General Issues *188*
2. Combat Ground Forces, Army *189*
Infantry, *189*; Armor, *190*; Air
Cavalry, *191*; Support, *191*
3. Combat Ground Forces, Marines *192*
4. Theater Air Power, Air Force and
Army *193*
5. General Naval Forces, Including Naval and Marine Air Power *196*
6. Submarines and Anti-Submarine Warfare *198*
7. Amphibious Forces *200*
8. Chemical and Biological Warfare *200*

E. Tactical Nuclear Forces   *202*

F. Air and Sea Lift   *203*

G. Guard and Reserve Forces   *205*

H. Military Intelligence and Communications   *206*

I. Science, Technology, Research and Development   *209*
1. General Issues *209*
2. Weapons Systems *218*
3. Military Space Programs *221*

J. Manpower, General Support, Supply and
Logistics   *223*
1. General Manpower Requirements *223*
2. Draft, Volunteer Army *228*
3. Supply and Logistics *233*

K. Regional Defense Policies, Including
Military Assistance   *237*

1. General Issues *237*
2. North America, Western Europe,
   Mediterranean *246*
3. Middle East, North Africa *262*
4. South Asia, Indian Ocean *262*
5. Southeast Asia, Vietnam War *262*
6. North Asia and Pacific, Korean War
   273
7. Latin America and Caribbean *281*
8. Africa *283*

VI. THE DOMESTIC EFFECTS OF DEFENSE POLICY *285*

A. General Economic, Social, and Political
   Impact of U.S. Defense Policy *285*

B. The Opportunity Costs of Arms Control
   and Disarmament *297*

VII. PERIODICALS THAT REGULARLY INCLUDE ARTI-
CLES ON AMERICAN DEFENSE POLICY *305*

Introduction

As originally conceived, this bibliography was intended to be an updating of the last Jackson Subcommittee bibliography, published in 1963,[1] and an expansion of it to cover the broad field of national security affairs. During the process of editing, however, it was discovered that several areas within the overall national security affairs field had already been treated in existing bibliographies. Arms control and civil-military relations are but two cases in point.[2] Redoing the bibliography in such areas would be redundant and of little substantive help to students in the field.

As a result, the focus of this bibliography was narrowed to encompass—and not exhaustively—only

---

[1]U.S. Congress, Senate Committee on Government Operations, Subcommittee on National Security Staffing and Operations, *Administration of National Security: A Bibliography* (Washington, D.C.: Government Printing Office, 1963).

[2]Arthur D. Larson, *Civil-Military Relations: A World-Wide Bibliography*. Kansas State University Library Bibliography Series, No. 9 (Manhattan, Kansas, 1971); and also see U.S. Library of Congress, Reference Department, General Reference and Bibliography Division, Arms Control and Disarmament Bibliography Section, *Arms Control and Disarmament: A Quarterly Bibliography with Abstracts and Annotations* (Washington: Government Printing Office, 1965 to date).

American defense policy since 1945. In general terms, this includes topical areas that are reasonably connected to United States military programs and military security in the post-World War II era. Not included are such topics as American foreign policy, the security policies of other countries, domestic uses of violence (except in guerrilla warfare), psychological warfare, the role of the military in underdeveloped countries, ethical and legal problems of war, military history, and others. By excluding such worthy topics we were enabled to present, albeit in limited fashion, a more tightly organized research tool.

There are six major subdivisions under which material is herein arranged:

1. Bibliography of Bibliographies
2. The Factual Context: Data and Descriptive Material
3. Strategic Thought and Military Doctrine in the Nuclear Age
4. The Defense Policy Making Process in the United States
5. Defense Output, Weapons Systems, and Military Programs
6. The Domestic Effects of Defense Policy

In some respects the organization of this preliminary edition might be viewed as a framework for collecting sources for subsequent editions. About three-thousand items are contained in this bibliography; but, as suggested above, this is by no means an exhaustive listing of sources. Future editions will add to the number of selections and will further subdivide several of the major categories for easier reference use. We encourage the users of this bibliography to recommend additions, deletions, or conceptual modifications that may help the editors in preparing the next edition. The reader will discover that some sections are "thinner" than others. It is in these areas, especially, that we will welcome suggestions.

Future editions of this bibliography will also be integrated with two other reference projects that have been initiated by the National Security Program of New York University. The first will be an annotated bibliography of hearings of the House and Senate armed forces committees and the House and Senate subcommittees on defense appropriations. The period covered will be 1945 to the present. The second will be a statistical abstract of United States and Soviet force structures and deployment data since 1945. These projects along with the current bibliography should provide an integrated research tool of considerable value to both beginning students and advanced scholars in the defense policy field.

The compiler, Dr. John Greenwood, his editorial adviser, Professor Robin Higham, and the undersigned editors are grateful to those who assisted in but are not responsible for this bibliography. Several scholars examined the manuscript and offered valuable criticism. A special word of thanks is due to Sam C. Sarkesian for his comments on successive drafts. We are also indebted to Ann Riotto for patient and skillful editing and to Marilyn J. King and Mary A. Parker for their administrative expertise. We hope that the response of the bibliography's users will justify the "toil and trouble" of bibliography-making.

C.M.
G.K.
F.L.S.

I

Bibliography of Bibliographies

A. General Literature
B. Military Policy, Doctrine, and Strategy
    1. General, Nuclear, and Conventional Warfare
    2. Guerrilla Warfare
    3. Arms Control and Disarmament
C. Defense Policy Making and Administration
D. U.S. Armed Forces
E. Weapons and Weapon Systems
F. Support Elements
    1. Science, Technology, Research, Development
    2. Logistics, Supply, Manpower, the Draft
    3. Civil Defense
G. Space Programs
H. Military History; Korean War; Vietnam War
I. Political, Social, and Economic Impact of Defense Policies
J. Defense Policy in the U.S.S.R. and China
K. Regional U.S. Defense Policies
L. Institutional Publications and Indices to Periodicals

Bibliographies are inherently hard to classify because so many of them deal with multiple areas. As a result, the twelve-part breakdown in Section I can

only be viewed as an approximate division of the titles into rough categories. The user of the Bibliography should consult all parts which seem to be relevant to his research interest.

A. GENERAL LITERATURE

Body, Alexander C. *Annotated Bibliography of Bibliog-
raphies on Selected Government Publications and
Supplementary Guides to the Superintendent of Docu-
ments Classification System.* Kalamazoo, Mich.:
Western Michigan University, 1967. 181 pp. *First
Supplement.* 1968. 115 pp.

Craig, Hardin, Jr., comp. *A Bibliography of Encyclo-
pedias and Dictionaries Dealing with Military, Naval and Maritime Affairs, 1577-1965.* 3d ed. Hous-
ton, Texas: Fondren Library, Rice University,
1965. 101 pp.

Gray, Charles H.; Gray, Leslie B.; and Gregory, Glen
W., comps. *A Bibliography of Peace Research: In-
dexed by Key Words.* Eugene, Ore.: General Research Analysis Methods, 1968.

Great Britain, Ministry of Defence. *Recent Military
Books.* Monthly. Changed to *Accessions to the War
Office Library,* to June 1964; then to *Accessions to
the Ministry of Defence, Army Department Library,*
June-September 1964; and to *Accessions to the Min-
istry of Defence Libraries,* from September 1964.

Heckler, Ellen L. *Defense Analysis Center Bibliography and Abstracts.* Menlo Park, Calif.: Stanford
Research Institute, 1963.

Huntington, Samuel P. "Recent Writing in Military
Policies: Foci and Corpora." In *Changing Patterns
of Military Politics,* edited by Samuel P. Huntington, pp. 235-66. New York: Free Press, 1962.

Jacobson, Harold K. "Scholarship and Security Policy: A Review of Recent Literature." *Journal of Conflict Resolution* 3 (1959):394-400.

Millett, Alan R., and Cooling, B. Franklin. *Doctoral Dissertations in Military Affairs*. Kansas State University Library Bibliography Series, no. 10. Manhattan, Kan., 1971.

U.S. Department of Defense, Defense Supply Agency, Defense Documentation Center. *Bibliography of Bibliographies: A Report Bibliography*. Compiled by Katye M. Gibbs and Elizabethe H. Hall. Arlington, Va.: Armed Services Technical Information Agency, 1962. 268 pp.

_____. *Bibliography of Bibliographies. Supplement*. Compiled by Elizabethe H. Hall. Arlington, Va.: Armed Services Technical Information Agency, 1963. 106 pp.

U.S. Department of the Air Force, Air University. *Guide to Air War College Theses, 1947-1956*. Montgomery, Ala., 1956. 156 pp.

U.S. Department of the Air Force, USAF Historical Division. *Studies and Histories by the USAF Historical Division, Aerospace Studies Institute, Air University*. Maxwell Air Force Base, Ala., 1968. 13 pp.

U.S. Department of the Army, Army Library. *Theses and Dissertations in the Holdings of the Army Library: A List of Titles*. 3d ed., rev. Washington, D.C.: Adjutant General's Office, 1966. 101 pp.

U.S. Department of the Army, Headquarters. *1970 Contemporary Military Reading List*. Circular no. 1-26. Washington, D.C.: Government Printing Office, 1970. 9 pp.

U.S. Historical Documents Institute. *Checklist of*

United States Public Documents, 1789-1970. Washington, D.C., 1970.

U.S. National War College. *Bibliography for "Conduct of National Security Affairs."* Washington, D.C., 1970-71, and 1971-72.

University of Wisconsin Law School National Security Studies Group. *Bibliography of Selected Periodical Literature Relevant to Military Policy and Administration.* Madison, Wis., 1960. 39 pp.

B. MILITARY POLICY, DOCTRINE, AND STRATEGY

1. General, Nuclear, and Conventional Warfare

"Aviation Literature." In *American Aviation Historical Society Journal.* 1956-date. Quarterly.

Brody, Richard A. "Deterrence Strategies: An Annotated Bibliography." *Journal of Conflict Resolution* 4 (1960):443-57.

Conway, E. A. *Survey of Significant Thought on a Strategy for Peace.* Washington, D.C.: Georgetown University, 1960. 18 pp.

Halperin, Morton H. *Limited War: An Essay on the Development of the Theory and an Annotated Bibliography.* Cambridge, Mass.: Harvard University Center for International Affairs, 1962.

Miller, William Robert. *Bibliography of Books on War, Pacifism, Nonviolence and Related Studies.* Rev. ed. Nyack, N.Y.: Fellowship of Reconciliation, 1961.

Newcombe, Hanna. *Bibliography on War and Peace.* Dundas, Ontario: Canadian Peace Research Institute, 1963.

Popper, Robert D., and Lybrand, William A. *An Inventory of Selected Source Materials Relevant to Integration of Physical and Social Effects of Air Attack.* Arlington, Va.: Human Sciences Research, 1960.

Santelli, James S., comp. *An Annotated Bibliography of the United States Marine Corps' Concept of Close Air Support.* Washington, D.C.: Historical Branch, G-3 Division, Headquarters, U.S. Marine Corps, 1968. 24 pp.

U.S. Armed Services Technical Information Agency. *Undersea Warfare: An ASTIA Report Bibliography.* Arlington, Va., 1961. 1102 pp.

U.S. Department of Defense, Defense Supply Agency, Defense Documentation Center. *Amphibious Operations.* Vol. 1, March 1944–July 1968. AD 685-900. Alexandria, Va., 1969.

U.S. Department of the Air Force, Air University. *An Aerospace Bibliography 1962.* Compiled by Raymond Estep. Maxwell Air Force Base, Ala., 1962. 158 pp.

———. *An Air Power Bibliography.* 2 vols. Compiled by Raymond Estep. Maxwell Air Force Base, Ala., 1956. 200 pp.

U.S. Department of the Air Force, Air University, Library. *A Bibliography of Periodical Literature Commemorating 50 Years of Powered Flight, 1903–1953.* Maxwell Air Force Base, Ala., 1954. 27 pp.

———. *National Air Power and International Politics.* Compiled by Eugene M. Emme. Maxwell Air Force Base, Ala., 1950. 191 pp.

———. *War: Selected References.* Special Bibliography, no. 190. Rev. ed. Compiled by Mary Louise Pitts. Maxwell Air Force Base, Ala., 1969. 61 pp.

U.S. Department of the Army, Army Library. *Bibliography on Limited War*. D.A. Pamphlet 20-60. Washington, D.C.: Government Printing Office, 1958. 53 pp.

_____. *Military Power and National Objectives: A Selected List of Titles*. Special Bibliography, no. 15. Washington, D.C.: Government Printing Office, 1957. 181 pp.

_____. *Mobility in Modern Warfare: A Selected List of Titles*. Special Bibliography, no. 13. Washington, D.C.: Government Printing Office, 1957. 175 pp.

_____. *United States National Security: A Bibliography*. Special Bibliography, no. 7. Washington, D.C.: Government Printing Office, 1956. 218 pp.

_____. *United States National Security and the Communist Challenge: The Spectrum of East-West Conflict*. D.A. Pamphlet 20-60. Washington, D.C.: Government Printing Office, 1961. 93 pp.

U.S. Department of the Army, Military Academy Library. *Subject Catalog of Selected Works Pertaining to the Military Arts and Sciences, with Selected Author and Added Entries, Including a Preliminary Guide to the Manuscript Collection*. 4 vols. Westport, Conn.: Greenwood Press, 1970.

U.S. Strategic Bombing Survey. *Index to Records of the United States Strategic Bombing Survey*. Washington, D.C.: Government Printing Office, 1947. 317 pp.

Weiler, Daniel. "Selected Bibliography." In *The Dispersion of Nuclear Weapons: Strategy and Politics*, edited by R. N. Rosecrance, pp. 319-36. New York: Columbia University Press, 1954.

Werner, H. O. "Paperbacks on Modern Warfare." *U.S.*

Naval Institute Proceedings, August 1959, pp. 110–16.

2. Guerrilla Warfare

American University, Center for Research in Social Systems. *Internal Defense: An Annotated Bibliography.* Washington, D.C., 1968. 66 pp.

American University, Special Operations Research Office. *A Counterinsurgency Bibliography.* Prepared by D. M. Condit, *et al.* Washington, D.C., 1963. 332 pp.

_____. *A Selected Bibliography on Unconventional Warfare, Part 1.* Prepared by Hope Miller and William A. Lybrand, *et al.* Washington, D.C., 1961. 123 pp.

_____. *Unconventional Warfare: An Interim Bibliography.* Prepared by D. M. Condit, *et al.* Washington, D.C., 1961. 288 pp.

Condit, D. M. *A System for Handling Data on Unconventional Warfare: Including a Bibliography of Open Sources.* Chevy Chase, Md.: Operations Research Office, Johns Hopkins University, 1956. 185 pp.

Currier, Nancy; Gosier, Dennis; and Berry, Heidi. *Bibliography on Counterinsurgency, Unconventional Warfare, and Psychological Operations: Supplement no. 8.* Washington, D.C.: Counterinsurgency Information Analysis Center, Special Operations Research Office, 1966. 91 pp.

Human Resources Research Office. *Bibliography on Counterinsurgency, Unconventional Warfare, Guerrilla, and Counterguerrilla Operations.* Washington, D.C., 1962.

Johns Hopkins University Operations Research Office.

Asian Guerrilla Movements: Annotated Bibliography of Source Materials on Guerrilla Movements in East and Southeast Asia. ORO-T-244. Washington, D.C., 1953.

Mughisuddin, Margaret; Butler, Barbara Reason; and Gardner, Nancy Ann. *Jungle Warfare Bibliography.* Washington, D.C.: Special Operations Research Office, 1964. 46 pp.

Ney, Virgil. "Guerrilla Warfare: Annotated Bibliography." *Military Review,* November 1961, pp. 97-112.

Osanka, Franklin Mark, ed. "Research Bibliography on Guerrillas and Unconventional Warfare." In *Modern Guerrilla Warfare: Fighting Communist Guerrilla Movements 1941-1961,* pp. 475-508. Glencoe, Ill.: Free Press, 1962.

U.S. Army Artillery and Missile School. *Jungle Warfare. An Annotated Bibliography.* Fort Sill, Okla., 1961. 16 pp.

U.S. Central Intelligence Agency. *Bibliography: Guerrilla, Underground, and Resistance Movements.* Washington, D.C., 1950.

U.S. Central Intelligence Agency, Curator of Historical Intelligence Collection. *A Selected Reading List on Guerrilla Warfare and Counterinsurgency.* Bibliography CR-L-3, 025, 212. Typescript. Washington, D.C., 1962. 11 pp.

U.S. Department of the Air Force, Air University Library. *Insurgency and Counterinsurgency: Annotated Bibliography.* Maxwell Air Force Base, Ala., 1962.

U.S. Department of the Navy, Library. *Bibliography on Guerrilla and Anti-Guerrilla Warfare, 1942-1962, in East and Southeast Asia, with Special Reference to the Navy*. Typescript. Washington, D.C., 1962. 6 pp.

U.S. Marine Corps, Headquarters. *Selected Bibliography on Counterinsurgency*. 3 pts. Marine Corps Bulletin 1500. Washington, D.C., 1962.

U.S. National Bureau of Standards. *Unconventional Warfare: A Selected Annotated Bibliography of Bibliographies*. Washington, D.C., 1964.

Vigneras, Marcel. *Bibliography on Counterinsurgency and Allied Subjects*. McLean, Va.: Research Analysis Corporation, 1965.

_____. *Preliminary Bibliography on Counterinsurgency and Related Matters*. TP-73. Bethesda, Md.: Research Analysis Corporation, 1962.

3. Arms Control and Disarmament

"Bibliography on Arms Control and Disarmament." *Intercom*, February–March 1963, pp. 61–72.

Collart, Yves. *Disarmament: A Study Guide and Bibliography on the Efforts of the United Nations*. The Hague: Martinus Nijhoff, 1958. 110 pp.

Coward, H. Roberts. "Bibliography on Arms Control and Related Problems." In *Collected Papers*, Summer Study on Arms Control, Dedham, Mass., 1960, pp. 441–59. Boston: American Academy of Arts and Sciences, 1961.

Dougherty, James E. "The Disarmament Debate: A Review of Current Literature." *Orbis* 5 (1961):342–69.

Green, Henrietta H. *Disarmament and Peace: A Selected, Annotated Bibliography*. Bethesda, Md.: Johns

Hopkins University Operations Research Office,
1960. 45 pp.

Harrison, S. L. *Selected Bibliography: Arms Control.*
Washington, D.C.: Institute for Defense Analyses
Weapons Systems Evaluation Group, 1962. 28 pp.

Lefever, Ernest W., ed. *Arms and Arms Control: A*
Symposium. New York: Frederick A. Praeger, 1962.

Oboler, Eli M. "World Disarmament: A Selected Reading List." *Choice* 6 (1969):630-32.

United Nations Dag Hammerskjold Library. *Disarmament:*
A Select Bibliography, 1962-1967. New York: Columbia University Press, 1967. 38 pp.

U.S. Arms Control and Disarmament Agency. *Documents*
on Disarmament. Washington, D.C.: Government
Printing Office, 1961-date. Annual.

_____. *External Research Reports.* Washington, D.C.,
1970. 15 pp.

U.S. Department of State. *Documents on Disarmament,*
1945-1959. 2 vols. Washington, D.C.: Government
Printing Office, 1960. 1644 pp.

U.S. Department of State, Disarmament Administration.
A Basic Bibliography: Disarmament, Arms Control,
and National Security. Department of State Publication 7193. Washington, D.C.: Government Printing Office, 1961. 29 pp.

U.S. Department of State, External Research Staff,
Bureau of Intelligence and Research, for the Arms
Control and Disarmament Agency. *Studies in Prog-*
ress or Recently Completed: Arms Control and Dis-
armament. Washington, D.C.: Government Printing
Office, 1963-68.

U.S. Department of the Air Force, Air Force Academy

Library. *Arms Control.* Special Bibliographical
Series, no. 20. Colorado Springs, Colo., 1962.

U.S. Department of the Army, Army Library. *Disarmament: A Bibliographical Record, 1916-1960.* Prepared by Harry Moskowitz and Jack Roberts. Washington, D.C.: Joint Chiefs of Staff Office, 1960.
66 pp.

_____. *United States Security, Arms Control, and
Disarmament, 1960-1961.* Compiled by Harry Moskowitz and Jack Roberts. Washington, D.C.: Government Printing Office, 1961. 144 pp.

_____. *United States Security, Arms Control, and
Disarmament, 1961-1965.* Compiled by Harry Moskowitz and Jack Roberts. Washington, D.C.: Government Printing Office, 1965. 140 pp.

U.S. Library of Congress, General Reference and Bibliography Division, Arms Control and Disarmament Bibliography Section. *Arms Control and Disarmament.*
Washington, D.C.: Government Printing Office,
1964-date.

C. DEFENSE POLICY MAKING AND ADMINISTRATION

Batchelor, James H. *Operations Research: An Annotated Bibliography.* St. Louis: St. Louis Academy
Press, 1952.

Larson, Arthur D. *Civil-Military Relations: A World-
Wide Bibliography.* Kansas State University Library
Bibliography Series, no. 9. Manhattan, Kan., 1971.

Pearman, Elizabeth H. *Bibliography on Cost-Benefit
Analysis and Planning, Programming, Budgeting.*
McLean, Va.: Research Analysis Corporation, 1966.

Social Science Research Council, Committee on

Civil-Military Relations Research. *Civil-Military Relations: An Annotated Bibliography, 1940-1952.* Edited by William T. R. Fox. New York: Columbia University Press, 1954. 140 pp.

Tompkins, Dorothy C. *Congressional Investigation of Lobbying: A Selected Bibliography.* Berkeley: University of California Bureau of Public Administration, 1956. 32 pp.

U.S. Bureau of the Budget Library. *Executive Office of the President: An Annotated Bibliography.* Washington, D.C., 1960. 44 pp.

U.S. Congress, Senate Committee on Government Operations, Subcommittee on National Policy Machinery. *Organizing for National Security: A Bibliography.* Washington, D.C.: Government Printing Office, 1959.

U.S. Congress, Senate Committee on Government Operations, Subcommittee on National Security Staffing and Operations. *Administration of National Security: A Bibliography.* Washington, D.C.: Government Printing Office, 1963. 89 pp.

U.S. Department of Defense, Defense Supply Agency, Defense Documentation Center. *Cost Effectiveness Analysis, January 1967-January 1968.* AD 675 900. Alexandria, Va., 1968.

U.S. Department of State, Library Division. *Executive-Congressional Relations and Foreign Policy: A Bibliographical Survey.* Department of State Bibliography BL-21. Washington, D.C., 1949.

U.S. Library of Congress, General Reference and Bibliography Division. *Military Administration: A Partial Bibliography with Special Reference to the Unification of the Armed Services.* Washington, D.C.: Government Printing Office, 1946.

Van Riper, Paul P. "A Survey of Materials for the
    Study of Military Management." *American Political
    Science Review* 49 (1955):828–50.

D. U.S. ARMED FORCES

Dollen, Charles. *Bibliography of the United States
    Marine Corps.* New York: Scarecrow Press, 1963.
    115 pp.

Dupre, Flint O., ed. *U.S. Air Force Biographical Dic-
    tionary.* New York: Franklin Watts, 1965.

Estep, Raymond. "Notes on Air Force Bibliography with
    a List of Basic Reference Guides." *Air University
    Quarterly Review,* Spring 1959, pp. 113–20.

Johnstone, Maj. John A. *An Annotated Bibliography of
    the United States Marines in Guerrilla, Anti-
    Guerrilla, and Small War Actions.* Washington,
    D.C., 1966. 58 pp.

Lang, Kurt. *Military Sociology: A Trend Report and
    Bibliography.* London: Basil Blackwell & Mott,
    1965.

_____. *Sociology of the Military: A Selected and
    Annotated Bibliography.* Chicago: Center for So-
    cial Organization Studies, 1969. 96 pp.

Little, Roger W., ed. *Handbook of Military Institu-
    tions.* Beverly Hills, Calif.: Sage, 1970.

Moran, John B. *Marine's Handbook of Writing about
    Marines: The Definitive Bibliography of the U.S.
    Marine Corps.* Chicago: Moran/Andrews, 1971.

Ney, Virgil. "Military Sociology--A Select Bibliog-
    raphy." *Military Affairs* 46 (1966):234–37.

Sells, S. B. *Military Small Group Performance under Isolation and Stress--An Annotated Bibliography.* 6 vols. Fort Wainwright, Alas.: Arctic Aeromedical Laboratory, Alaska Air Command, 1961.

Sunderman, Maj. James F. "Documentary Collections Related to the U.S. Air Force: A Guide for Military Writers." *Air University Quarterly Review* 12 (1961):110-26.

U.S. Department of the Air Force, Air University. *An Aerospace Bibliography, 1962.* Compiled by Raymond Estep. Maxwell Air Force Base, Ala., 1962. 158 pp.

_____. *Armed Forces: Segregation.* Special Bibliography, no. 92. Maxwell Air Force Base, Ala., 1955. 4 pp.

U.S. Department of the Air Force, Historical Division, Directorate of Information Services, Strategic Air Command. *Bibliography of SAC Sources.* Offutt Air Force Base, Nebr., 1959. 7 pp.

U.S. Department of the Army, Army Library. *Civilian in Peace, Soldier in War: A Bibliographic Survey of the Army and Air National Guard.* D.A. Pamphlet 130-2. Washington, D.C.: Government Printing Office, 1967. 192 pp.

_____. *Strength in Reserve: A Bibliographic Survey of the United States Army Reserve.* D.A. Pamphlet 140-3. Washington, D.C.: Government Printing Office, 1968. 119 pp.

U.S. Superintendent of Documents. *Army: Field Manuals and Technical Manuals.* Price List 19. Washington, D.C.: Government Printing Office, current issue.

_____. *Defense. Veterans' Affairs.* Price List 85.

Washington, D.C.: Government Printing Office, current issue.

U.S. Superintendent of Documents. *Navy, Marine Corps and Coast Guard.* Price List 63. Washington, D.C.: Government Printing Office, current issue.

U.S. Veterans' Administration. *Medical Care of the Veteran in the United States, 1870-1960. A Bibliography.* Washington, D.C.: Government Printing Office, 1963. 106 pp.

U.S. War Department, Field Artillery School. *Officer Reserve Corps: A Bibliography.* Fort Sill, Okla., 1946.

Van Riper, Paul P. "A Survey of Materials for the Study of Military Management." *American Political Science Review* 49 (1955):828-50.

E. WEAPONS AND WEAPON SYSTEMS

Anderson, Frank J. *Submarines, Submariners, Submarining: A Checklist of Submarine Books in the English Language, Principally of the Twentieth Century, Arranged by Author, Title, and Subject.* Hamden, Conn.: Shoe String Press, 1963. 140 pp.

"Bibliography." In *Why ABM?,* edited by Johan J. Holst and William Schneider, Jr., pp. 295-302. New York: Pergamon Press, 1969.

Brown, Willis C. *Bibliography of Recent Books about Jets, Rockets and Space Exploration, 1953-1958.* Washington, D.C.: Department of Health, Education, and Welfare, 1958.

Donnelly, Ralph W., comp. *An Annotated Bibliography of United States Marine Corps Artillery.*

Washington, D.C.: Government Printing Office,
1970. 68 pp.

Kemp, E. N., and Hall, P. B. *Study of Human Element
in Future Anti-Ballistic Missile Systems: Annotated Bibliography.* San Diego, Calif.: Convair,
1960. 87 pp.

Sunderman, Maj. James F. "A Missile and Space Bibliography." *Air Force and Space Digest,* April 1962,
pp. 175-83.

U.S. Department of the Air Force, Headquarters, Eighth
Air Force. *An Annotated Bibliography of Missile
Science, Rocket Technology and Space Exploration
for Professional Reading.* Mimeographed. Westover
Air Force Base, Mass., 1961. 57 pp.

U.S. Department of the Army, Army Library. *Guided
Missiles.* Special Bibliography, no. 4. Washington,
D.C.: Government Printing Office, 1956. 91 pp.

_____. *Guided Missiles, Rockets and Artificial Sat-
ellites, Including Project Vanguard: A Selected
List of Titles.* Special Bibliography, no. 11.
Washington, D.C.: Government Printing Office,
1957. 153 pp.

_____. *Missiles and Ventures into Space: 1960-1961.*
D.A. Pamphlet 70-5-9. Washington, D.C.: Government Printing Office, 1960. 81 pp.

_____. *Missiles, Rockets and Satellites.* 5 vols.
D.A. Pamphlets 70-1-1 to 70-5-5. Washington, D.C.:
Government Printing Office, 1958.

_____. *Missiles, Rockets and Satellites, 1959-1960.*
D.A. Pamphlet 70-5-7. Washington, D.C.: Government Printing Office, 1960. 81 pp.

_____. *Missiles, Rockets and Space in War and Peace.*
D.A. Pamphlet 70-5-6. Washington, D.C.:

Government Printing Office, 1959. 94 pp.

U.S. Department of the Army, U.S. Army Engineering
School Library. *Guided Missiles and Rockets: A
Bibliography, 1946-1956.* Fort Belvoir, Va., 1956.
50 pp.

U.S. Library of Congress, Legislative Reference Service. *Controlling the Further Development of Nuclear Weapons: A Collection of Excerpts and a Bibliography.* Prepared for the Subcommittee on Disarmament, Senate Committee on Foreign Relations. Washington, D.C.: Government Printing Office, 1958.
54 pp.

U.S. Library of Congress, Science and Technology Division. *Aeronautical and Space Science Serial Publications: A World List.* Washington, D.C.: Government Printing Office, 1962.

Wasan, R. P. "Chemical and Biological Warfare: A
Select Bibliography." *Journal of the Institute for
Defense Studies and Analyses* (Delhi, India) 2
(1970):365-78.

F. SUPPORT ELEMENTS

1. Science, Technology, Research, Development

Caldwell, Lynton K., ed. *Science, Technology, and
Public Policy: A Selected and Annotated Bibliogra-
phy.* 2 vols. Bloomington: Indiana University
Department of Government, 1969.

Hines, Theodore C., ed. *McGraw-Hill Bibliography of
Science and Technology: Recent Titles on More Than
7,000 Subjects* . . . . New York, 1966. 738 pp.

Holmfield, John D. *Independent Research and Development: A Bibliography.* Congressional Memorandum

70-59-SP. Washington, D.C.: Library of Congress
Legislative Reference Service, 1970.

National Science Foundation. *A Selected Bibliography
of Research and Development and Its Impact on the
Economy.* NSF-58-18. Washington, D.C., 1958.

U.S. Congress, House Committee on Foreign Affairs,
Subcommittee on National Security Policy and Scientific Developments. 91st Cong., 2d Sess. *Science,
Technology, and American Diplomacy. A Selected,
Annotated Bibliography of Articles, Books, Documents, Periodicals, and Reference Guides.* Prepared
by the Science Policy Research and Foreign Affairs
Divisions, Legislative Reference Service, Library
of Congress. Washington, D.C.: Government Printing Office, March 1970. 69 pp.

U.S. Congress, House Committee on Science and Astro-
nautics. 91st Cong., 1st Sess. *Publication of the
Committee on Science and Astronautics, U.S. House
of Representatives, from February 1959-August 1969.*
Committee Print. Washington, D.C.: Government
Printing Office, 1969. 12 pp.

U.S. Congress, Joint Committee on Atomic Energy. *Current Membership of the Joint Committee on Atomic
Energy, Congress of the United States; Joint Committee on Atomic Energy Membership, Publications,
and Other Pertinent Information through the 91st
Congress, 1st Session.* Washington, D.C.: Government Printing Office, 1970. 57 pp.

U.S. Congress, Senate Committee on Government Operations, Subcommittee on Government Research. *An Inventory of Congressional Concern with Research and
Development.* Washington, D.C.: Government Printing Office, 1966-.

U.S. Department of Commerce, National Technical Information Service. *Government Reports Announcements.*
Springfield, Va., 1946-. Semi-monthly.

Formerly issued by the U.S. Clearinghouse for
Federal Scientific and Technical Information
with the title *U.S. Government Research and Development Reports*.

U.S. Department of the Air Force, Office of Aerospace
Research. *Air Force Research Resumes*. December
1959-.
Annually, except 1961-62 issued in one vol-
ume. Titles and series designations vary:
e.g., 1959, *Basic Research Resumes: A Survey of
Basic Research Activities . . . .* (AFOSR TR 59-
204); 1960 to 1961-62, *Basic Research Resumes:
A Survey of Basic Research Activities in the Office of Aerospace Research* (AFOSR 925 and OAR-
9); vol. 4, 1963, OAR-016; etc.

U.S. Department of the Air Force, Air Force Office of
Scientific Research. *Air Force Scientific Research
Bibliography (1950-1959)*. Compiled by G. Vernon
Hooker, *et al.* 4 vols. Washington, D.C.: Govern-
ment Printing Office, 1961, 1964, 1965.

U.S. Department of the Army, Army Library. *Military
and Strategic Implications of Technological Progress: A Selected List of Titles*. Special Bibliography, no. 17. Washington, D.C.: Government
Printing Office, 1958. 23 pp.

U.S. Department of the Navy, Bureau of Naval Personnel, Psychological Research Division. *Abstracts
of Research Reports*. Washington, D.C.: Government Printing Office, 1963. 137 pp.

Wayne State University Center for Application of Sciences and Technology. *Bibliography of Aerospace
Bibliographies: A Key-Word-In-Context Index*. Compiled by Robert E. Booth, *et al.* Detroit, 1965.

2. Logistics, Supply, Manpower, the Draft

Moskowitz, Harry, and Roberts, Jack, comps. *The College Graduate and National Security: Utilization
of Manpower by the U.S. Armed Services, a Bibliographic Survey*. Washington, D.C.: Government
Printing Office, 1968. 74 pp.

_____. *Military Manpower Policy: A Bibliographic
Survey*. Washington, D.C.: Government Printing Office, 1964. 142 pp.

Plant, William H. *Scientific Manpower, 1940-1959: A
Selected and Annotated Bibliography*. Washington,
D.C.: Department of Defense Research and Develop-
ment Board, 1951.

Richardson, Helen, comp. *Railroads in Defense and
War: A Bibliography*. Washington, D.C.: Association of American Railroads, Bureau of Railway Economics Library, 1953. 262 pp.

U.S. Armed Services Technical Information Agency.
Logistics: An ASTIA Report Bibliography. Compiled
by Herman W. Miles. Arlington, Va., 1962. 30 pp.

U.S. Industrial College of the Armed Forces. *Manpower: An Annotated Reading List*. Washington, D.C.,
1955. 32 pp.

U.S. Library of Congress, General Reference and Bibliography Division. *Universal Military Training: A
Selected and Annotated List of References*. Compiled by Francis Cheney. Washington, D.C., 1945.

3. Civil Defense

"Bibliography," in *Effective Civil Defense,* pp. 305-
23. Cambridge, Mass.: Harvard Graduate School of
Business Administration, 1962.

"Civil Defense Against Nuclear Attack: A Selected
    Bibliography." *Bulletin of the Atomic Scientists*,
    September 1962, pp. 33-34.

Human Sciences Research, Inc. *Civil Defense Bibliog-
    raphy*. McLean, Va., 1966. 76 pp.

Kaiser, E. R., and Tolciss, J. *A Selective Bibliogra-
    phy on Environment Control and Habitability of Sur-
    vival Shelters*. New York: American Society of
    Heating, Refrigerating and Air Conditioning Engi-
    neers, 1962. 44 pp.

Moll, Kendall D. *Bibliography: Reports Related to
    Civil and Nonmilitary Defense at SRI*. Menlo Park,
    Calif.: Stanford Research Institute, 1963. 48 pp.

U.S. Department of Commerce, Office of Technical Serv-
    ices. *Civil Defense: OTS Selective Bibliography*.
    Publication SB-501. Washington, D.C.: Department
    of Commerce, 1962. 11 pp.

U.S. Department of Defense, Defense Supply Agency.
    Defense Documentation Center. *Civil Defense: A
    Report Bibliography*. Alexandria, Va., 1965.

_____. *Civil Defense Systems: Pre-attack and Post-
    attack (Nuclear Warfare)*. AD 705 900, DDC-TAS-70-
    13. Alexandria, Va., 1970.

_____. *Civil Defense Systems: Shelters*. AD 704
    500, DDD-TAS-70-12. Alexandria, Va., 1970.

U.S. Department of the Army, Army Library. *Civil De-
    fense: 1960-1967. A Bibliographic Survey*. D.A.
    Pamphlet 500-3. Washington, D.C.: Government
    Printing Office, 1967. 124 pp.

U.S. Federal Civil Defense Administration. *Civil De-
    fense and Atomic Warfare: A Selected Reading List*.
    Washington, D.C.: Government Printing Office,
    1953. 48 pp.

U.S. Superintendent of Documents. *Atomic Energy and Civil Defense*. Price List 84. Washington, D.C.: Government Printing Office, current issue.

G. SPACE PROGRAMS

Emme, Eugene M. "History in the National Aeronautics and Space Administration." In *Official Histories*, edited by Robin D. S. Higham, pp. 633-38. Manhattan: Kansas State University Library, 1970.

John F. Kennedy Space Center Library. *A Selective Bibliography, 1949-1965*. Cape Kennedy, Fla., 1966. 24 pp.

National Aerospace Education Council. *A Bibliography of Adult Aerospace Books and Materials*. Washington, D.C.: Government Printing Office, 1961.

U.S. Congress, House Committee on Science and Astronautics. 87th Cong., 1st Sess. *Military Astronautics: Preliminary Report*. Washington, D.C.: Government Printing Office, 1961. 37 pp.

U.S. Department of the Air Force, Air University. *A Space Bibliography through 1958*. Compiled by Raymond Estep. Maxwell Air Force Base, Ala., 1959. 109 pp.

U.S. Department of the Army, Army Library. *Military Aspects of Space Exploration: A Selected List of Titles*. Special Bibliography, no. 16. Washington, D.C.: Government Printing Office, 1958. 55 pp.

U.S. Library of Congress, Science and Technology Division. *History of Aeronautics and Astronautics: A Preliminary Bibliography*. Compiled by Katherine Murphy Dickson. NASA HHR-29. Washington, D.C.: National Aeronautics and Space Administration, Historical Division, 1968. 420 pp.

U.S. National Aeronautics and Space Administration.
Aerospace Bibliography. 5th ed. Washington, D.C.:
Government Printing Office, 1970. 102 pp.

_____. *List of Doctoral Theses since 1961 on the
Management of Aerospace Activities.* NASA HHN-67.
Compiled by Howard McCurdy. Washington, D.C.,
1967. 6 pp.

U.S. National Bureau of Standards. *Bibliography of
Books and Published Reports . . . on Rocket Power
Plants . . . .* Washington, D.C.: Government
Printing Office, 1949. 53 pp.

U.S. Superintendent of Documents. *Space. Missiles,
The Moon, NASA, and Satellites: Space Education,
Exploration, Research and Technology.* Price List
79A. Washington, D.C.: Government Printing Office, current issue.

H. MILITARY HISTORY; KOREAN WAR; VIETNAM WAR

Albion, Robert Greenhalgh. *Naval and Maritime History: An Annotated Bibliography.* 3d ed. Mystic,
Conn.: Marine Historical Association, 1963. 230
pp.

Blanchard, Carroll H., Jr. *Korean War Bibliography
and Maps of Korea.* Albany, N.Y.: Korean Conflict
Research Foundation, 1964. 181 pp.

Conn, Stetson. "The Army's World War II History and
Related Publications." In *Official Histories,* ed-
ited by Robin D. S. Higham, pp. 553-64. Manhattan:
Kansas State University Library, 1970.

Cook, Blanche W. *Bibliography on Peace Research in
History.* Santa Barbara, Calif.: ABC-Clio, 1969.

Dornbusch, C. E. *Histories, Personal Narratives,*

United States Army: A Checklist. Cornwallville,
N.Y.: Hope Farm Press, 1967. 400 pp.

Dornbusch, C. E., comp. *Unit Histories of the United
States Air Forces: Including Privately Printed
Personal Narratives.* Hampton Bays, N.Y.: Hampton
Books, 1958. 56 pp.

Eiler, Rear Adm. E. M. "United States Naval History
Division Documentary Publications." In *Official
Histories,* edited by Robin D. S. Higham. Manhat-
tan: Kansas State University Library, 1970.

Higham, Robin D. S. *An Introduction to Maritime, Naval, and Aeronautical History.* Library Study Out-
lines, vol. 1, no. 3. Chapel Hill: University of
North Carolina Library, 1960. 48 pp.

Shaw, Henry I., Jr. "The Historical Publications of
the U.S. Marine Corps." In *Official Histories,* edited by Robin D. S. Higham, pp. 543-50. Manhattan:
Kansas State University Library, 1970.

U.S. Department of the Air Force, Office of Air Force
History. *United States Air Force History: An Annotated Bibliography.* Washington, D.C., forthcom-
ing.

U.S. Department of the Air Force, USAF Historical Division. *Studies and Histories by the USAF Historical Division, Aerospace Studies Institute, Air University.* Maxwell Air Force Base, Ala., 1968. 13
pp.

U.S. Department of the Army, Military Academy Library.
*Doctoral Dissertations in American Military Histo-
ry, 1961-1970.* Compiled by Stetson Conn. Washington, D.C.: Government Printing Office, 1971. 29
pp.

U.S. Department of the Army, Military History Research
Collection. *The U.S. Army and the Negro: A*

Military History Research Collection Bibliography.
Compiled by John Slonaker. Special Bibliography,
no. 2. Carlisle Barracks, Pa., 1971. 95 pp.

U.S. Department of the Navy, Library. *United States
Naval History: A Bibliography.* 5th ed. Washington, D.C.: Government Printing Office, 1969. 33
pp.

U.S. Department of the Navy, Library, Naval History
Division. *United States Naval History, Naval Biog-
raphy, Naval Strategy, and Tactics: A Selected and
Annotated Bibliography.* 3d ed., rev. Washington,
D.C., 1963. 29 pp.

_____. *U.S. Naval History Sources in the Washington
Area and Suggested Research Subjects.* Rev. ed.
Washington, D.C.: Government Printing Office,
1965. 26 pp.

U.S. Marine Corps, Headquarters, Historical Division.
*An Annotated Bibliography of the United States Ma-
rine Corps in the Korean War.* Prepared by Michael
O'Quinlivan and James S. Santelli. Washington,
D.C., 1962; rev. ed., 1970. 32 pp.

U.S. National Aeronautics and Space Administration.
*List of Academic Theses since 1961 Related to the
History of Aeronautics and Astronautics.* NASA HHN-
61. Compiled by Charles M. Atkins. Washington,
D.C., 1966. 11 pp.

I. POLITICAL, SOCIAL, AND ECONOMIC IMPACT OF DEFENSE
POLICIES

Dutko, Theodore F. *Current Works on Economic and Social Aspects of National Security: A Selected Bibliography.* Washington, D.C.: Industrial College
of the Armed Forces, 1962.

Friends Committee on National Legislation. *Some Published Materials on the Economics of Disarmament.* Washington, D.C., 1960. 5 pp.

Sica, Geraldine P. *A Preliminary Bibliography of Studies of the Economic Effects of Defense Policies and Expenditures.* RAC Technical Paper 314. McLean, Va.: Research Analysis Corporation, 1968.

U.S. Library of Congress, Legislative Reference Service. *Economic Aspects of Disarmament: A Bibliography.* Compiled by Ellen C. Collier. Washington, D.C.: Government Printing Office, 1963. 7 pp.

J. DEFENSE POLICY IN THE U.S.S.R. AND CHINA

Clemens, Walter C., Jr., comp. *Soviet Disarmament Policy, 1917-1963: An Annotated Bibliography of Soviet and Western Sources.* Stanford, Calif.: Hoover Institution on War, Revolution, and Peace, 1966. 151 pp.

Garthoff, Raymond L. "Source Materials on Soviet Strategy: A Bibliography and Interpretive Guide." In *Soviet Strategy in the Nuclear Age,* pp. 253-74. New York: Frederick A. Praeger, 1958.

Parrish, Michael. *The Soviet Armed Forces: Books in English, 1950-1967.* Hoover Institution Bibliographical Series, no. 47. Stanford, Calif.: Hoover Institution on War, Revolution, and Peace, 1970. 128 pp.

Rhoads, Edward J. M. *The Chinese Red Army, 1927-1963: An Annotated Bibliography.* Harvard East Asia Monographs. Cambridge, Mass.: Harvard University Press, 1964.

U.S. Department of the Air Force, Air University, Research Studies Institute. *Soviet Air Power--An*

Annotated Bibliography (Secret). AU 215-53-RSI.
Maxwell Air Force Base, Ala., 1954.

U.S. Department of the Army. *Communist China: A
Strategic Survey, A Bibliography.* D.A. Pamphlet
20-67. Washington, D.C.: Government Printing Office, 1966. 143 pp.

_____. "Special Bibliographic Supplement. Nuclear
Strategy and Red China's A-Bomb: A New Dimension."
In *Nuclear Weapons and the Atlantic Alliance: A
Bibliographic Survey,* pp. 143-51. Washington,
D.C.: Government Printing Office, 1965.

U.S. Department of the Army, Army Library. *Soviet
Military Power: A Bibliography.* D.A. Pamphlet
20-65. Washington, D.C.: Government Printing Office, 1959. Reprinted by the Greenwood Press,
1969. 186 pp.

_____. *Soviet Russia: Strategic Survey. A Bibliog-
raphy.* D.A. Pamphlet 20-64. Washington, D.C.:
Government Printing Office, 1963. 217 pp.

_____. *U.S.S.R.: Missiles, Rockets, and Space Ef-
forts: A Bibliographic Record, 1956-1960.* D.A.
Pamphlet 70-5-8. Washington, D.C.: Government
Printing Office, 1960. 49 pp.

_____. *U.S.S.R.: Strategic Survey.* D.A. Pamphlet
550-6. Washington, D.C.: Government Printing Office, 1969. 237 pp.

U.S. Department of the Army, Office of the Assistant
Chief of Staff, Intelligence. *Catalog of Soviet
Military Publications, Unclassified.* Washington,
D.C., 1957. Compiled in conjunction with the War
Office, London, and Army Headquarters, Ottawa.
944 pp.

U.S. Library of Congress. *Nuclear Science in Main-
land China: A Selected Bibliography.* Washington,

D.C.: Government Printing Office, 1968.   70 pp.

U.S. Library of Congress, Aerospace Technology Division. *U.S.S.R. Missile and Rocket Program: Bibliography*. Report 61-12. Washington, D.C., 1961.
66 pp.

U.S. Library of Congress, Reference Department. *Aero-
nautical Sciences and Aviation in the Soviet Union:
A Bibliography*. Compiled by Bertha Kucherov.
Washington, D.C., 1955.   274 pp.

K. REGIONAL U.S. DEFENSE POLICIES

"Bibliography." In *Proposal: The North Atlantic
Treaty Organization and Arms Control*, pp. 43-59.
Washington, D.C.: American University Center for
the Studies of Approaches to Peace, 1962.

Conference on North Atlantic Community. *The Atlantic
Community: An Introductory Bibliography*. 2 vols.
Leiden: A. W. Sythoff, 1961.

North Atlantic Treaty Organization, Information Service. *Bibliography*. Paris, 1964.   205 pp.

Pass, David J. "A Selective Bibliography on the Atlantic Community." *American Academy of Political
Science Proceedings* 29 (1968):153-56.

U.S. Department of the Army, Army Library. *Nuclear
Weapons and NATO: An Analytical Survey of Literature*. D.A. Pamphlet 50-1. Washington, D.C.: Government Printing Office, 1970.   450 pp.

_____. *Nuclear Weapons and the Atlantic Alliance:
A Bibliographic Survey*. D.A. Pamphlet 20-66.
Washington, D.C.: Government Printing Office,
1965.   189 pp.

U.S. Department of the Army, Army Library. *U.S. Over-
    seas Bases: Present Status and Future Prospects.*
    D.A. Pamphlet 20-63. Washington, D.C.: Govern-
    ment Printing Office, 1963. 133 pp.

L. INSTITUTIONAL PUBLICATIONS AND INDICES TO
   PERIODICALS

American University, Special Operations Research Of-
    fice. *Annotated Bibliography of SORO Publications.*
    Washington, D.C., February 1966.

Breese, E., and Graham, Tan C. C. *Publication of the
    Social Science Division, Rand Corporation, 1948-
    1967.* RAND Memorandum RM-3600-4. Santa Monica,
    Calif.: RAND Corporation, May 1967.

Brown, Emma E. *Abstracts of USAPRO Research Publica-
    tions--Fiscal Year 1963.* Technical Research Note
    138. Washington, D.C.: U.S. Army Personnel Re-
    search Office, 1963.

_____. *Abstracts of USAPRO Research Publications--
    Fiscal Year 1964.* Technical Research Note 149.
    Washington, D.C.: U.S. Army Personnel Research Of-
    fice, 1964.

*Consolidated Author and Subject Index to the Journal
    of the Royal United Service Institution.* Ann
    Arbor, Mich.: University Microfilms, 1964.

Corbin, Doris, comp. *Open Literature Publications of
    the Social Science Department: 1966-1969.* RAND
    Memorandum RM-3600-6. Santa Monica, Calif.: RAND
    Corporation, March 1970.

Graham, Tan C. C., and Lieb, Bonnie. *Publications of
    the Social Science Department, Rand Corporation,
    1948-1965.* RAND Memorandum RM-3600-2. Santa
    Monica, Calif.: RAND Corporation, 1965.

Military Affairs: Cumulative Indices, 1937-1969.
    Manhattan: Kansas State University Library, 1969.

RAND Corporation. *A Bibliography of Selected RAND*
    Publications: USSR. Santa Monica, Calif., Octo-
    ber 1970. 52 pp.

_____. *Index of Selected Publications of the RAND*
    Corporation. Vol. 1, 1946-1962. Santa Monica,
    Calif., 1962.

_____. *Selected List of Unclassified Publications of*
    the Economics Division of the RAND Corporation.
    RAND Memorandum EM-821-6. Santa Monica, Calif.,
    1958.

U.S. Department of the Air Force, Air University, Li-
    brary. *Air University Library Index to Military*
    Periodicals. Maxwell Air Force Base, Ala., 1967-.
    Quarterly.
        Preceded by the quarterly *Air University Li-*
    brary Index (1949-1962) and triennial *Air Uni-*
    versity Periodical Index (1962-1967).

U.S. Department of the Army. *Military Publications:*
    Index of Administrative Publications. D.A. Pam-
    phlet 310-1. Washington, D.C.: Government Print-
    ing Office, 1969.

U.S. Department of the Navy, Naval War College. *Naval*
    War College Review Index: September 1948-June
    1968. Newport, R.I., 1970. 50 pp.

Wing, Mark, and Wing, Karen. *Subject and Author Index*
    to Military Review 1922-1965. Fort Leavenworth,
    Kan.: U.S. Army Command and General Staff College,
    1967. 679 pp.

II

The Factual Context:
Data and Descriptive Material

Section II is primarily a reference section. Included are statistical and descriptive materials on
defense programs, weapon systems, budgets, force levels, defense organization, and the like. Important
pieces of legislation in the defense field, such as
the National Security Act, are also to be found here.
Although the focus is on post-World War II American
defense policy, some of the selections are broader in
scope, providing like information on the armed forces
and defense policies of other countries.

The best descriptive materials are:
1. *Military Balance* and *Strategic Survey* of
   the International Institute for Strategic
   Studies and *Brassey's Annual* for statistics on the world's armed forces;
2. *Jane's Fighting Ships, Jane's All the
   World's Aircraft,* and *Jane's Weapon Systems* for performance and production characteristics of world armaments.
3. The annual posture statements of the Secretary of Defense, the various Hearings
   and Reports of the four basic Congressional committees (House and Senate Appropriations and Armed Forces), and the
   continuous reports by the Jackson subcommittee (under various names) for
   statement of American strategic policy
   and defense programs.

31

Air Force Bases: A Directory of U.S. Air Force In-stallations, Both in the Continental U.S. and Over-seas. Harrisburg, Pa.: Stackpole, 1965. 224 pp.

Alexander, Archibald S. "The Cost of World Arma-ments." *Scientific American,* October 1969, pp. 21-27.

Bombers and Reconnaissance Aircraft. MacDonald Air-craft Pocketbook, vol. 2. London: MacDonald, 1964.

Brassey's Annual: The Armed Forces Year-Book. New York: Macmillan, 1886-date.

Brassey's Naval Annual. New York: Macmillan, 1886-date.

Brodie, Bernard, and Brodie, Fawn. *From Crossbow to H-Bomb: The Evolution of the Weapons and Tactics of Warfare in the Light of Science and Invention.* New York: Dell, 1962. 288 pp.

Brunner, E. D. *The Cost of Basic Scientific Research in Europe: Department of Defense Experience, 1956-1966.* RAND Memorandum RM-5275-PR. Santa Monica, Calif.: RAND Corporation, 1967.

Burgess, Eric. *Guided Weapons.* New York: Macmillan, 1957.

Bussard, R. W., and De Lauer, R. D. *Nuclear Rocket Propulsion.* New York: McGraw-Hill, 1958.

Calder, Nigel, ed. *Unless Peace Comes: A Scientific Forecast of New Weapons.* New York: Viking, 1968. 243 pp.

Committee for World Development and World Disarmament. *The Economics of Disarmament: Fact Sheet.* United Nations Plaza, New York, 1959.

Democratic Study Group of the House of Representatives. *Fact Book on the FY 1970 Defense Budget.* Washington, D.C., 1969.

Dupuy, R. Ernest, and Dupuy, Trevor N. *The Encyclopedia of Military History from 3500 B.C. to the Present.* New York: Harper & Row, 1969.

Dupuy, Trevor N. *The Almanac of World Military Power.* Harrisburg, Pa.: Stackpole, 1970.

Eggenberger, David. *A Dictionary of Battles.* New York: Thomas Y. Crowell, 1967. 526 pp.

Esposito, Col. Vincent J. *The West Point Atlas of American Wars.* 2 vols. New York: Frederick A. Praeger, 1959.

Fighters. MacDonald Aircraft Pocketbook, vol. 1. London: MacDonald, 1964.

Gatland, Kenneth W. *Development of the Guided Missile.* Philadelphia: Philosophical Library, 1958.

Gurney, Gene. *Rocket and Missile Technology.* New York: Franklin Watts, 1964. 394 pp.

Hoagland, John H. *World Combat Aircraft Inventories and Production, 1970-75: Implications for Arms Transfers.* M.I.T. Publication, no. C/70-4. Cambridge, Mass.: M.I.T. Press, 1970.

International Institute for Strategic Studies. *Military Balance.* London, 1959-date. Annual.

_____. *Strategic Survey.* London, 1967-date. Annual.

Jane's All the World's Aircraft. New York: McGraw-Hill, 1945-date. Annual.

Jane's Fighting Ships. New York: McGraw-Hill, 1945–date. Annual.

Jane's Weapon Systems. New York: McGraw-Hill, 1969–date. Annual.

Keesing's Publications. *Treaties and Alliances of the World: An International Survey Covering Treaties in Force and Communities of States.* New York: Charles Scribner's Sons, 1968. 214 pp.

Leckie, Robert. *The Wars of America.* New York: Harper & Row, 1968. 1052 pp.

Loosbrock, John F., *et al.*, eds. *Space Weapons: A Handbook of Military Astronautics.* New York: Frederick A. Praeger, 1959. 245 pp.

McDonnell-Douglas Corporation, Aerospace System Analysis Division. *Cost of War Index.* Publication no. DAC-58166, September 1968.

Mydans, Carl, and Mydans, Shelley. *The Violent Peace: A Report on Wars in the Postwar World.* New York: Atheneum, 1968. 478 pp.

Remington, Owen J. "Army Contributions to the Space Age." *Army Digest,* November 1969, pp. 2–35.

Roy, Elizabeth C. *U.S. Military Commitments.* Research Paper P-79. Washington, D.C.: Institute for Defense Analyses, 1963. 40 pp.

Schwiebert, Ernest G. *A History of the United States Air Force Ballistic Missiles.* New York: Frederick A. Praeger, 1965.

Sheldon, Charles S., II. *Review of the Soviet Space Program: with Comparative United States Data.* New York: McGraw-Hill, 1968. 152 pp.

Shuon, Karl. *U.S. Navy Biographical Dictionary.* New

York: Franklin Watts, 1965.   180 pp.

Simons, Howard.   "World-Wide Capabilities for Produc-
    tion and Control of Nuclear Weapons." *Daedalus* 88
    (1959):385-409.

Singer, J. David, and Small, Melvin. *The Wages of
    War: A Statistical Handbook, 1816-1965*. New York:
    Wiley, 1970.

Smart, Ian. *Advanced Strategic Missiles: A Short
    Guide*. Adelphi Papers, no. 63. London: Institute
    for Strategic Studies, 1969.

Stockholm International Peace Research Institute.
    *SIPRI Yearbook of World Armaments and Disarmaments,
    1968-69*. New York: Humanities Press, 1969.

_____. *SIPRI Yearbook of World Armaments and Disarma-
    ments, 1969-70*. New York: Humanities Press, 1970.

Taylor, John W. R., ed. *Combat Aircraft of the World,
    1909-1968*. London: Michael Joseph Ebury Press, 1970.

Ulanoff, Stanley. *Illustrated Guide to United States
    Missiles and Rockets*. Garden City, N.Y.: Double-
    day, 1959.

U.S. Arms Control and Disarmament Agency. *World Mili-
    tary Expenditures and Related Data, Calendar Year
    1966 and Summary Trends, 1962-1967*. Research Re-
    port 68-52. Washington, D.C.: Government Printing
    Office, 1969.   24 pp.

_____. *World Military Expenditures 1969*. ACDA Pub-
    lication, no. 53. Washington, D.C.: Government
    Printing Office, 1970. 26 pp.

_____. *World-Wide Defense Expenditures and Related
    Data for Calendar Year 1965*. Research Report 67-6.
    Washington, D.C.: Government Printing Office,
    1967.

U.S. Army Armor School. *Armor Reference Data.* Fort
Knox, Ky., May 1962.

U.S. Army Artillery and Missile School. *Field Artillery Data.* Fort Sill, Okla., July 1967.

U.S. Army Command and General Staff College. *Organizational Data for the Army in the Field.* Fort
Leavenworth, Kan., April 1967.

U.S. Army Infantry School. *Infantry Reference Data.*
Fort Benning, Ga., July 1964.

U.S. Bureau of the Budget. *Budget of the United
States Government: Fiscal Years 1945-1972.* Washington, D.C.: Government Printing Office, annual.

U.S. Congress, House of Representatives. 85th Cong.,
1st Sess. *United States Defense Policies since
World War II.* Prepared by Charles H. Donnelly.
House Doc. 100. Washington, D.C.: Government
Printing Office, 1957.

_____. 85th Cong., 2d Sess. *United States Defense
Policies in 1957.* Prepared by Charles H. Donnelly.
House Doc. 436. Washington, D.C.: Government
Printing Office, 1958.

_____. 86th Cong., 1st Sess. *United States Defense
Policies in 1958.* Prepared by the Library of Congress, Legislative Reference Service. House Doc.
227. Washington, D.C.: Government Printing Office, 1959.

_____. 86th Cong., 2d Sess. *United States Defense
Policies in 1959.* Prepared by Charles H. Donnelly.
House Doc. 432. Washington, D.C.: Government
Printing Office, 1960.

_____. 87th Cong., 1st Sess. *United States Defense
Policies in 1960.* Prepared by Charles H. Donnelly.

House Doc. 207. Washington, D.C.: Government
Printing Office, 1961.

U.S. Congress, House of Representatives. 87th Cong.,
2d Sess. *United States Defense Policies in 1961.*
Prepared by Charles H. Donnelly. House Doc. 502.
Washington, D.C.: Government Printing Office,
1962.

_____. 88th Cong., 1st Sess. *A Compilation of Mate-
rial Relating to United States Defense Policies in
1962.* Compiled by Charles H. Donnelly. House Doc.
155. Washington, D.C.: Government Printing Office, 1963.

_____. 88th Cong., 2d Sess. *Index to United States
Defense Policies from World War II through 1963.*
Prepared by Charles H. Donnelly. House Doc. 371.
Washington, D.C.: Government Printing Office,
1964.

_____. 88th Cong., 2d Sess. *United States Defense
Policies in 1963.* Prepared by Charles H. Donnelly.
House Doc. 335. Washington, D.C.: Government
Printing Office, 1964.

_____. 89th Cong., 1st Sess. *United States Defense
Policies in 1964.* Prepared by Charles H. Donnelly.
House Doc. 285. Washington, D.C.: Government
Printing Office, 1965.

U.S. Congress, House Committee on Appropriations. *Department of Defense Appropriations for 19--. Hearings* . . . . Washington, D.C.: Government Printing Office, 1947-. Annual.

_____. 80th Cong., 2d Sess. *Military Functions, Na-
tional Military Establishment Appropriations.
Hearings.* 3 pts. Washington, D.C.: Government
Printing Office, 1948.

_____. 84th Cong., 2d Sess. *Department of Defense*

Appropriations for 1957: Procurement Policies and Practices . . . . Charles G. Haynes Report. Washington, D.C.: Government Printing Office, 1956.

U.S. Congress, House Committee on Appropriations. 87th Cong., 1st Sess. *Report, Air Force Intercontinental Ballistic Missile Construction Program.* Washington, D.C.: Government Printing Office, 1961.

U.S. Congress, House Committee on Armed Services. 85th Cong., 2d Sess. *Hearings: Reorganization of the Department of Defense.* Washington, D.C.: Government Printing Office, 1958.

_____. 87th Cong., 1st Sess. *Military Posture Briefings. Hearings* . . . . Washington, D.C.: Government Printing Office, 1961.

_____. 89th Cong., 2d Sess. *United States Defense Policies in 1965.* Prepared by Charles H. Donnelly. Washington, D.C.: Government Printing Office, 1966. 223 pp.

_____. 90th Cong., 1st Sess. *The Changing Strategic Balance: U.S.A. vs. U.S.S.R.* Prepared for the American Security Council. Washington, D.C.: Government Printing Office, 1967.

_____. 90th Cong., 2d Sess. *The Changing Strategic Naval Balance, U.S.S.R. vs. U.S.A.* Prepared for the American Security Council. Washington, D.C.: Government Printing Office, 1968.

U.S. Congress, House Committee on Armed Services, Special Subcommittee no. 6. 85th Cong., 2d Sess. *Hearings on Investigation of National Defense Establishment. Study of Procurement and Utilization of Scientists, Engineers and Technical Skills.* Washington, D.C.: Government Printing Office, 1958.

U.S. Congress, House Committee on Foreign Affairs.
90th Cong., 1st Sess. *Collective Defense Treaties
with Maps, Texts of Treaties, a Chronology, Status
of Force Agreements, and Comparative Chart, April
10, 1967.* Washington, D.C.: Government Printing
Office, 1967.

U.S. Congress, House Committee on Government Operations. 80th Cong., 1st Sess. *National Security
Act of 1947. Hearings before the Committee on Expenditures in the Executive Departments . . . .*
Washington, D.C.: Government Printing Office,
1947.

U.S. Congress, Joint Committee on Atomic Energy. *The
Hydrogen Bomb and International Control: Technical
and Background Information.* Washington, D.C.:
Government Printing Office, 1950. 41 pp.

U.S. Congress, Senate Committee on Appropriations.
*Department of Defense Appropriations. Hearings
. . . .* [title varies.] Washington, D.C.: Government Printing Office, 1949-. Annual.

U.S. Congress, Senate Committee on Armed Services.
80th Cong., 1st Sess. *Hearings . . . . National
Defense Establishment.* 3 pts. Washington, D.C.:
Government Printing Office, 1947.

_____. 85th Cong., 2d Sess. *Department of Defense
Reorganization Act of 1958. Hearings . . . .*
Washington, D.C.: Government Printing Office,
1958. 444 pp.

_____. 85th Cong., 2d Sess. *National Security Act
of 1947 As Amended Through December 31, 1958
. . . .* Washington, D.C.: Government Printing Office, 1959.

U.S. Congress, Senate Committee on Foreign Relations,
Subcommittee on National Security Policy and Scientific Developments. 91st Cong., 2d Sess.

Background Information on the Use of United States Armed Forces in Foreign Countries. Compiled by Library of Congress, Legislative Reference Service. Washington, D.C.: Government Printing Office, 1970. 61 pp.

U.S. Congress, Senate Committee on Government Operations, Subcommittee on National Security and International Operations. 89th Cong., 1st Sess. *Conduct of National Security Policy: Selected Readings.* Washington, D.C.: Government Printing Office, 1965. 155 pp.

U.S. Department of Defense. *Annual Report Including Reports of the Secretary of Defense, Secretary of the Army, Secretary of the Navy, Secretary of the Air Force, for the Fiscal Year 19-- [various titles].* Washington, D.C.: Government Printing Office, 1946-70.

_____. *Department of Defense Semiannual Report of the Secretary of Defense and the Semiannual Reports of the Secretary of the Army, Secretary of the Navy, Secretary of the Air Force, January 1 to June 30, 1956.* Washington, D.C.: Government Printing Office, 1957.

_____. *Dictionary of United States Military Terms for Joint Usage.* Washington, D.C.: Government Printing Office, 1968. 322 pp.

_____. *Effects of Nuclear Weapons.* Edited by Samuel Glasstone. Rev. ed. Washington, D.C.: U.S. Atomic Energy Commission, 1962. 730 pp.

_____. *Fact Sheet on United States Guided Missiles.* Washington, D.C.: Government Printing Office, 1962. 101 pp.

_____. *Five Year Trends in Defense Procurement, FY 1958-FY 1962.* Washington, D.C.: Government Printing Office, 1963.

U.S. Department of Defense. *Military Assistance and Foreign Military Sales Facts*. Washington, D.C.: Government Printing Office, 1967.

_____. *Statement of Secretary of Defense Melvin R. Laird on the Fiscal Year 1972-76 Defense Program and the 1972 Defense Budget* [title varies]. Washington, D.C.: Government Printing Office, 1971-. Annual.

U.S. Department of State. *Issues in United States Foreign Policy, No.3: Commitments of U.S. Power Abroad*. Publication no. 8488. Washington, D.C.: Government Printing Office, 1969. 20 pp.

U.S. Department of the Air Force. *Fundamentals of Aerospace Weapon Systems*. Washington, D.C.: Government Printing Office, 1961. 402 pp.

_____. *Guided Missiles: Operations, Design and Theory*. New York: McGraw-Hill, 1958. 575 pp.

U.S. Department of the Air Force, Historical Division. *A Chronology of American Aviation Events from 1903 through 1964*. AF Pamphlet 190-2-2. Washington, D.C., 1965. 85 pp.

U.S. Department of the Navy. *Naval Fighting Ships*. 5 vols. Washington, D.C.: Government Printing Office, 1959-70.

U.S. Department of the Navy, Bureau of Naval Weapons. *Proceedings of the Bureau of Naval Weapons' Missiles and Rockets Symposium, April 1961*. Washington, D.C.: Government Printing Office, 1962. 344 pp.

U.S. President. *Public Papers of the Presidents of the United States, Containing Public Messages, Speeches, and Statements of the President*. Washington, D.C.: Government Printing Office, annually.

U.S. President. *U.S. Foreign Policy for the 1970's: A New Strategy for Peace. A Report to the Congress by Richard Nixon, President of the United States, February 18, 1970.* Washington, D.C.: Government Printing Office, 1970.

Worley, Marvin L., Jr. *A Digest of New Developments in Army Weapons, Tactics, Organization and Equipment.* Harrisburg, Pa.: Stackpole, 1959.

III

Strategic Thought and Military Doctrine in the Nuclear Age

A. General Strategic Thought
   1. Strategic Theory Applicable to All Types of Warfare
   2. Land Power
   3. Air Power
   4. Sea Power
B. Nuclear Weapons, Deterrence, and General War
C. Limited War, Including Guerrilla Warfare and Counterinsurgency

Section III is concerned primarily with theory--the theory of warfare in the 1945-1972 time frame. It is somewhat arbitrarily divided into three major subsections: General Strategic Thought; Nuclear Weapons, Deterrence, and General War; and Limited War, including Guerrilla War and Counterinsurgency. There are, of course, many overlaps among these areas, and no classification scheme could neatly allocate works on strategic theory among watertight compartments. Some subdivision is necessary, however, to make the search for material a manageable task. This conventional three-part division was selected because it is familiar and because it roughly reflects the types of warfare possible in today's world.

The materials in Part A-1 (General Strategic Thought) cover in a broad way the more specific subsections A-2 through A-4, B, and C. The interfaces

43

between subsections are also to be found in A-1.
Since the major strategic problem of the 1945-1972
period has been the nuclear confrontation between the
United States and the Soviet Union, a number of selections on Soviet strategic theory have been sprinkled
throughout Section III. Older strategic works, such
as Mahan or Douhet, have not been included; but strategic theory by non-Americans written since 1945 will
be found here if it is at all relevant to American defense policy.

The distinction between strategic theory and defense policy (Section V) may seem ambiguous. In general, Section III is concerned with inputs to policy
making, while Section V contains policy output. Or,
in other words, the materials of Section V deal with
the application of the theoretical works of Section
III to concrete situations. For example, a book on
the nature and tactical doctrine of tank warfare would
be found in III A-2, while an account of the American
use of tanks in Korea would be in V K-6 or V D-2(b).
Sorting materials along these lines is not always
easy; and the student interested in strategic theory
should check the selections in Section V, especially
part A.

A. GENERAL STRATEGIC THOUGHT

1. Strategic Theory Applicable to All Types of
   Warfare

Abshire, David M., and Allen, Richard V. *National Security: Political, Military, and Economic Strategies in the Decade Ahead.* New York: Frederick A.
Praeger, 1963. 1039 pp.

Aron, Raymond. *On War: Atomic Weapons and Global Diplomacy.* New York: Doubleday, 1959. 143 pp.

Austin, Bernard L. "Military Considerations in Grand

Strategy." *Naval War College Review*, December 1962, pp. 1-16.

Austin, Bernard L. "Military Considerations in National Strategy." *Naval War College Review*, December 1963, pp. 1-15.

Baldwin, Hanson W. *Power and Politics: The Price of Security in the Atomic Age*. Claremont, Calif.: Claremont College Press, 1950. 117 pp.

_____. *Strategy for Tomorrow*. New York: Harper & Row, 1970. 377 pp.

Beaufre, Gen. André. *Deterrence and Strategy*. Translated by Maj. Gen. R. H. Barry. New York: Frederick A. Praeger, 1966. 174 pp.

_____. "The Dimensions of Strategy." *Intercollegiate Review*, January-March 1968.

_____. *An Introduction to Strategy with Particular Reference to Problems of Defense, Politics, Economics, and Diplomacy of the Nuclear Age*. Translated by Maj. Gen. R. H. Barry. New York: Frederick A. Praeger, 1966. 174 pp.

_____. *Strategy of Action*. Translated by Maj. Gen. R. H. Barry. New York: Frederick A. Praeger, 1967. 136 pp.

Blackett, P. M. S. *Studies of War: Nuclear and Conventional*. New York: Hill & Wang, 1962. 242 pp.

Brodie, Bernard. "Characteristics of a Sound Strategy." *Naval War College Review*, June 1952, pp. 65-83.

_____. *Escalation and the Nuclear Option*. Princeton, N.J.: Princeton University Press, 1966. 160 pp.

Brodie, Bernard. "Strategy as a Science." *World Politics* 1 (1959):467-88.

_____. *Strategy in the Missile Age.* Princeton, N.J.: Princeton University Press, 1959. 433 pp.

_____. *Strategy Versus Tactics in a Nuclear Age.* RAND Paper P-841. Santa Monica, Calif.: RAND Corporation, 1956.

Buchan, Alastair, ed. *Problems of Modern Strategy.* New York: Frederick A. Praeger, 1970.

Burke, Adm. Arleigh A. "National Strategy." *Naval War College Review*, October 1965, pp. 21-40.

Burns, Arthur L. "The New Weapons and International Relations." *Australian Outlook*, June 1958, pp. 32-42.

Calder, Nigel, ed. *Unless Peace Comes: A Scientific Forecast of New Weapons.* New York: Viking, 1968. 243 pp.

Cerf, Jay H., and Pozen, Walter, eds. *Strategy for the 60's.* New York: Frederick A. Praeger, 1961.

Coats, Brig. Gen. Wendell J. *Armed Force as Power: The Theory of War Reconsidered.* New York: Exposition Press, 1966. 432 pp.

Coffey, Joseph I. "Strategies and Realities." *U.S. Naval Institute Proceedings*, February 1966, pp. 34-41.

Cohen, Saul B. "Geography and Strategy: Their Interrelationship." *Naval War College Review*, December 1957, pp. 1-31.

Dinerstein, H. S. *War and the Soviet Union: Nuclear Weapons and the Revolution in Soviet Military and Political Thinking.* Rev. ed. New York: Frederick A. Praeger, 1962. 265 pp.

Donnelly, Col. Charles H. "Evolution of United States Military Strategic Thought." *Military Review,* October 1959, pp. 12-24.

Dorsey, Laurens. "A Concept of National Strategy." *Naval War College Review,* September 1959, pp. 35-83.

Earle, Edward Meade, ed. *Makers of Modern Strategy: Military Thought from Machiavelli to Hitler.* Princeton, N.J.: Princeton University Press, 1943.

Eccles, Rear Adm. Henry E. *Military Concepts and Philosophy.* New Brunswick, N.J.: Rutgers University Press, 1965. 339 pp.

Eliot, George Fielding. "Current U.S. Military Strategy." *Naval War College Review,* April 1959, pp. 15-31.

Emerson, David F. "The Principles of War." *Naval War College Review,* March 1964, pp. 1-22.

Emerson, William R. "American Concepts of Peace and War." *Naval War College Review,* May 1958, pp. 1-28.

Erickson, John, ed. *The Military-Technical Revolution: Its Impact on Strategy and Foreign Policy.* New York: Frederick A. Praeger, 1966.

Fair, Charles. *From the Jaws of Victory: The Bad Generals from Crassus to Westmoreland.* New York: Harper & Row, 1971.

Fisher, Ernest F. "A Strategy of Flexible Response." *Military Review,* March 1967, pp. 41-55.

Foster, William C. "Toward a Balanced Defense." *Orbis* 3 (1959):26-37.

Fuller, Maj. Gen. J. F. C. *The Conduct of War,*

1789-1961. New Brunswick, N.J.: Rutgers University Press, 1961. 352 pp.

Galbraith, John K. "The Illusion of National Security." In *The Affluent Society*, pp. 161-80. Boston: Houghton Mifflin, 1958.

Garthoff, Raymond L. *Soviet Military Doctrine*. Glencoe, Ill.: Free Press, 1953.

_____. *Soviet Strategy in the Nuclear Age*. Rev. ed. New York: Frederick A. Praeger, 1962.

Gavin, Lt. Gen. James M. *War and Peace in the Space Age*. New York: Harper & Row, 1958. 304 pp.

Ginsburgh, Robert N. *U.S. Military Strategy in the Sixties*. New York: W. W. Norton, 1965. 160 pp.

Goffmann, Irving. *Doubts at Play: The Strategic Perspective on Interaction*. Philadelphia: University of Pennsylvania Press, 1969.

Hahn, Walter F., and Neff, John C., eds. *American Strategy for the Nuclear Age*. Garden City, N.Y.: Doubleday, 1960.

Halle, Louis J. "Lessons of the Nuclear Age." *Encounter*, March 1968, pp. 17-25.

Halperin, Morton H. *Contemporary Military Strategy*. Boston: Little, Brown, 1967. 156 pp.

_____. *Defense Strategies for the Seventies*. Boston: Little, Brown, 1971. 149 pp.

Haskins, Caryl P. "Atomic Energy and American Foreign Policy." *Foreign Affairs* 24 (1946):591-609.

Heilbrunn, Otto. *Conventional Warfare in the Nuclear Age*. New York: Frederick A. Praeger, 1965. 164 pp.

Historical Evaluation and Research Organization. *National Strategic Concepts and the Changing Nature of Modern War*. 3 vols. Washington, D.C., 1966.

Hoffmann, Stanley. *The State of War. Essays in the Theory and Practice of International Politics*. New York: Frederick A. Praeger, 1965. 276 pp.

Holst, Johan J. *Comparative U.S. and Soviet Deployments Doctrines and Arms Limitations*. Chicago: University of Chicago Press, 1971.

Horelick, Arnold, and Rush, Myron. *Strategic Power in Soviet Foreign Policy*. Chicago: University of Chicago Press, 1968.

Howard, Michael. "Military Power and International Order." *International Affairs* 40 (1964):397-408.

_____. "Strategy in the Nuclear Age." *Royal United Service Institution Journal*, November 1957, pp. 473-82.

Hoxie, R. Gordon. "The Calculated Risk in Strategy." *Naval War College Review*, December 1960, pp. 1-17.

Huntington, Samuel P. "Radicalism and Conservatism in National Defense Policy." *Journal of International Affairs* 8 (1954):206-22.

_____. "To Choose Peace or War: Is There a Place for Preventive War in American Policy?" *U.S. Naval Institute Proceedings*, 1957, pp. 359-69.

Huszar, George B., ed. *National Strategy in an Age of Revolution*. New York: Frederick A. Praeger, 1959. 282 pp.

Iklé, Fred C. *Every War Must End*. New York: Columbia University Press, 1971.

International Institute for Strategic Studies.

Problems of Modern Strategy. 2 pts. Adelphi Papers, nos. 54 and 55. London, February and March 1969.

Jackson, Henry M. *Fact, Fiction and National Security.* New York: Macfadden-Bartell, 1964. 128 pp.

_____. "To Forge a Strategy for Survival." *Public Administration Review,* Summer 1959, pp. 157-63.

Jordan, Col. Amos A., Jr., ed. *Issues of National Security in the 1970's.* New York: Frederick A. Praeger, 1967. 336 pp.

Kahn, Herman. *On Escalation: Metaphors and Scenarios.* New York: Frederick A. Praeger, 1965. 208 pp.

Kaufmann, William W., ed. *Military Policy and National Security.* Princeton, N.J.: Princeton University Press, 1956. 274 pp.

Kecskemeti, Paul. *Strategic Surrender: The Politics of Victory and Defeat.* Stanford, Calif.: Stanford University Press, 1958.

King, James E., Jr. "Nuclear Weapons and Foreign Policy." *New Republic,* 1 July 1957, pp. 18-21; 15 July 1957, pp. 16-18.

King-Hall, Stephen. *Defense in the Nuclear Age.* London: Victor Gollancz, 1958.

Kingston-McCloughry, Air Vice-Marshall E. J. *Defense: Policy and Strategy.* New York: Frederick A. Praeger, 1960.

_____. *The Spectrum of Strategy: A Study of Policy and Strategy in Modern War.* London: Jonathan Cape, 1964. 223 pp.

Kintner, William R. *Peace and the Strategy Conflict.*

New York: Frederick A. Praeger, 1967.

Kintner, William R. *The Politicalization of Strategy in National Security: Political, Military, and Economic Strategies in the Decade Ahead.* New York: Frederick A. Praeger, 1963.

Kissinger, Henry A. "American Policy and Preventing War." *Yale Review* 44 (1955):321-39.

_____. "American Strategic Doctrine and Diplomacy." In *The Theory and Practice of War: Essays Presented to Captain B. H. Liddell Hart,* ed. Michael Howard, pp. 271-92. London: Cassell, 1965.

_____. "Force and Diplomacy in the Nuclear Age." *Foreign Affairs* 34 (1956):349-66.

_____. *The Necessity for Choice: Prospects of American Foreign Policy.* New York: Harper & Row, 1961. 370 pp.

_____. *Nuclear Weapons and Foreign Policy.* New York: Harper for the Council on Foreign Relations, 1957. 455 pp.

Knorr, Klaus. "American Security and World Security." *Fifteen Nations,* April 1960, pp. 6-15.

_____. *Military Power and Potential.* Lexington, Mass.: D. C. Heath, 1970.

_____. *On the Uses of Military Power in the Nuclear Age.* Princeton, N.J.: Princeton University Press, 1966. 185 pp.

Lasswell, Harold D. "Political Factors in the Formulating of Strategy." *Naval War College Review,* June 1952, pp. 49-64.

_____. "Political Factors in the Foundation of

National Strategy." *Naval War College Review,*
March 1954, pp. 19-38.

Lerner, Max. *The Age of Overkill: A Preface to
World Politics.* New York: Simon & Schuster, 1962.
329 pp.

Levine, Robert A. *The Arms Debate.* Cambridge, Mass.:
Harvard University Press, 1963. 347 pp.

Liddell Hart, B. H. *Defense of the West.* New York:
William Morrow, 1950.

_____. *Deterrent or Defense: A Fresh Look at the
West's Military Position.* New York: Frederick A.
Praeger, 1960. 267 pp.

_____. "The Objective in War." *Naval War College
Review,* December 1952, pp. 1-30.

_____. *The Revolution in Warfare.* New Haven: Yale
University Press, 1947.

_____. *Strategy.* New York: Frederick A. Praeger,
1954. 424 pp.

Lincoln, George A. "The Nature of War." *Naval War
College Review,* October 1954, pp. 1-20.

Lincoln, George A., and Jordan, Amos A., Jr. "Technology and the Changing Nature of General War."
Military Review, May 1957, pp. 3-13.

Mao Tse-tung. *Selected Military Writings.* Peking:
Foreign Language Press, 1963.

Matloff, Maurice. "The Evolution of Strategic
Thought." *National War College Forum,* Spring 1971,
pp. 69-81.

Miller, Raphael. "The Metaphysical World of Strategic

Systems." *Bulletin of the Atomic Scientists,* December 1968, pp. 18-22.

Morgenstern, Oskar. *The Question of National Defense.* 2d rev. ed. New York: Random House, 1961. 306 pp.

Mrazek, Col. James. *The Art of Winning Wars.* New York: Walker, 1968. 193 pp.

Nitze, Paul H. *Political Aspects of a National Strategy.* Washington, D.C.: Washington Center for Foreign Policy Research, 1960.

O'Brien, William V. *War and/or Survival.* Garden City, N.Y.: Doubleday, 1969. 289 pp.

O'Connor, Raymond G. "Current Concepts and Philosophy of Warfare." *Naval War College Review,* January 1968.

Osgood, Charles E. *An Alternative to War or Surrender.* Chicago: University of Chicago Press, 1962. 183 pp.

_____. "Questioning Some Unquestioned Assumptions about National Security." *Social Problems* 11 (1963):6-12.

Osgood, Robert E. "Stabilizing the Military Environment." *American Political Science Review* 55 (1961):24-39.

Pace, Frank. "American Strategy: Goals and Tactics." *Naval War College Review,* December 1954, pp. 21-38.

Palit, Maj. Gen. D. K. *War in the Deterrent Age.* Cranbur, N.J.: A. A. Barnes, 1969. 224 pp.

Parson, Nels A., Jr. *Missiles and the Revolution in Warfare.* Cambridge, Mass.: Harvard University Press, 1962. 245 pp.

Payne, James L. *The American Threat: The Fear of War as an Instrument of Foreign Policy.* Chicago: Markham, 1970. 241 pp.

Perkins, Dexter. "Political Factors in National Strategy." *Naval War College Review,* January 1955, pp. 1-22.

Posvar, Col. Wesley W. "National Security Policy: The Realm of Obscurity." *Orbis* 9 (1965):694-713.

Power, Gen. Thomas S. *Design for Survival.* New York: Coward-McCann, 1965. 255 pp.

Powers, Lt. Col. Patrick W. *A Guide to National Defense.* New York: Frederick A. Praeger, 1964. 326 pp.

Reinhardt, George C. *American Strategy in the Atomic Age.* Norman: University of Oklahoma Press, 1955.

Roberts, Adam, ed. *Civilian Resistance as National Defense.* Harrisburg, Pa.: Stackpole, 1968. 320 pp.

Rosinski, Herbert. *The Evolution of the Conduct of War and of Strategic Thinking.* Newport, R.I.: Naval War College, 1955.

Schelling, Thomas C. *Arms and Influence.* New Haven: Yale University Press, 1966. 293 pp.

_____. *The Strategy of Conflict.* Cambridge, Mass.: Harvard University Press, 1960. 309 pp.

Schelling, Thomas C., and Halperin, Morton H. *Strategy and Arms Control.* New York: Twentieth Century Fund, 1961. 148 pp.

Sharp, Gene. "The Political Equivalent of War--Civilian Defense." *International Conciliation,* November 1965, entire issue.

Shulman, Marshall D. "What Does Security Mean Today?" *Foreign Affairs* 49 (1971):607-18.

Sokolovskii, Marshal V. D., ed. *Soviet Military Strategy*. Santa Monica, Calif.: RAND Corporation, 1963.

Stewart, Charles T., Jr. "Time as a Concept in Military Strategy." *Military Review*, April 1959, pp. 3-15.

Strachey, John. *On the Prevention of War*. New York: St. Martin's Press, 1963. 334 pp.

Strausz-Hupé, Robert, *et al*. *Protracted Conflict*. New York: Harper & Row, 1963.

Strausz-Hupé, Robert, and Kintner, William R. "A Forward Strategy Beyond Survival." *Orbis* 4 (1960): 141-58.

Strother, Lydia, and Strother, Claude L. *Prepare for Armageddon: Survival in the Nuclear Age*. Cardiff-by-the-Sea, Calif.: Lee Press, 1969. 276 pp.

Taylor, Gen. Maxwell D. *Responsibility and Response*. New York: Harper & Row, 1967. 84 pp.

_____. *The Uncertain Trumpet*. New York: Harper & Bros., 1960.

Teller, Edward. "Alternatives for Security." *Foreign Affairs* 36 (1958):201-08.

Ten Eyck, John C. *The Law of Diminishing War Power: From Troy to Vietnam*. New York: Pageant Press International, 1970. 273 pp.

Turner, Gordon B. "Diplomatic Aspects of Unbalanced Military Force." *Naval War College Review*, December 1957, pp. 33-56.

Turner, Gordon B., and Challener, Richard D., eds. *National Security in the Nuclear Age: Basic Facts and Theories*. New York: Frederick A. Praeger, 1960. 303 pp.

U.S. Congress, House Committee on Foreign Affairs. 91st Cong., 1st Sess. *Strategy and Science: Toward a National Security Policy for the 1970's. Hearings* . . . . Washington, D.C.: Government Printing Office, 1969. 283 pp.

U.S. Congress, Senate Committee on Foreign Relations. 86th Cong., 1st Sess. *Developments in Military Technology and Their Impact on United States Strategy and Foreign Policy*. Prepared by Arnold Wolfers, *et al*. Study no. 8 prepared by the Washington Center of Foreign Policy Research. Washington, D.C.: Government Printing Office, 1959.

U.S. Library of Congress, Legislative Reference Section. *Armaments Policy in the Postwar World*. Public Affairs Bulletin, no. 34. Washington, D.C.: Government Printing Office, 1945.

Walkowicz, T. F. "Strategic Concepts for the Nuclear Age." *Annals of the American Academy of Political and Social Science*, May 1955, pp. 118–27.

Waskow, Arthur I. *The Limits of Defense*. Garden City, N.Y.: Doubleday, 1962.

Whaley, Barton. *Stratagem: Deception and Surprise in War*. Cambridge, Mass.: M.I.T. Center for International Studies, 1969.

Wolfe, Thomas W. *Soviet Strategy at the Crossroads*. Cambridge, Mass.: Harvard University Press, 1964. 342 pp.

_____. *Trends in Soviet Thinking on Theatre Warfare, Conventional Operations, and Limited War*. RAND

Memorandum RM–4305–PR. Santa Monica, Calif.:   RAND
    Corporation, 1964.

Wolfers, Arnold. *Discord and Collaboration: Essays
    on International Politics*. Baltimore: Johns Hop-
    kins Press, 1962.

Wriston, Henry M. "The Validity of Limited Objec-
    tives." *Naval War College Review*, November 1951,
    pp. 1-32.

Wylie, Rear Adm. J. C. *Military Strategy: A General
    Theory of Power Control*. New Brunswick, N.J.:
    Rutgers University Press, 1967. 111 pp.

Wyman, Gen. Willard G. "The United States Army: Its
    Doctrine and Influence on U.S. Military Strategy."
    Military Review, March 1958, pp. 3-13.

Zuckerman, Sir Solly. "Judgment and Control in Modern
    Warfare." *Foreign Affairs* 40 (1962):196-212.

2. Land Power

"Army Requirements for Strategic Mobility." *Army In-
    formation Digest*, June 1958, pp. 31-40.

Baldwin, Hanson W. "Land Power as an Element of Na-
    tional Power." *Army Combat Forces Journal*, January
    1956, pp. 16-21.

Gleason, Lt. Col. F. A. "Unconventional Forces—The
    Commander's Untapped Resources." *Military Review*,
    October 1959, pp. 25-33.

Ortner, E. H. "U.S. Special Forces—The Faceless Ar-
    my." *Popular Science*, August 1961, pp. 56ff.

Page, Thornton. "National Policy and the Army." *Ar-
    my*, June 1956, pp. 30-33.

"Peace or P-i-e-c-e-m-e-a-l? A Special Issue on the Army's Role in Limited War." *Army Information Digest,* June 1958.

Pezzelle, R. M. "Special Forces." *Infantry,* April-June 1959.

Taylor, Gen. Maxwell D. "The Army in the Atomic Age." *Quartermaster Review,* January-February 1956.

Yale, Wesley W.; White, I. D.; and von Manteuffel, Hasso E. *Alternative to Armageddon: The Peace Potential of Lightning War.* New Brunswick, N.J.: Rutgers University Press, 1970.

3. Air Power

Brodie, Bernard. "Some Notes on the Evolution of Air Doctrine." *World Politics* 7 (1955):349-70.

_____. "Strategic Bombing: What It Can Do." *Reporter,* 15 August 1950, pp. 28-31.

Brown, Grover C. "Concepts and Nature of Air Warfare." *Naval War College Review,* November 1953, pp. 25-45.

Brown, Harold. "Air Power in Limited War." *Air University Review,* May-June 1969, pp. 2-15.

De Seversky, Alexander P. *Air Power: Key to Survival.* New York: Simon & Schuster, 1950.

Emme, Eugene M., ed. *The Impact of Air Power: National Security and World Politics.* Princeton, N.J.: Van Nostrand Reinhold, 1959. 914 pp.

Erwin, W. H. Bruce. *Air Power, Political Realities, and the Cold War.* Air War College Study, no. 9. Maxwell Air Force Base, Ala.: Air University, 1956. 94 pp.

Finletter, Thomas K. "New Look at Air Policy." *At-lantic*, September 1953, pp. 25-30.

Lee, Asher. *Air Power*. New York: Frederick A. Prae-ger, 1958.

Martin, Col. Donald F. "View on Aerospace Power." *Air University Review*, March-April 1968, pp. 30-39.

Saundby, Air Marshall Sir Robert. "Air Power in Lim-ited Wars." *Royal United Service Institution Journal*, August 1958, pp. 378-87.

Sleeper, Raymond S. "Air Power, Cold War, and Peace." *Air University Quarterly Review*, Winter 1951-52, pp. 3-18.

Slessor, Marshal Sir John. "Air Power and World Strategy." *Foreign Affairs* 33 (1954):43-53.

Strausz-Hupé, Robert, and Possony, Stefan T., eds. "Air Power and National Security." *Annals of the American Academy of Political and Social Sciences*, May 1955, pp. 1-140.

Tarr, Curtis W. "The Air Force as a National Re-source." *Air University Review*, May-June 1970, pp. 32-40.

U.S. Congress, Senate Committee on Armed Services. 84th Cong., 2d Sess. *Airpower. Hearings* . . . . 2 vols. Washington, D.C.: Government Printing Of-fice, 1956.

———. 85th Cong., 1st Sess. *Airpower. Report* . . . . Washington, D.C.: Government Printing Of-fice, 1957. 128 pp.

U.S. Congress, Senate Committee on Armed Services, Subcommittee on the Air Force. 84th Cong., 2d Sess. *Study of Airpower, Hearings* . . . . 23 pts.

Washington, D.C.: Government Printing Office, 1956.

U.S. Department of the Air Force, Air University, Documentary Research Division. *Readings on the Functions of Military Air Power.* Maxwell Air Force Base, Ala., 1957.

Verrier, Anthony. "Strategic Bombing—The Lessons of World War II and the American Experience in Vietnam." *Royal United Service Institution Journal,* May 1967, pp. 157-61.

Wilson, Eugene E. *Air Power for Peace.* New York: McGraw-Hill, 1945. 184 pp.

4. Sea Power

Amme, Carl H., Jr. "Perspectives on Naval Strategy." *U.S. Naval Institute Proceedings,* May 1969, pp. 12-24.

Austin, Bernard L. "Naval Strategy." *Naval War College Review,* January-February 1962, pp. 22-45.

Brodie, Bernard. *A Guide to Naval Strategy.* 5th ed. New York: Frederick A. Praeger, 1965.

Burke, Adm. Arleigh A. "The U.S. Navy's Role in General War and Conflict Short of General War." *Naval War College Review,* April 1959, pp. 1-12.

Cable, James. *Gunboat Diplomacy: Political Applications of Limited Naval Force.* New York: Frederick A. Praeger, 1971. 251 pp.

Carney, Adm. Robert B. "Principles of Sea Power." *U.S. Naval Institute Proceedings,* September 1955, pp. 967-86.

_____. "Role of the Navy in a Future War." *Naval*

War College Review, June 1954, pp. 1-14.

Cohen, Paul. "The Erosion of Surface Naval Power." *Foreign Affairs* 49 (1971):330-41.

Craven, John P. "Sea Power and the Seabed." *U.S. Naval Institute Proceedings,* April 1966, pp. 36-51.

Eliot, George Fielding. "Sea Power and Current U.S. Military Strategy." *Naval War College Review,* April 1961, pp. 1-14.

Field, James A., Jr. "The Influence of Sea Power on Modern Strategy." *Naval War College Review,* September 1957, pp. 31-53.

_____. "Origins of Maritime Strategy and the Development of Sea Power." *Naval War College Review,* March 1955, pp. 1-24.

_____. "Seapower and Military Strategy Today." *Naval War College Review,* April 1956, pp. 21-40.

Georgetown University Center for Strategic and International Studies. *Soviet Sea Power.* Special Report Series, no. 10. Washington, D.C., 1969. 131 pp.

Gretton, Vice-Adm. Sir Peter. *Maritime Strategy: A Study of Defense Problems.* New York: Frederick A. Praeger, 1965. 210 pp.

Herrick, Comdr. Robert Waring. *Soviet Naval Strategy.* Annapolis: U.S. Naval Institute, 1968. 157 pp.

Hezlet, Vice-Adm. Sir Arthur. *Aircraft and Sea Power.* New York: Stein & Day, 1970. 370 pp.

Howe, Jonathan Trumbull. *Multicrises: Sea Power and Global Politics in the Missile Age.* Cambridge, Mass.: M.I.T. Press, 1971. 412 pp.

James, Harry R. "An Analysis of Limited Maritime
    War." *Naval War College Review*, February 1967, pp.
    33-75.

Larkin, James R. "Modern Technology and Sea Power."
    Naval War College Review, May 1963, pp. 19-36.

McInteer, James F., Jr. "The Significance of Seapower
    to the United States." *Naval War College Review*,
    September 1959, pp. 1-33.

Martin, L. W. *The Sea in Modern Strategy*. New York:
    Frederick A. Praeger, 1967.

Mitchell, Donald W. "The Soviet Naval Challenge."
    Orbis 14 (1970):129-53.

Phelan, George R. "Sea Power and Strategies for the
    Control of the Seas." *Naval War College Review*,
    June 1954, pp. 15-37.

Sokol, Anthony E. *Seapower in the Nuclear Age*. Wash-
    ington, D.C.: Public Affairs Press, 1961.

Williams, Comdr. Ralph E. "Task for Today: Security
    through Seapower." *U.S. Naval Institute Proceed-
    ings*, March 1958, pp. 23-35.

Wright, Quincy. *Prevention of the Expansion of Lim-
    ited Wars and Preservation of International Order
    with Special Reference to the Role of Seaborne
    Weapons Systems*. NOTS TP 2668. China Lake,
    Calif.: U.S. Naval Ordnance Test Station, 1961.

B. NUCLEAR WEAPONS, DETERRENCE, AND GENERAL WAR

Afheldt, Horst, and Sonntag, Philipp. *Stability and
    Strategic Nuclear Arms*. New York: World Law Fund,
    1971. 65 pp.

Amster, Warren. "Design for Deterrence." *Bulletin of the Atomic Scientists,* May 1956, pp. 164-65.

Archibald, Kathleen, ed. *Strategic Interaction and Conflict.* Berkeley: University of California Press, 1966. 227 pp.

Aron, Raymond. *The Great Debate: Theories of Nuclear Strategy.* Translated by Ernst Pawel. New York: Doubleday, 1965.

_____. *On War: Atomic Weapons and Global Diplomacy.* Translated by Terence Kilmartin. Garden City, N.Y.: Doubleday, 1959.

Aron, Raymond; Knorr, Klaus; and Buchan, Alastair. "The Future of Western Deterrent Power." *Bulletin of the Atomic Scientists* 16 (1960):266-82.

Aronow, Saul, *et al. The Fallen Sky: Medical Consequences of Thermonuclear War.* New York: Hill & Wang, 1963. 134 pp.

_____. "The Medical Consequences of Nuclear War." *New England Journal of Medicine* 266 (1962):1126-58.

Backus, P. H. "Finite Deterrence, Controlled Retaliation." *U.S. Naval Institute Proceedings,* March 1959, pp. 22-29.

Bader, William B. *The United States and the Spread of Nuclear Weapons.* New York: Pegasus, 1968. 176 pp.

Beaton, Leonard. "Implications of the Non-Proliferation Treaty on Deterrence and the Prospects for Disarmament." *Royal United Service Institution Journal,* June 1969, pp. 34-39.

_____. *Must the Bomb Spread?* London: Penguin Books, 1966.

Beaton, Leonard, and Maddox, John. *The Spread of Nuclear Weapons*. Studies in International Security, no. 5. New York: Frederick A. Praeger, 1962. 216 pp.

Beaufre, Gen. André. *Deterrence and Strategy*. Translated by Maj. Gen. R. H. Barry. New York: Frederick A. Praeger, 1966. 174 pp.

Bendix Corporation Aerospace Systems Division. *Problems of U.S. Defense Policy in a World of Nuclear Proliferation*. 2 vols. Ann Arbor, Mich., 1966.

Blackett, P. M. S. *Atomic Weapons and East-West Relations*. Cambridge: Cambridge University Press, 1956. 107 pp.

_____. *Fear, War and the Bomb: Military and Political Consequences of Atomic Energy*. New York: Whittlesey House, 1949. 244 pp.

_____. "Nuclear Weapons and Defense: Comments on Kissinger, Kennan and King-Hall." *International Affairs* 34 (1958):421-34.

Bothwell, Frank E. "Deterrence and Counterforce." In *Short Essays on National Defense*. Chicago: University of Chicago Laboratories for Applied Sciences, 1961.

Bretscher, Willy. "The Case for Conventional Armaments." *Orbis* 1 (1958):235-47.

Brodie, Bernard, ed. *The Absolute Weapon: Atomic Power and World Order*. New York: Harcourt, Brace, 1946. 214 pp.

_____. "The Anatomy of Deterrence." *World Politics* 11 (1959):173-92.

_____. *The Atomic Bomb and American Security*. Memorandum, no. 18. New Haven: Yale University

Institute of International Studies, 1945.   28 pp.

Brodie, Bernard. *Implications of Nuclear Weapons in Total War*. RAND Memorandum RM-1842. Santa Monica, Calif.: RAND Corporation, 1957.

_____. "Influence of Mass Destruction Weapons on Strategy." *Naval War College Review*, June 1956, pp. 27-44.

_____. *Nuclear Weapons and Changing Strategic Outlooks*. RAND Paper P-811. Santa Monica, Calif.: RAND Corporation, 1956.

_____. "Nuclear Weapons: Strategic or Tactical?" *Foreign Affairs* 32 (1954):217-29.

Brodie, Bernard, and Galloway, Eilene. *The Atomic Bomb and the Armed Services*. Public Affairs Bulletin, no. 55. Washington, D.C.: Government Printing Office, 1947.   177 pp.

Brody, Richard A. "Some Systemic Effects of the Spread of Nuclear Weapons Technology: A Study through Simulation of a Multi-nuclear Future." *Journal of Conflict Resolution* 7 (1963):663-753.

Brown, Harold. "Strategic Weapons: Security Through Limitations." *Foreign Affairs* 47 (1969):422-32.

Brown, Neville. *Nuclear War: The Impending Strategic Deadlock*. New York: Frederick A. Praeger, 1964.   238 pp.

Bryerton, Gene. *Nuclear Dilemma*. New York: Ballantine Books, 1970.

Bull, Hedley. *The Control of the Arms Race. Disarmament and Arms Control in the Missile Age*. Rev. ed. New York: Frederick A. Praeger, 1965.

Burns, Arthur Lee. *Ethics and Deterrence: A Nuclear*

Balance Without Hostage Cities? Adelphi Papers, no. 69. London: Institute for Strategic Studies, 1970.

Burns, Arthur Lee. "From Balance to Deterrence: A Theoretical Analysis." *World Politics* 9 (1957): 494-529.

_____. *The Rationale of Catalytic War.* Research Memo, no. 3. Princeton, N.J.: Princeton University Center of International Studies, 1959.

_____. *Two Essays on Deterrence.* Tempo RM-60-TMP-86. Santa Barbara, Calif.: General Electric, 1960.

Buzzard, Rear Adm. Sir Anthony W. "Massive Retaliation and Graduated Deterrence." *World Politics* 8 (1956):228-37.

Buzzard, Rear Adm. Sir Anthony W., *et al.* "The H-Bomb: Massive Retaliation or Graduated Deterrence?" *International Affairs,* April 1956, pp. 148-65.

_____. *On Limiting Atomic War.* London: Royal Institute of International Affairs, 1956. 46 pp.

_____. "On Limiting Atomic War." *Bulletin of the Atomic Scientists* 13 (1957):216-22.

Church, A. T., Jr. "Deterrence and Delusion." *Orbis* 3 (1959):141-53.

Coffey, Joseph I. *Strategic Power and National Security.* Pittsburgh: University of Pittsburgh Press, 1971. 214 pp.

_____. *Strategy, Strategic Forces and Arms Control.* Ann Arbor, Mich.: Bendix Systems Division, 1964.

Cottrell, Alvin J., and Dougherty, James E. "Nuclear

Weapons, Policy, and Strategy." *Orbis* 1 (1957): 138-60.

Cummins, David E., *et al*. *Accidental War: Some Dangers in the 1960's*. Columbus: Ohio State University Press, 1960. 19 pp.

Dahr, S. N. *Atomic Weapons in World Politics*. Calcutta: Das Gupta, 1957.

Dulles, John Foster. "Policy for Security and Peace." *Foreign Affairs* 32 (1954):353-64.

Enthoven, Alain. "American Deterrent Policy." *Survival*, May-June 1963, pp. 94-101.

Fergus, Martin C. "The Massive Retaliation Doctrine: A Study in United States Military Policy Formation." *Public Policy* 17 (1968):231-57.

Ferguson, Allen R. *Disarmament and Deterrence*. RAND Paper P-2553. Santa Monica, Calif.: RAND Corporation, 1962.

Fink, Clinton F. "More Calculations about Deterrence." *Journal of Conflict Resolution* 9 (1965): 54-65.

Fink, Daniel J. "Strategic Warfare." *Science and Technology*, October 1968, pp. 54-68.

Foye, Raymond, and Phelps, John B. *Counterforce Calculations: Attack and Retaliation with Mixed Weapons Systems*. Mershon Research Paper, no. 2. Columbus: Mershon National Security Program, Ohio State University, 1959.

Gallois, Pierre. *The Balance of Terror: Strategy for the Nuclear Age*. Boston: Houghton Mifflin, 1961. 234 pp.

Green, Philip. *Deadly Logic: The Theory of Nuclear*

Deterrence. Columbus: Ohio State University
Press, 1966. 361 pp.

Hadley, Arthur T. "Low-Yield Atomic Weapons: A New
Military Dimension." *Reporter,* 19 April 1956, pp.
23-25.

Hall, John A. "Atoms for Peace, or War." *Foreign Affairs* 43 (1965):602-15.

Halperin, Morton H. *Deterrence and Local War.* China
Lake, Calif.: U.S. Naval Ordnance Test Station,
1963.

_____. *Nuclear Weapons and Limited War.* Cambridge,
Mass.: Harvard University Center for International
Affairs, 1960.

Harkabi, Y. *Nuclear War and Nuclear Peace.* Jerusa-
lem: Israel Program for Scientific Translations,
1966.

Hughes, H. Stuart. "The Strategy of Deterrence: A
Dissenting Statement." *Commentary,* March 1961, pp.
185-92; July 1961, pp. 64-65, 67.

Huntington, Samuel P. "Arms Races: Prerequisites and
Results." *Public Policy* 8 (1958):41-86.

International Institute for Strategic Studies.
*Soviet-American Relations and World Order: Arms
Limitations and Policy.* Adelphi Papers, no. 65.
London, 1970.

Intriligator, Michael D. "The Debate over Missile
Strategy: Targets and Rates of Fire." *Orbis* 11
(1968):1138-59.

Kahn, Herman. "Can the Nuclear Deterrent Still Pro-
tect the Western World?" *Fifteen Nations,* June
1961, pp. 38-41.

Kahn, Herman. *The Nature and Feasibility of War and Deterrence*. RAND Paper P-1888. Santa Monica, Calif.: RAND Corporation, 1960.

_____. *On Thermonuclear War*. Princeton, N.J.: Princeton University Press, 1960.

_____. *Thinking about the Unthinkable*. New York: Horizon Press, 1962. 254 pp.

Kaplan, Morton A. "The Calculus of Nuclear Deterrence." *World Politics* 11 (1958):20-43.

_____. *The Strategy of Limited Retaliation*. Policy Memo, no. 19. Princeton, N.J.: Princeton University Center of International Studies, 1959.

Karber, Phillip A. "Nuclear Weapons and 'Flexible Response.'" *Orbis* 14 (1970):284-97.

Kaufmann, William W. *The Requirements of Deterrence*. Memorandum no. 7. Princeton, N.J.: Princeton University Center of International Studies, 1954. 23 pp.

Kaysen, Carl. "Keeping the Strategic Balance." *Foreign Affairs* 46 (1968):665-75.

_____. "The Vulnerability of the U.S. to Atomic Attack." *World Politics* 6 (1954):190-208.

King, James E., Jr. "Nuclear Plenty and Limited War." *Foreign Affairs* 35 (1957):238-56.

Kintner, William R. "A Reappraisal of the Proposed Nonproliferation Treaty." *Orbis* 10 (1966):138-51.

Kissinger, Henry A. "Arms Control, Inspection and Surprise Attack." *Foreign Affairs* 38 (1960):557-75.

Knorr, Klaus. "Nuclear Weapons: 'Haves' and

'Have-Nots.'" *Foreign Affairs* 36 (1957):167-78.

Knorr, Klaus, and Read, Thornton, eds. *Limited Strategic War. Essays on Nuclear Strategy.* New York: Frederick A. Praeger, 1962.

Kolkowicz, Roman, *et al. The Soviet Union and Arms Control: A Superpower Dilemma.* Baltimore: Johns Hopkins Press, 1970.

Kuzmack, Arnold M. "Technological Change and Stable Deterrence." *Journal of Conflict Resolution* 9 (1965):304-17.

Lang, Daniel. *An Inquiry into Enoughness of Bombs and Men and Staying Alive.* New York: McGraw-Hill, 1965.

Lapp, Ralph E. *Arms Beyond Doubt.* New York: Cowles, 1969.

_____. "Fear of a First-Strike." *New Republic,* 28 June 1969, pp. 21-24.

_____. *Kill and Overkill: The Strategy of Annihilation.* New York: Basic Books, 1962. 179 pp.

LeGhait, Edward. *No Carte Blanche to Capricorn: The Folly of Nuclear War Strategy.* New York: Bookfield House, 1960. 115 pp.

Leghorn, Richard S. "No Need to Bomb Cities to Win War." *U.S. News and World Report,* 28 January 1955, pp. 79-94.

_____. "The Problem of Accidental War." *Bulletin of the Atomic Scientists* 14 (1958):205-9.

Liddell Hart, B. H. *Defense of the West.* New York: William Morrow, 1950.

_____. *Deterrent or Defense: A Fresh Look at the*

West's Military Position. New York: Frederick A. Praeger, 1960. 267 pp.

Lowe, George E. *The Age of Deterrence.* Boston: Little, Brown, 1964. 324 pp.

McClelland, Charles A., ed. *Nuclear Weapons, Missiles, and Future War: Problem for the Sixties.* San Francisco, Calif.: Chandler, 1960. 235 pp.

McGuire, Martin C. *Secrecy and the Arms Race. A Theory of the Accumulation of Strategic Weapons and How Secrecy Affects It.* Harvard Economic Studies, no. 125. Cambridge, Mass.: Harvard University Press, 1965. 256 pp.

McMahon, Brien E. "Atomic Weapons and Defense." *Bulletin of the Atomic Scientists* 7 (1951):297-301.

May, Michael M. "Some Advantage of a Counterforce Deterrence." *Orbis* 14 (1970):271-83.

Miksche, Ferdinand Otto. *The Failure of Atomic Strategy--And a New Proposal for the Defense of the West.* New York: Frederick A. Praeger, 1958.

_____. "The Nuclear Deterrent and Western Strategy." *Orbis* 8 (1964):221-37.

_____. *The Nuclear Impasse.* New York: Frederick A. Praeger, 1959.

Milburn, T. W. "What Constitutes Effective Deterrence?" *Journal of Conflict Resolution* 3 (1959): 138-45.

Moore, William C. "History, Vietnam, and the Concept of Deterrence." *Air University Review,* September-October 1969, pp. 58-63.

Morgenstern, Oskar. "Nuclear Stalemates? Some

Comments on P. M. S. Blackett." *Encounter,* June 1961, pp. 70-71.

Morgenthau, Hans J. "The Four Paradoxes of Nuclear Strategy." *American Political Science Review* 58 (1964):23-35.

_____. "Has Atomic War Really Become Impossible?" *Bulletin of the Atomic Scientists* 12 (1956):7-9.

Morse, John H., and Van Cleave, W. R. *Problems Posed by Conflicting Views Concerning Nuclear Weapons.* Menlo Park, Calif.: Stanford Research Institute, 1965.

Moulton, Harland B. "The McNamara General War Strategy." *Orbis* 8 (1964):238-54.

Murray, Thomas E. *Nuclear Policy for War and Peace.* Cleveland, Ohio: World, 1960. 241 pp.

Nitze, Paul H. "Atoms, Strategy and Policy." *Foreign Affairs* 34 (1956):187-98.

Oppenheimer, J. Robert. "Atomic Weapons and American Policy." *Foreign Affairs* 31 (1953):525-35.

_____. "Comments on the Military Value of the Atom." *Bulletin of the Atomic Scientists* 7 (1951):43-45.

Osgood, Robert E. "Concepts of General and Limited War." *Naval War College Review,* December 1959, pp. 1-18.

Panofsky, W. K. H. "Roots of the Strategic Arms Race: Ambiguity and Ignorance." *Bulletin of the Atomic Scientists,* June 1971, pp. 15-20.

Peeters, Paul. *Massive Retaliation: The Policy and Its Critics.* Chicago: Henry A. Regnery, 1959.

Phelps, John B.; Foye, Raymond; and Howland, Daniel.

Some Calculations on Counterforce Strategies in a General Nuclear War. Columbus: Mershon National Security Program, Ohio State University, 1959.

Pitman, George R., Jr. *Arms Races and Stable Deterrence.* Los Angeles: University of California Security Studies Project, 1969.

Plate, Thomas G. *Understanding Doomsday: A Guide to the Arms Race for Hawks, Doves and People.* New York: Simon & Schuster, 1970.

Rabinowitch, Eugene. "Editorial: Atomic Weapons and the Korean War." *Bulletin of the Atomic Scientists* 6 (1950):194, 217.

Rapoport, Anatol. *Strategy and Conscience.* New York: Harper & Row, 1964.

Raser, John R. "Deterrence Research: Past Progress and Future Needs." *Journal of Peace Research* 4 (1966):297-327.

Raymond, Jack. "The Influence of Nuclear Weapons on National Strategy and Policy." *Naval War College Review,* April 1967, pp. 55-74.

Reinhardt, George C. *Guerrilla-Combat, Strategy, and Deterrence in Asia.* RAND Report P-2706. Santa Monica, Calif.: RAND Corporation, 1963.

_____. "Notes on the Tactical Employment of Atomic Weapons." *Military Review,* September 1952, pp. 28-37.

_____. *Nuclear Weapons and Limited Warfare: A Sketchbook History.* RAND Report P-3011. Santa Monica, Calif.: RAND Corporation, 1964. 13 pp.

Reinhardt, Col. George C., and Lt. Col. Kintner, William R. *Atomic Weapons in Land Combat.*

Harrisburg, Pa.: Military Service Publishing Company, 1954.

Reinhardt, Col. George C., and Lt. Col. Kintner, William R. "The Tactical Side of Atomic Warfare." *Bulletin of the Atomic Scientists* 11 (1955):53–58.

Research Analysis Corporation. *Optimal Allocation of Missiles Against Area and Point Defenses*. McLean, Va., 1969.

Riukin, Steven R. *The Hobbled Weapon: Second-Strike-Only Force*. Boston: M.I.T. Center for International Studies, 1961.

Rosecrance, R. N., ed. *The Dispersion of Nuclear Weapons: Strategy and Politics*. New York: Columbia University Press, 1964.

Rosow, S. M., and Phelps, John B. *Measures of Destruction: Some Observations on Damage Levels in a General Nuclear War*. Mershon Research Paper, no. 3. Columbus: Mershon National Security Program, Ohio State University, 1959.

Schelling, Thomas C. "Deterrence: Military Diplomacy in the Nuclear Age." *Virginia Quarterly Review* 39 (1963):531–47.

_____. "Dispersal, Deterrence, and Damage." *Operations Research*, May–June 1961, pp. 363–70.

_____. *Nuclear Weapons and Limited War*. RAND Report P-1620. Santa Monica, Calif.: RAND Corporation, 1959.

_____. *The Reciprocal Fear of Surprise Attack*. RAND Paper P-1342. Santa Monica, Calif.: RAND Corporation, 1958.

Scowcroft, Brent. "Deterrence and Strategic Superiority." *Orbis* 13 (1969):435–54.

Shils, E. A. *The Atomic Bomb in World Politics.*
Peace Aims Pamphlet, no. 45. London: National
Peace Council, 1948.

Singer, Joel David. *Deterrence, Arms Control, and
Disarmament: Toward a Synthesis in National Secu-
rity Policy.* Columbus: Ohio State University
Press, 1962. 279 pp.

_____, ed. *Weapons Management in World Politics.*
Proceedings of the International Arms Control Symposium. Ann Arbor, Michigan, 1963.

Slocombe, Walter. *The Political Implications of Strategic Parity.* Adelphi Papers, no. 77. London:
Institute for Strategic Studies, 1971.

Snyder, Glenn H. *Deterrence and Defense: Toward a
Theory of National Security.* Princeton, N.J.:
Princeton University Press, 1961. 294 pp.

_____. "Deterrence and Power." *Journal of Conflict
Resolution* 4 (1960):163-78.

_____. *Deterrence by Denial and Punishment.* Re-
search Monograph, no. 1. Princeton, N.J.: Princeton University Center of International Studies,
1959.

Spaight, J. M. "Limited War and Unlimited War." *Royal Air Force Quarterly,* January 1952, p. 608.

Strausz-Hupé, Robert. "Limits of Limited War." *Reporter,* 29 November 1957, pp. 30-34.

_____. "Nuclear Blackmail and Limited War." *Yale
Review* 28 (1959):177-81.

Szilard, Leo. "'Minimal Deterrent' vs. Saturation
Parity." *Bulletin of the Atomic Scientists,* March
1964, pp. 6-12.

Taynton, Lt. Col. Lewis C. "Impact of Atomic Weapons on Defense." *Military Review,* September 1956, pp. 49-57.

Toynbee, Philip, ed. *Fearful Choice: A Debate on Nuclear Policy.* Detroit: Wayne State University Press, 1959. 112 pp.

Tucker, Robert C. *Proposal for No First Use of Nuclear Weapons: Pros and Cons. Four Essays.* Policy Memorandum, no. 28. Princeton, N.J.: Princeton University Center of International Studies, 1963.

Turner, Gordon B. "The Influence of Modern Weapons on Strategy." *Naval War College Review,* March 1957, pp. 21-42.

U.S. Arms Control and Disarmament Agency. *Arms Control and Nation   Security.* Publication no. 49. Washington, D.C.: Government Printing Office, 1968.

Van Cleave, William R. "The Nuclear Weapons Debate." *U.S. Naval Institute Proceedings,* May 1966, pp. 26-38.

Watson, Mark S. *The U.S. and Armaments.* Headline Series, no. 143. New York: Foreign Policy Association World Affairs Center, 1960. 63 pp.

Willrich, Mason. "No First Use of Nuclear Weapons: An Assessment." *Orbis* 9 (1965):299-315.

Wohlstetter, Albert. "The Delicate Balance of Terror." *Foreign Affairs* 37 (1959):211-34.

Wolfers, Arnold. "Superiority in Nuclear Weapons: Advantages and Limitations." *Annals of the American Academy of Political and Social Science,* November 1953, pp. 7-15.

Woodward, Ernest Llewellyn. *Some Political*

Consequences of the Atomic Bomb. New York and London: Oxford University Press, 1946. 30 pp.

York, Herbert. *Race to Oblivion: A Participant's View of the Arms Race.* New York: Simon & Schuster, 1970.

C. LIMITED WAR, INCLUDING GUERRILLA WARFARE AND COUNTERINSURGENCY

Ahmad, Eqbal. "Revolutionary War and Counter Insurgency." *Journal of International Affairs,* March 1971, pp. 1-27.

Allison, Graham; May, Ernest; and Yarmolinsky, Adam. "U.S. Military Policy: Limits to Intervention." *Foreign Affairs* 48 (1970):245-61.

American University, Special Operations Research Office. *Casebook on Insurgency and Revolutionary Warfare: 23 Summary Accounts.* Prepared by Paul A. Jureidini, *et al.* Washington, D.C., 1962.

Aron, Raymond. "Can War in the Atomic Age Be Limited?" *Confluence,* July 1956, pp. 99-114.

_____. "A Half-Century of Limited War?" *Bulletin of the Atomic Scientists* 12 (1956):99-104.

Baldwin, Hanson W. "Limited War." *Atlantic,* May 1959, pp. 35-43.

Beavers, Cmdr. Roy. "A Doctrine for Limited War." *U.S. Naval Institute Proceedings,* October 1970, pp. 26-34.

Biorkland, Adm. Elis. "Countering Revolutionary Wars." *NATO's Fifteen Nations,* December-January 1965, pp. 40-47.

Bjelajac, Slavko N. "Principles of Counterinsurgency." *Orbis* 8 (1964):655-69.

_____. "Unconventional Warfare: American and Soviet Approaches." *Annals of the American Academy of Political and Social Science,* May 1962, pp. 74-81.

Bloomfield, Lincoln P. "Future Small Wars: Must the United States Intervene?" *Orbis* 12 (1968):669-84.

Bloomfield, Lincoln P., and Leiss, Amelia C. *Controlling Small Wars: A Strategy for the 1970's.* New York: Alfred A. Knopf, 1969. 421 pp.

Brennan, Donald G.; Strausz-Hupé, Robert; Wiesner, Jerome B.; and Yarmolinsky, Adam. "The Great Nuclear Debate: Parity vs. Superiority." *War-Peace Report,* October 1968, pp. 3-10.

Brodie, Bernard. *The Meaning of Limited War.* RAND Memorandum RM-2224. Santa Monica, Calif.: RAND Corporation, 1958.

_____. "More about Limited War." *World Politics* 10 (1957):112-22.

_____. "Unlimited Weapons and Limited War." *Reporter,* 15 November 1954, pp. 16-21.

Cagle, Comdr. Malcolm W. "Sea Power and Limited War." *U.S. Naval Institute Proceedings,* July 1958, pp. 23-27.

Cagle, Comdr. Malcolm W., and Manson, Comdr. Frank A. *The Sea War in Korea.* Annapolis, Md.: U.S. Naval Institute, 1957.

Campbell, Arthur. *Guerrillas: A History and Analysis.* New York: John Day, 1968. 344 pp.

Clutterbuck, Brig. Richard L. *The Long, Long War: Counterinsurgency in Malaya and Vietnam.* Foreword by Gen. Harold K. Johnson. New York: Frederick A. Praeger, 1966. 206 pp.

Condit, D. M. *Case Study in Guerrilla War: Greece during World War II.* Washington, D.C.: Special Operations Research Office, 1961.

Cottrell, Alvin J., and Dougherty, James E. "The Lessons of Korea: War and the Power of Man." *Orbis* 2 (1958):39–65.

Critchfield, Richard. *The Long Charade: Political Subversion in the Vietnam War.* New York: Harcourt, Brace & World, 1968. 401 pp.

Deitchman, Seymour J. "Limited War." *Military Review,* July 1971, pp. 3–16.

_____. *Limited War and American Defense Policy: Building and Using Military Power in a World at War.* 2d ed., rev. Cambridge, Mass.: M.I.T. Press, 1969. 302 pp.

DeWeerd, Harvey A. "Lessons of the Korean War." *Yale Review* 40 (1951):592–603.

Dupuy, Trevor M. "Can America Fight a Limited Nuclear War?" *Orbis* 5 (1961):31–42.

Durst, Jay B. "Limited Conventional War." *Military Review,* January 1970, pp. 56–63.

Eccles, Rear Adm. Henry E. "Suez 1956—Some Military Lessons." *Naval War College Review,* March 1969, pp. 28–56.

Fall, Bernard B. "The Theory and Practice of Insurgency and Counterinsurgency." *Naval War College Review,* April 1965, pp. 21–38.

Fisher, Thomas L. "'Limited War'—What Is It?" *Air*

University Quarterly Review, Winter 1957-58, pp. 127-42.

Galula, David. *Counterinsurgency Warfare: Theory and Practice.* New York: Frederick A. Praeger, 1965.

Gann, Lewis. *Guerrillas in History.* Stanford, Calif.: Hoover Institution, 1970.

Garthoff, Raymond L. "Unconventional Warfare in Communist Strategy." *Foreign Affairs* 40 (1962):566-75.

Geneste, Marc E. "Vietnam . . . A New Type of War?" *U.S. Naval Institute Proceedings,* May 1968, pp. 66-77.

Giap, Vo Nguyen. *People's War, People's Army.* New York: Frederick A. Praeger, 1962.

Glick, Edward Bernard. "Conflict, Civic Action and Counterinsurgency." *Orbis* 10 (1966):899-910.

_____. "Isolating the Guerrilla: Some Latin American Examples." *Orbis* 12 (1968):873-86.

Greene, Lt. Col. T. N., ed. *The Guerrilla--and How to Fight Him: Selections from the Marine Corps Gazette.* New York: Frederick A. Praeger, 1962.

Guevara, Che. *On Guerrilla Warfare.* New York: Frederick A. Praeger, 1961.

Halperin, Morton H. *Deterrence and Local War.* China Lake, Calif.: U.S. Naval Ordnance Test Station, 1963.

_____. *Limited War in the Nuclear Age.* New York: John Wiley, 1963. 191 pp.

_____. *Nuclear Weapons and Limited War.* Cambridge, Mass.: Center for International Affairs, 1960.

Hamlett, B. "Special Forces: Training for Peace and War." *Army Information Digest,* June 1961, pp. 2-9.

Hampton, Ephraim M. "Unlimited Confusion over Limited War." *Air University Quarterly Review,* Spring 1957, pp. 28-47.

Heilbrunn, Otto. *Conventional Warfare in the Nuclear Age.* New York: Frederick A. Praeger, 1965. 164 pp.

Higgins, Trumbull. *Korea and the Fall of MacArthur: A Précis in Limited War.* New York: Oxford University Press, 1960.

Hoag, Malcolm W. *On Local War Doctrine.* RAND Paper P-2433. Santa Monica, Calif.: RAND Corporation, 1961.

_____. *The Place of Limited War in NATO Strategy.* RAND Paper P-1566. Santa Monica, Calif.: RAND Corporation, 1958. 48 pp.

Huntington, Samuel P. *Instability at the Non-Strategic Level of Conflict.* Study Memorandum, no. 2. Washington, D.C.: Institute for Defense Analyses, Special Studies Group, 1961.

Janos, Andrew C. "Unconventional Warfare: A Framework and Analysis." *World Politics* 15 (1963):636-46.

Johnson, C. "The Third Generation of Guerrilla Warfare." *Asian Survey,* June 1968, pp. 435-47.

Jones, Adrian, *et al. Internal Defense against Insurgency: Six Cases.* Washington, D.C.: American University Special Operations Research Office, 1966.

Kahn, E. J., Jr. *The Peculiar War.* New York: Random House, 1952.

Kecskemeti, Paul. *Insurgency as a Strategic Problem.* RAND Report RM-5160-PR. Santa Monica, Calif.: RAND Corporation, 1967.

King, James E., Jr. "Nuclear Plenty and Limited War." *Foreign Affairs* 35 (1957):238-56.

Kinkead, Eugene. *In Every War But One.* New York: W. W. Norton, 1959.

Kissinger, Henry A. "Controls, Inspection and Limited War." *Reporter,* 13 June 1957, pp. 14-19.

_____. "Limited War: Conventional or Nuclear?--A Reappraisal." *Daedalus* 89 (1960):800-18.

_____. "Military Policy and Defense of the 'Grey Areas.'" *Foreign Affairs* 33 (1955):416-28.

Knorr, Klaus. "Unconventional Warfare." *Annals of the American Academy of Political and Social Science,* May 1962, pp. 53-64.

La Charite, Norman A. *Case Study in Insurgency and Revolutionary Warfare: Guatemala, 1944-54.* Washington, D.C.: American University Human Resources Research Office, 1964.

Lansdale, Maj. Gen. Edward G. "Viet Nam: Do We Understand Revolution?" *Foreign Affairs* 43 (1964): 75-86.

Larrabee, E. "Korea: The Military Lesson." *Harper's,* November 1950, pp. 51-57.

Leighton, Richard M., and Sanders, Ralph, eds. *Insurgency and Counterinsurgency: An Anthology.* Washington, D.C.: Industrial College of the Armed Forces, 1962.

Leites, Nathan, and Wolf, Charles, Jr. *Rebellion and*

*Authority: An Analytic Essay on Insurgent Con-
flicts.* Chicago: Markham, 1970.

Liddell Hart, B. H. "War, Limited." *Harper's,* March
1946, pp. 193-203.

Lindsay, Franklin A. "Unconventional Warfare." *Foreign Affairs* 40 (1962):264-74.

McClintock, Robert. *The Meaning of Limited War.* Boston: Houghton Mifflin, 1967. 239 pp.

MacCloskey, Munro. *Alert the Fifth Force: Counterinsurgency, Unconventional Warfare, and Psychological
Operations of the United States Air Force in Special Air Warfare.* New York: R. Rosen, 1969. 190
pp.

McCuen, John J. *The Art of Counter-Revolutionary War:
The Strategy of Counter-Insurgency.* Harrisburg,
Pa.: Stackpole, 1966.

Mao Tse-tung on Guerrilla Warfare. Translated by
S. B. Griffith. New York: Frederick A. Praeger,
1961.

Marshall, C. B. "Unconventional Warfare as a Concern
for American Foreign Policy." *Annals of the American Academy of Political and Social Science,* May
1962, pp. 93-101.

Methvin, Eugene H. "Ideology and Organization in
Counterinsurgency." *Orbis* 8 (1964):106-24.

Moore, William C. "History, Vietnam, and the Concept
of Deterrence." *Air University Review,* September-
October 1969, pp. 58-63.

Ney, Virgil. "Guerrilla War and Modern Strategy."
Orbis 2 (1958):66-82.

Ney, Virgil. *Notes on Guerrilla War.* Washington, D.C.: Command Publications, 1961.

Nickerson, Hoffman. "Limited War 1957." *Ordnance,* November–December 1957, pp. 428–30.

O'Brien, Conor C. "The Counterrevolutionary Reflex." *Columbia University Forum,* Spring 1966, pp. 21–24.

Oppenheimer, Martin. *The Urban Guerrilla.* Chicago: Quadrangle Books, 1969.

Orlov, Alexander. *Handbook of Intelligence and Guerrilla Warfare.* Ann Arbor: University of Michigan Press, 1963.

Osanka, Franklin M., ed. *Guerrilla Warfare Readings.* Washington, D.C.: George Washington University Human Resources Research Office, 1962. 196 pp.

_____, ed. *Modern Guerrilla Warfare.* New York: Free Press, 1960.

Osgood, Robert E. *Limited War: The Challenge to American Strategy.* Chicago: University of Chicago Press, 1957. 315 pp.

Paret, Peter. "Guerrilla Warfare and U.S. Military Policy: A Study." In *Components of Defense Policy,* edited by Davis B. Bobrow, pp. 259–71. Chicago: Rand McNally, 1965.

Paret, Peter, and Shy, John W. *Guerrillas in the 1960's.* New York: Frederick A. Praeger, 1962.

Pustay, Maj. John S. *Counter-insurgency Warfare.* New York: Free Press, 1965. 245 pp.

"Readiness for the Little War: Optimum 'Integrated Strategy.'" *Military Review,* April 1957, pp. 14–26.

Reid, William R. "Tactical Air in Limited War." *Air University Quarterly Review*, Spring 1956, pp. 40-48.

Reinhardt, George C. "Notes on the Tactical Employment of Atomic Weapons." *Military Review*, September 1952, pp. 28-37.

_____. *Nuclear Weapons and Limited Warfare: A Sketchbook History*. RAND Paper P-3011. Santa Monica, Calif.: RAND Corporation, 1964. 13 pp.

Robinson, Donald, ed. *The Dirty Wars: Guerrilla Actions and Other Forms of Unconventional Warfare*. New York: Delacorte Press, 1968. 356 pp.

Royal United Service Institution. *Lessons from the Vietnam War*. London, 1970.

_____. *Strategy in South-East Asia*. London, 1970.

Saundby, Air Marshal Sir Robert. "War--Limited or Unlimited?" *Air Power*, January 1955, pp. 100-102.

Schelling, Thomas C. *Nuclear Weapons and Limited War*. RAND Research Memorandum RM 2510. Santa Monica, Calif.: RAND Corporation, 1959.

Schwartz, David C. "Toward a New Knowledge-Base for Military Development Operations during Insurgencies." *Orbis* 12 (1968):73-86.

Scott, Andrew M., *et al*. *Insurgency*. Chapel Hill: University of North Carolina Press, 1970. 139 pp.

Somit, Albert. "Theory and Practice of Insurgency and Counterinsurgency." *Naval War College Review*, October 1962, pp. 44-56.

Spaight, J. M. "Limited War and Unlimited War." *Royal Air Force Quarterly*, January 1952, pp. 6-8.

Speier, Hans. *Revolutionary War.* RAND Paper P-3445. Santa Monica, Calif.: RAND Corporation, 1966. 23 pp.

Stilwell, Lt. Gen. R. G. "Evolution in Tactics: The Vietnam Experience." *Army,* February 1970, pp. 14-23.

Strausz-Hupé, Robert. "Nuclear Blackmail and Limited War." *Yale Review* 28 (1959):177-81.

Swenson, Mark E. [pseud.]. "Vietnam: Limited-War Strategy at a Dead End?" *Air Force and Space Digest,* April 1968, pp. 60-62.

Taber, Robert. *The War of the Flea.* New York: Citadel, 1965.

Tanham, George K. *Communist Revolutionary Warfare-- The Vietminh in Indo-China.* New York: Frederick A. Praeger, 1961. 166 pp.

Tanham, George K., and Duncanson, Dennis J. "Some Dilemmas of Counterinsurgency." *Foreign Affairs* 48 (1969):113-22.

Taylor, Gen. Maxwell D. "Improving Our Capabilities for Limited War." *Army Information Digest,* February 1959, pp. 2-9.

_____. "On Limited War." *Army Information Digest,* June 1958, pp. 4-5.

Thompson, Sir Robert. *Defeating Communist Insurgency: The Lessons of Malaya and Vietnam.* New York: Frederick A. Praeger, 1966. 176 pp.

_____. *Revolutionary War in World Strategy, 1945-1969.* New York: Taplinger, 1970.

Traverso, Edmund. *Korea and the Limits of Limited*

War. Menlo Park, Calif.: Addison-Wesley, 1970.
81 pp.

U.S. Arms Control and Disarmament Agency. *Control of
Local Conflict*. 4 vols. Washington, D.C.: Government Printing Office, 1967.

U.S. Department of the Air Force, Aerospace Studies
Institute, Air University. *Guerrilla Warfare and
Airpower in Korea, 1950-1953*. Maxwell Air Force
Base, Ala., 1964. 248 pp.

U.S. Department of the Army. *Undergrounds in Insur-
gent, Revolutionary, and Resistance Warfare*. D.A.
Pamphlet 550-104. Washington, D.C.: Government
Printing Office, 1966.

U.S. Department of the Army, Army Special Warfare
School. *Readings in Counter-Guerrilla Operations*.
Fort Bragg, N.C., 1961.

_____. *Readings in Counterinsurgency*. ST 31-177.
Fort Bragg, N.C., January 1965.

_____. *Readings in Guerrilla Warfare*. Fort Bragg,
N.C., 1960.

Wayland, Otto P. "Air Power in Limited War." *Ordnance*, July-August 1959, pp. 40-43.

Wolf, Charles. *Insurgency and Counterinsurgency:
New Myths and Old Realities*. RAND Paper P-3132.
Santa Monica, Calif.: RAND Corporation, 1965.

Wolfers, Arnold. "Could a War in Europe Be Limited?"
Yale Review 45 (1956):214-28.

Zawodny, J. K. "Unconventional Warfare." *American
Scholar*, Summer 1962, pp. 384-94.

_____. "Unconventional Warfare." *Annals of the*

American Academy of Political and Social Science
341 (1962): Special Issue.

IV

The Defense Policy Making Process

A. General Literature, Including Civil-
   Military Relations
B. The Department of Defense
   1. The Pentagon and Office of the Sec-
      retary of Defense
   2. Inter-service Relations and the
      Joint Chiefs of Staff
   3. The Military Departments
      a. General Literature on the Armed
         Forces
      b. U.S. Army
      c. U.S. Navy
      d. U.S. Air Force
      e. U.S. Marine Corps
      f. Reserve and National Guard
         Forces
   4. Budgeting, Planning, Systems Analy-
      sis, Operations Research
C. The President and Other Executive
   Agencies
   1. The Presidential Office
   2. National Security Council
D. Congress and Executive-Legislative Relations
E. Non-Governmental Inputs into Policy
   Making
   1. Defense Industries, the "Military-
      Industrial Complex"
   2. Private Interest Groups, Public Opin-
      ion, Defense Research Organizations

Section IV contains materials on institutions and
policy making in the United States. Part A covers in
a general way the specific topics found in the rest of
the section. Part A also lists materials on civil-
military relations where these bear on defense policy
making. Part B is concerned with the Department of
Defense and with defense management. Parts C, D, and
E cover actors, agencies, or groups that have a direct
influence on defense policy but are not solely in the
defense field and are not part of the Department of
Defense itself.

This section is basically concerned with administration rather than with the substance of policy.
But, as with the rest of this bibliography, the distinction is somewhat arbitrary. Many works in this
section are concerned with both the substance and administration of policy. The user should also examine
the relevant portions of Section V for policy-oriented
materials with an administrative input.

A. GENERAL LITERATURE, INCLUDING CIVIL-MILITARY RELATIONS

Armacost, Michael H. *The Politics of Weapons Innovation: The Thor-Jupiter Controversy.* New York:
Columbia University Press, 1969. 304 pp.

Batchelder, Robert C. *The Irreversible Decision,
1939-1950.* Boston: Houghton Mifflin, 1962. 306
pp.

Bobrow, Davis B. "Soldiers and the Nation-State."
*Annals of the American Academy of Political and So-
cial Science,* March 1965, pp. 65-76.

Boguslaw, Robert; Davis, Robert H.; and Glick,
Edward B. "A Simulation Vehicle for Studying Na-
tional Policy Formation in a Less Armed World."
Behavioral Science 11 (1966):43-61.

Bottome, Edgar M. *The Missile Gap: A Study of the Formulation of Military and Political Policy.* Cranbury, N.Y.: Fairleigh Dickinson University Press, 1970. 264 pp.

Brown, Fred R., ed. *Management: Concepts and Practice.* Washington, D.C.: Industrial College of the Armed Forces, 1967.

Brown, Harold. "Planning Our Military Forces." *Foreign Affairs* 45 (1967):277-90.

"Changing Patterns in Defense Management." *Armed Forces Management Association Journal* 11, no. 5 (1965): Twelfth National Conference Issue. 71 pp.

Cline, John B. "Defense Management: The Navy's Position." *U.S. Naval Institute Proceedings,* January 1965, pp. 43-51.

Committee for Economic Development. *The Problem of National Security: Some Economic and Administrative Aspects. . . .* New York, 1958.

Coser, Lewis. "The Dysfunctions of Military Secrecy." *Social Problems* 11 (1963):13-22.

Dawson, Raymond H. "Political Pressures and American National Strategy." *Naval War College Review,* April 1963, pp. 1-18.

"Decision Making in Defense: A Symposium." *Public Administration Review,* Summer 1958, pp. 169-207.

Donovan, John C. *The Policy Makers.* New York: Pegasus, 1970. 255 pp.

Duffield, Eugene S. "Organizing for Defense." *Harvard Business Review,* September-October 1953, pp. 29-42.

Eberstadt, Ferdinand. "The Historical Evolution of

Our National Security Organization." *Naval War College Review,* January 1954, pp. 1-17.

Enke, Stephen, ed. *Defense Management.* Englewood Cliffs, N.J.: Prentice-Hall, 1967. 385 pp.

Enthoven, Alain C., and Rowen, Harry S. "Defense Planning and Organization." In *Public Finances: Needs, Sources, and Utilization,* pp. 365-417. Princeton, N.J.: Princeton University Press, 1961.

Falk, Stanley L. *The National Security Structure.* Washington, D.C.: Industrial College of the Armed Forces, 1967. 166 pp.

Feld, Maury D. "Information and Authority: The Structure of Military Organization." *American Sociological Review,* February 1959, pp. 15-22.

_____. "A Typology of Military Organization." *Public Policy* 8 (1958):3-40.

Fergus, Martin C. "The Massive Retaliation Doctrine: A Study in United States Military Policy Formation." *Public Policy* 17 (1968):231-57.

Fox, William T. R. "Civilians, Soldiers, and American Military Policy." *World Politics* 7 (1955):402-18.

_____. "Representatives and Efficiency: Dual Problem of Civil-Military Relations." *Political Science Quarterly* 76 (1961):354-66.

Fulbright, J. W. "The Governance of the Pentagon." *Saturday Review,* 7 November 1970, pp. 22-25, 57-58.

Galbraith, John K. *How to Control the Military.* Garden City, N.Y.: Doubleday, 1969. 69 pp.

Gard, Col. Robert G., Jr. "The Military and American Society." *Foreign Affairs* 49 (1971):698-710.

Gimbel, John. *The American Occupation of Germany: Politics and the Military, 1945-1949.* Stanford, Calif.: Stanford University Press, 1968. 335 pp.

Goldwin, Robert A., ed. *America Armed: Essays on United States Military Policy.* Chicago: Rand McNally, 1963. 140 pp.

Goulding, Phil G. *Confirm or Deny: Informing the People on National Security.* New York: Harper & Row, 1970. 368 pp.

Guttmann, Allen. "Political Ideas and the Military Ethic." *American Scholar,* Spring 1965, pp. 221-37.

Hammond, Paul Y. "Effects of Structure on Policy." *Public Administration Review,* Summer 1958, pp. 175-79.

Hays, Samuel H. *Essays on American Military Institutions.* West Point, N.Y.: Office of Military Psychology and Leadership, U.S. Military Academy, 1969.

Hewlett, Richard G., and Anderson, Oscar E., Jr. *A History of the United States Atomic Energy Commission.* 2 vols. University Park: Pennsylvania State University Press, 1962, 1969.

Hilsman, Roger. "Planning for National Security. A Proposal." *Bulletin of the Atomic Scientists* 16 (1960):93-96, 112.

_____. *The Politics of Policy Making in Defense and Foreign Affairs.* New York: Harper, 1970.

Hoag, Malcolm W. "Some Complexities in Military Planning." *World Politics* 11 (1959):553-76.

Hoopes, Townsend. "Civilian-Military Balance." *Yale Review* 43 (1953):218-34.

Hoopes, Townsend. *The Limits of Intervention.* New
   York: David McKay, 1969. 245 pp.

Horowitz, Irving Louis. "United States Policy and the
   Military Establishment." *Correspondent,* no. 32
   (1964), pp. 45-60.

Howard, Michael. "Civil-Military Relations in Great
   Britain and the United States, 1945-1958." *Political Science Quarterly* 75 (1960):35-46.

Huntington, Samuel P. "Civilian Control and the Constitution." *American Political Science Review* 50
   (1956):676-99.

_____. "Civilian Control of the Military: A Theo-
   retical Statement." In *Political Behavior: A
   Reader in Theory and Research,* edited by Heinz
   Eulau, *et al.,* pp. 380-85. New York: Free Press,
   1956.

_____. *The Common Defense: Strategic Programs in
   National Politics.* New York: Columbia University
   Press, 1961.

_____. "Recent Writing in Military Politics: Foci
   and Corpora." In *Changing Patterns of Military
   Politics,* edited by Samuel P. Huntington, pp. 235-
   66. New York: Free Press, 1962.

_____. *The Soldier and the State: The Theory and
   Politics of Civil-Military Relations.* Cambridge,
   Mass.: Harvard University Press, 1957; Vintage
   Paperback ed., 1964.

_____. "Strategic Planning and the Political Proc-
   ess." *Foreign Affairs* 38 (1960):285-99.

Huzar, Elias. "Reorganization for National Security."
   Journal of Politics 12 (1950):128-52.

Jackson, Henry M. "Organizing for Survival." *Foreign Affairs* 38 (1960):446-56.

Katzenbach, Edward L., Jr. "The Horse Cavalry in the Twentieth Century: A Study in Policy Responses." *Public Policy* 8 (1958):120-50.

Kaufmann, William W. *The McNamara Strategy.* New York: Harper & Row, 1964.

Kerwin, Jerome G., ed. *Civil-Military Relations in American Life.* Chicago: University of Chicago Press, 1948.

Kissinger, Henry A. "Strategy and Organization." *Foreign Affairs* 35 (1957):379-94.

Knorr, Klaus, and Morgenstern, Oskar. *Political Conjecture in Military Planning.* Policy Memorandum, no. 35. Princeton, N.J.: Princeton University Center of International Studies, 1968.

Kraft, Joseph. "The War Thinkers." *Esquire,* September 1962, pp. 102ff.

Lambright, W. Henry. *Shooting Down the Nuclear Plane.* Indianapolis: Bobbs-Merrill, 1967.

Laurent, Francis W. *Control of Expenditures for National Defense.* Madison: University of Wisconsin Law School National Security Studies Group, 1960.

_____. *Organization for Military Defense of the United States, 1789-1959.* Madison: University of Wisconsin Law School National Security Studies Group, 1959; 1960. 113 pp.; 115 pp.

Lee, Gus C. "The Organization for National Security." *Public Administration Review* 9 (1949):36-50.

Lilienthal, David E. *The Journals of David E. Lilienthal.* Vol. 2: *The Atomic Energy Years, 1945-1950.*

New York: Harper & Row, 1964. 666 pp.

Lyons, Gene M. "The New Civil-Military Relations."
    American Political Science Review 55 (1961):53-63.

McClendon, Robert Earl. *Changes in Organization for
    National Defense, 1949-1953.* Maxwell Air Force
    Base, Ala.: U.S. Air University, Research Studies
    Institute, Documentary Research Division, 1956.   86
    pp.

McNamara, Robert S. "American Strategy Now." *Surviv-
    al,* May-June 1965, pp. 98-107.

_____. *The Essence of Security: Reflections in Of-
    fice.* New York: Harper & Row, 1968. 176 pp.

Mangrum, Richard C. "Organization for National Secu-
    rity." *Naval War College Review,* October 1949, pp.
    13-34.

Mansfield, Harvey C. "Civil-Military Relations in the
    United States." *Current History* 38 (1960):228-33.

May, Ernest R. "The Development of Political-Military
    Consultation in the United States." *Political Sci-
    ence Quarterly* 70 (1955):161-80.

Millis, Walter; with Mansfield, Harvey C.; and Stein,
    Harold. *Arms and the State: Civil-Military Ele-
    ments in National Policy.* New York: Twentieth
    Century Fund, 1958.

Mosher, Frederick C., *et al.* "Decision-Making in De-
    fense: The Role of Organization." *Public Adminis-
    tration Review* 18 (1958):169-88.

Murphy, Charles J. V. "The Eisenhower Shift." *For-
    tune,* January 1956, pp. 82-87; February 1956, pp.
    110ff; March 1956, pp. 110ff.

"Organizing for Defense." *General Electric Defense*

Quarterly, January-March 1959, entire issue.

Perkins, James A. "Administration of the National Security Program." *Public Administration Review*, Spring 1953, pp. 80-86.

Phillips, David C. *Ballistic Missile Defense: Evolution of the Decision-Making Process*. SP-3462. Santa Monica, Calif.: Systems Development Corporation, 1969. 63 pp.

Posvar, Col. Wesley W. "The Impact of Strategy Expertise on National Security Policy." *Public Policy* 13 (1964):36-68.

Radway, Laurence I. *The Liberal Democracy in World Affairs: Foreign Policy and National Defense*. Glenview, Ill.: Scott, Foresman, 1969. 207 pp.

Ransom, Harry Howe. *Can American Democracy Survive the Cold War?* Garden City, N.Y.: Doubleday, 1963. 270 pp.

Reitzel, William A. "The National Higher Strategic Direction of War." *Naval War College Review*, March 1955, pp. 25-55.

Rodberg, Leonard, and Shearer, Derek, eds. *The Pentagon Watchers: Students Report on the National Security State*. Garden City, N.Y.: Doubleday, 1970.

Rosenberg, Herbert H. *ODM: A Study of Civil-Military Relations during the Korean Mobilization*. Washington, D.C.: Office of Defense Mobilization, 1953.

Sapin, Burton M., ed. *Contemporary American Foreign and Military Policy*. Glenview, Ill.: Scott, Foresman, 1970.

Schilling, Warner R. "The H-Bomb Decision: How to Decide Without Actually Choosing." *Political Science Quarterly* 76 (1961):24-46.

Schilling, Warner R., *et al.* *Strategy, Politics, and Defense Budgets.* New York: Columbia University Press, 1962. 532 pp.

Schlesinger, Arthur M., Jr., and Rovere, Richard H. *The General and the President.* New York: Farrar, Straus & Young, 1951.

Sheehan, Neil; Smith, Hendrick; Kenworthy, E. W.; and Butterfield, Fox. *The Pentagon Papers.* New York: Bantam, 1971. 667 pp.

Smalter, Donald J., and Ruggles, Rudy L., Jr. "Six Business Lessons from the Pentagon." *Harvard Business Review* 44 (1966):64-75.

Smith, Dale O. *The Eagle's Talons: A Military View of Civil Control of the Military.* Washington, D.C.: Spartan Books, 1966. 368 pp.

Stein, Harold, ed. *American Civil-Military Decisions: A Book of Case Studies.* Birmingham: University of Alabama Press, 1963. 705 pp.

Strohlein, John. *Defense Weapon Systems Management.* Washington, D.C.: Industrial College of the Armed Forces, 1968.

Swomley, John M. *The Military Establishment.* Boston: Beacon Press, 1964.

Tansill, William R. *The Concept of Civil Supremacy over the Military in the United States.* Public Affairs Bulletin, no. 94. Washington, D.C.: Library of Congress Legislative Reference Service, 1951. 59 pp.

Tarr, David. "Military Technology and the Policy Process." *Western Political Quarterly,* March 1965, pp. 135-48.

Taylor, Gen. Maxwell D. *Responsibility and Response.*
New York: Harper & Row, 1967.

_____. *The Uncertain Trumpet.* New York: Harper &
Bros., 1960.

Tucker, Samuel A., ed. *A Modern Design for Defense
Decision: A McNamara-Hitch-Enthoven Anthology.*
Washington, D.C.: Industrial College of the Armed
Forces, 1966.

U.S. Commission on the Organization of the Executive
Branch of the Government (1947-49). *The National
Security Organization: A Report to Congress.* Her-
bert Clark Hoover Commission. Washington, D.C.:
Government Printing Office, 1949.

_____. *Task Force Report on National Security Organ-
ization, Appendix G.* Washington, D.C.: Government
Printing Office, 1949.

U.S. Congress, House Committee on Armed Services, Special Subcommittee no. 6. 85th Cong., 2d Sess.
*Hearings on Investigation of National Defense Es-
tablishment. Study of Procurement and Utilization
of Scientists, Engineers and Technical Skills.*
Washington, D.C.: Government Printing Office,
1958.

U.S. Congress, House Committee on Government Operations. 80th Cong., 1st Sess. *National Security
Act of 1947. Hearings before the Committee on Expenditures in the Executive Departments . . . .*
Washington, D.C.: Government Printing Office,
1947.

U.S. Congress, Senate Committee on Government Operations, Permanent Subcommittee on Investigations.
88th Cong., 1st Sess. *Hearings on the TFX Contract
Investigation.* 10 vols. Washington, D.C.: Government Printing Office, 1963-64.

U.S. Congress, Senate Committee on Government Operations, Permanent Subcommittee on Investigations. 91st Cong., 2d Sess. *TFX Contract Investigation . . . . Report.* Washington, D.C.: Government Printing Office, 1970. 97 pp.

U.S. Congress, Senate Committee on Government Operations, Subcommittee on National Security and International Operations. 91st Cong., 1st Sess. *Political Advisers to U.S. Military Commanders: Analysis and Assessment.* Washington, D.C.: Government Printing Office, 1969. 18 pp.

U.S. Congress, Senate Special Committee Investigating the National Defense Program. 77th Cong., 1st Sess. to 80th Cong., 1st Sess. *Investigation of the National Defense Program. Hearings . . . .* 43 pts. Washington, D.C.: Government Printing Office, 1941-48.

U.S. Department of the Air Force, Air University, Aerospace Studies Institute. *Development of Organization for National Defense, 1898-1960.* Maxwell Air Force Base, Ala., 1963.

Vagts, Alfred. *Defense and Diplomacy.* New York: King's Crown Press, 1956.

Westerfield, H. Bradford. *Foreign Policy and Party Politics: Pearl Harbor to Korea.* New Haven: Yale University Press, 1955.

Wood, Marshall. "The National Security Dilemma: Challenge to Management Scientists." *Management Science,* April 1960, pp. 195-209.

Yarmolinsky, Adam. *The Military Establishment: Its Impact on American Society.* New York: Harper & Row, 1971.

_____. "The Military Establishment (or How Political Problems Become Military Problems)." *Foreign*

Policy, Winter 1970-71, pp. 78-97.

Yoshpe, Harry B., and Bauer, Theodore W., *et al.* *Defense Organization and Management.* *National Security Management Series.* Washington, D.C.: Industrial College of the Armed Forces, 1967. 251 pp.

B. THE DEPARTMENT OF DEFENSE

1. The Pentagon and Office of the Secretary of Defense

Art, Robert J. *The TFX Decision: McNamara and the Military.* Boston: Little, Brown, 1968.

Baldwin, Hanson W. "The McNamara Monarchy." *Saturday Evening Post,* 9 March 1963, pp. 8-11.

_____. "Slow-Down in the Pentagon." *Foreign Affairs* 43 (1965):262-80.

Bell, James A. "Defense Secretary Louis Johnson." *American Mercury,* June 1950, pp. 643-53.

"Blue Ribbon Defense Panel Proposals." *Navy,* September 1970, pp. 9-27.

Borklund, C. W. *The Department of Defense.* New York: Frederick A. Praeger, 1968. 311 pp.

_____. *Men of the Pentagon: From Forrestal to McNamara.* New York: Frederick A. Praeger, 1966. 236 pp.

Brodie, Bernard. "The McNamara Phenomenon." *World Politics* 17 (1965):672-87.

Brown, Alvin. *The Armor of Organization: A Rational Plan of Organization for the Armed Forces and, as a Preliminary Thereto, an Inquiry into the Origins of*

Existing Military Organization. New York: Hibbert, 1953. 597 pp.

Bryan, Stanley E. "TFX—A Case in Policy Level Decision-Making." *Academy of Management Journal* 7 (1964):54-70.

_____. "The TFX F-111 Aircraft: A Perspective in Military Command and Defense Management." *Naval War College Review,* April 1971, pp. 66-87.

Bush, Vannevar. "What's Wrong at the Pentagon?" *Collier's,* 15 December 1952, pp. 131-35.

Carlisle, Howard M. "Incentive Contracts: Management Strategy of the Department of Defense." *Public Administration Review* 24 (1964):21-28.

Church, Albert T., Jr., and Vasey, Floyd R. "Defense Organization Issues." *U.S. Naval Institute Proceedings,* February 1961, pp. 23-31.

Dawson, Raymond H. "The Blue Ribbon Panel Report: Unification Orthodoxy Revisited and Revised." *Aerospace Historian,* Spring 1971, pp. 4-11.

Drucker, Peter F. "Defense Organization: New Realities and Old Concepts." *General Electric Defense Quarterly,* January-March 1959, pp. 4-7.

Eberstadt, Ferdinand. *Unification of the War and Navy Departments and Postwar Organization for National Security. Report to Honorable James Forrestal, Secretary of the Navy . . . .* Washington, D.C.: Government Printing Office, 1945. 251 pp.

Enthoven, Alain C., and Smith, K. Wayne. *How Much Is Enough?: Shaping the Defense Program, 1961-1969.* New York: Harper & Row, 1970. 364 pp.

Frye, W. "National Military Establishment." *American Political Science Review* 43 (1949):543-55.

Fulbright, J. William. *The Pentagon Propaganda Machine.* New York: Liverwright, 1970.

George, Edwin B. "The Staggering Problems in Managing National Defense." *California Management Review,* Summer 1960, pp. 73-83.

Gilman, Col. Seymour I. "A New Concept in Military Organization." *Military Review,* April 1959, pp. 36-42.

Halberstam, David. "The Programming of Robert McNamara." *Harper's,* February 1971, pp. 37-71.

Hammond, Paul Y. "A Functional Analysis of Defense Department Decision-Making in the McNamara Administration." *American Political Science Review* 62 (1968):57-69.

Katzenbach, Edward L., Jr. "Some Thoughts on Department of Defense Organization." *Naval War College Review,* December 1956, pp. 23-48.

Kaufmann, William W. *The McNamara Strategy.* New York: Harper & Row, 1964.

Kiker, Douglas. "The Education of Robert McNamara." *Atlantic,* March 1967, pp. 49-56.

Kintner, William R. *Forging a New Sword: A Study of the Department of Defense.* New York: Harper & Bros., 1958.

_____. "Organizing for Conflict: A Proposal." *Orbis* 2 (1958):155-74.

_____. "Progress in Defense Organization." *Journal of Public Law* 43 (1960):73-95.

Knight, Archie J., and Herzberg, Allen F. "A Proposal for the Next Step in Defense Reorganization." *Air*

University Quarterly Review, Summer 1960, pp. 53-90.

Kushnerick, John P. "The Motives and Methods of McNamara." *Aerospace Management,* October 1962, pp. 13-18.

Leach, W. Barton, and Ransom, Harry Howe. *Department of Defense Reorganization--1958.* Harvard Defense Policy Seminar Serial, no. 131. Cambridge, Mass.: Harvard University Graduate School of Public Administration, 1958.

McGaffin, William, and Knoll, Erwin. *Scandal in the Pentagon: A Challenge to Democracy.* Greenwich, Conn.: Fawcett, 1969. 192 pp.

McNamara, Robert S. "Managing the Department of Defense." *Civil Service Journal,* April-June 1964, pp. 1-5.

Mann, Dean E., with Doig, Jameson W. *Assistant Secretaries: Problems and Processes of Appointment.* Washington, D.C.: Brookings Institution, 1965. 310 pp.

Millis, Walter, with Duffield, E. S., eds. *The Forrestal Diaries.* New York: Viking, 1951.

Mollenhoff, Clark R. *The Pentagon: Politics, Profits and Plunder.* New York: G.P. Putnam's Sons, 1967. 438 pp.

Murphy, Charles J. V. "The Education of a Defense Secretary." *Fortune,* May 1962, pp. 102ff.

Niskanen, William A. "Defense Management after McNamara." *Armed Forces Journal,* February 1969, pp. 17-21.

Perry, Robert L. *Innovation and Military Requirements: A Comparative Study.* RAND Memorandum

5182-PR. Santa Monica, Calif.: RAND Corporation, 1967.

Powers, Lt. Col. Patrick W. *Guide to National Defense: The Organization and Operation of the U.S. Military Establishment.* New York: Frederick A. Praeger, 1964. 326 pp.

"The Question of National Defense Organization: A Quarterly Review Study." *Air University Quarterly Review,* Summer 1960, pp. 52-134.

Raymond, Jack. "Mr. McNamara Remodels the Pentagon." *Reporter,* 18 January 1962, pp. 31-35.

_____. *Power at the Pentagon.* New York: Harper & Row, 1964. 363 pp.

Ries, John C. *The Management of Defense: Organization and Control of the U.S. Armed Services.* Baltimore: Johns Hopkins Press, 1964. 222 pp.

Rogow, Arnold A. *James Forrestal: A Study of Personality, Politics, and Policy.* New York: Macmillan, 1963.

Roherty, James M. *Decisions of Robert S. McNamara: A Study of the Role of the Secretary of Defense.* Coral Gables, Fla.: University of Miami Press, 1970. 192 pp.

Seligman, Daniel. "McNamara's Management Revolution." *Fortune,* July 1965, pp. 117-20, 246-50.

Sights, Albert P., Jr. "Major Tasks and Military Reorganization." *Air University Quarterly Review,* Winter 1957, pp. 3-26.

Smale, Capt. Gordon F., ed. *A Commentary on Defense Management.* Washington, D.C.: Industrial College of the Armed Forces, 1967.

Trewhitt, Henry L. *McNamara: His Ordeal in the Pentagon.* New York: Harper & Row, 1971.

U.S. Blue Ribbon Defense Panel. *Report to the President and the Secretary of Defense on the Department of Defense by the Blue Ribbon Defense Panel, 1 July 1970.* Gilbert W. Fitzburgh Report. Washington, D.C.: Government Printing Office, 1970.

U.S. Commission on Organization of the Executive Branch of the Government. *Business Organization of the Department of Defense.* Washington, D.C.: Government Printing Office, 1955.

U.S. Committee on Department of Defense Organization. *Report of the Rockefeller Committee on Department of Defense Organization.* Washington, D.C.: Government Printing Office, 1953. 25 pp.

U.S. Congress, House Committee on Appropriations. 80th Cong., 2d Sess. *Military Functions, National Military Establishment Appropriation Bill . . . . Hearings before the Subcommittee of the Committee on Appropriations.* 3 pts. Washington, D.C.: Government Printing Office, 1948.

U.S. Congress, House Committee on Armed Services. 81st Cong., 1st Sess. *Hearings, to Convert the National Military Establishment into an Executive Department of Government to be Known as the Department of Defense.* Washington, D.C.: Government Printing Office, 1949.

_____. 81st Cong., 1st Sess. *Hearings, to Reorganize Fiscal Management in the National Military Establishment to Promote Economy and Efficiency, and for other Purposes.* Washington, D.C.: Government Printing Office, 1949.

_____. 85th Cong., 2d Sess. *Reorganization of the Department of Defense. Hearings . . . .* Washington, D.C.: Government Printing Office, 1958.

U.S. Congress, House Committee on Government Operations. 83d Cong., 1st Sess. *Reorganization Plan
no. 6 of 1953: Department of Defense. Hearings
. . . .* Washington, D.C.: Government Printing Office, 1953.

_____. 86th Cong., 1st Sess. *Organization and Man-
agement of Missile Programs.* Hyde Gillette Report.
Washington, D.C.: Government Printing Office,
1959.

_____. 86th Cong., 2nd Sess. *Organization and Man-
agement of Missile Programs. Hearings.* Clark B.
Millikan Report. Washington, D.C.: Government
Printing Office, 1960.

U.S. Congress, Senate Committee on Armed Services.
80th Cong., 1st Sess. *National Defense Establishment. . . . Hearings . . . .* 3 pts. Washington,
D.C.: Government Printing Office, 1947.

_____. 85th Cong., 2d Sess. *Department of Defense
Reorganization Act of 1958, Hearings . . . .* Washington, D.C.: Government Printing Office, 1958.
444 pp.

_____. 85th Cong., 2d Sess. *Department of Defense
Reorganization Act of 1958. Report . . . .* Washington, D.C.: Government Printing Office, 1958.
23 pp.

U.S. Congress, Senate Committee on Military Affairs.
79th Cong., 1st Sess. *Department of Armed Forces,
Department of Military Security. Hearings . . . .*
Washington, D.C.: Government Printing Office,
1945.

_____. 79th Cong., 2d Sess. *Department of Common
Defense: Report . . . .* Washington, D.C.: Government Printing Office, 1946.

U.S. Congress, Senate Committee on Naval Affairs.

79th Cong., 2d Sess. *A Scientific Evaluation of the Proposal That the War and Navy Departments Be Merged into a Single Department of National Defense.* Washington, D.C.: Government Printing Office, 1946. 39 pp.

U.S. Department of Defense. *Comments on the Hoover Commission Report on Business Organization of the Department of Defense.* Mimeographed. Washington, D.C., 1956.

U.S. Department of the Air Force, Air University, Aerospace Studies Institute. *Defense Organizations and Management, 1958-1964.* Maxwell Air Force Base, Ala., 1966.

Waters, Ace L., Jr., and Rogers, Jack L. "The Reorganization of the Department of Defense." *Armor,* January-February 1959, pp. 17-21.

White, Theodore H. "Revolution in the Pentagon." *Look,* 23 April 1963, pp. 31-49.

Yarmolinsky, Adam. "How the Pentagon Works." *Atlantic,* March 1967, pp. 56-62.

2. Inter-service Relations and the Joint Chiefs of Staff

"Army-Air Force Agreements." *Army Information Digest,* November 1947, pp. 48-56.

Ballagh, Capt. Robert S., Jr. "The JCS Challenge." *Military Review,* April 1971, pp. 25-34.

Brannen, Philip B. "A Single Service: Perennial Issue in National Defense." *U.S. Naval Institute Proceedings,* December 1957, pp. 1280-87.

Caraley, Demetrios. *The Politics of Military Unification: A Study of Conflict and the Policy Process.*

New York: Columbia University Press, 1966. 345
pp.

Childs, Marquis W. "The Battle of the Pentagon."
Harper's, August 1949, pp. 47-53.

Cline, Ray S., and Matloff, Maurice. "Development of
War Department View on Unification." *Military Affairs*, Summer 1949, pp. 65-74.

Connery, Robert H. "Unification of the Armed Services: The First Year." *American Political Science
Review* 63 (1949):38-52.

Davis, Vincent. *The Admirals Lobby.* Chapel Hill:
University of North Carolina Press, 1967. 329 pp.

_____. *The Politics of Innovation: Patterns in Navy
Cases.* Denver, Colo.: University of Denver, 1967.
69 pp.

Dawson, Raymond H. "The Blue Ribbon Panel Report:
Unification Orthodoxy Revisited and Revised." *Aerospace Historian*, Spring 1971, pp. 4-11.

Eifler, Charles W. "Management by Conflict." *Army*,
March 1968, pp. 64-69.

Giffin, S. F. "Relationships among Military Forces."
Air University Quarterly Review, Winter 1957-58,
pp. 31-45.

Hammond, Paul Y. "Unification: The Continuing De-
bate." In *National Security in the Nuclear Age:
Basic Facts and Theories*, edited by Gordon B.
Turner and Richard D. Challener, pp. 199-223. New
York: Frederick A. Praeger, 1960.

Henry, A. F.; Masland, J. W.; and Radway, Laurence I.
"Armed Forces Unification and the Pentagon Officer." *Public Administration Review* 15 (1955):173-
80.

Hensel, H. Struve. "Changes inside the Pentagon."
    Harvard Business Review, January-February 1954, pp.
    98-108.

Hittle, James D. *The Military Staff: Its History and
    Development.* 3d ed. Harrisburg, Pa.: Stackpole,
    1961. 326 pp.

Hubbard, William H. "The Staff and Modern War." *Mil-
    itary Review,* February 1960, pp. 52-69.

Huie, William Bradford. *The Case against the Admi-
    rals: Why We Must Have a Unified Command.* New
    York: E. P. Dutton, 1946.

Huntington, Samuel P. "Interservice Competition and
    the Political Roles of the Armed Services." *Ameri-
    can Political Science Review* 55 (1961):40-52.

Huzar, Elias. "Notes on the Unification Controversy."
    Public Administration Review 6 (1946):297-314.

"Joint Chiefs of Staff: A Study of the Problems and
    Proposed Solutions." *Armed Forces Management,* Jan-
    uary 1962, pp. 16-23.

Lemnitzer, Lyman L. "The Joint Chiefs of Staff and
    National Security." *Naval War College Review,*
    March 1962, pp. 1-14.

Megee, Vernon E. "The Joint Staff." *Naval War Col-
    lege Review,* March 1951, pp. 1-17.

Olverson, John B. "Problems of Defense Unification
    under the National Security Act." *Federal Bar
    Journal* 18 (1958):3-20.

Ransom, Harry Howe. "The Politics of Airpower: A
    Comparative Analysis." *Public Policy* 7 (1958):87-
    119.

Reinhardt, George C., and Kintner, William R. "The

Need for a National Staff." *U.S. Naval Institute Proceedings*, July 1952, pp. 720-27.

"Should Congress Create a Single Department of Armed Forces: Pros and Cons." *Congressional Record*, December 1945, pp. 291-320.

Singh, Nagendra. *The Defence Mechanism of the Modern State: A Study of the Politico-Military Set-Up of National and International Organisations with Special Reference to the Chiefs of Staff Committee.* New York: Asia, 1964.

Sulzberger, Arthur O. *The Joint Chiefs of Staff, 1941-1954.* Washington, D.C.: U.S. Marine Corps Institute, 1954. 88 pp.

Tatum, Lawrence B. "The Joint Chiefs of Staff and Defense Policy Formulation." *Air University Review*, May-June 1966, pp. 40-45; July-August 1966, pp. 10-20.

Thompson, Carol L. "Can Unification Work? Who is Right? The Air Force? The Navy?" *Forum* 112 (1949):341-50.

U.S. Commission on Organization of the Executive Branch of the Government, Task Force on Procurement. *Defense Procurement: The Vital Roles of the National Security Council and the Joint Chiefs of Staff.* Mimeographed. Washington, D.C., 1955.

U.S. Congress, House Committee on Armed Services. 81st Cong., 1st Sess. *The National Defense Program: Unification and Strategy. Hearings* . . . . Washington, D.C.: Government Printing Office, 1949. 639 pp.

_____. 81st Cong., 2d Sess. *Unification and Strategy: A Report of Investigation.* Washington, D.C.: Government Printing Office, 1950. 59 pp.

U.S. Congress, House Select Committee on Post-War Military Policy (Woodrum Committee). 78th Cong., 2d Sess. *Proposal to Establish a Single Department of Armed Forces. Hearings* . . . . Washington, D.C.: Government Printing Office, 1944.

U.S. Congress, Senate Committee on Armed Services. 80th Cong., 1st Sess. *National Defense Establishment: Unification of the Armed Services. Hearings* . . . . Washington, D.C.: Government Printing Office, 1947.

U.S. Congress, Senate Committee on Military Affairs. 79th Cong., 1st Sess. *Unification of the Armed Services: Analytical Digest of Testimony Before the Senate Military Affairs Committee* . . . . Washington, D.C.: Government Printing Office, 1946. 132 pp.

U.S. Congress, Senate Committee on Naval Affairs. 79th Cong., 2d Sess. *Unification of the Armed Forces. Hearings.* Washington, D.C.: Government Printing Office, 1946. 351 pp.

U.S. Department of Defense. *Methods of Operations of the Joint Chiefs of Staff and their Relationships with Other Staff Agencies of the Office of the Secretary of Defense.* Washington, D.C.: Government Printing Office, 1954.

U.S. Department of the Air Force, Air University, Documentary Research Division. *Unification of the Armed Forces: Administrative and Legislative Developments, 1945-1949.* R. Earl McClendon. Maxwell Air Force Base, Ala., 1952. 169 pp.

U.S. Department of the Army. Office of the Chief of Military History. *Unification of the Armed Forces* by Lawrence J. Legere, Jr. Mimeographed. Washington, D.C., n.d.

U.S. Joint Chiefs of Staff. *Organization and*

Function of the Joint Chiefs of Staff. JCS Publication 4, rev. Washington, D.C., 1966.

U.S. Joint Chiefs of Staff, Historical Division. *Major Changes in the Organization of the Joint Chiefs of Staff, 1942-1969.* Washington, D.C., 1970. 47 pp.

Wermuth, Anthony L. "A General Staff for America in the Sixties." *Military Review,* February 1960, pp. 11-20.

3. The Military Departments

a. General Literature on the Armed Forces

Alexander, Richard G. "Command and Decision." *Naval War College Review,* June 1962, pp. 18-42.

Beishline, John R. *Military Management for National Defense.* New York: Prentice-Hall, 1950.

Bolles, Blair. "Influence of Armed Forces on U.S. Foreign Policy." *Foreign Policy Reports,* 1 October 1946, pp. 170-79.

Campbell, R. R. "Progress and Problems in the War Colleges." *U.S. Naval Institute Proceedings,* September 1968, pp. 52-59.

Carney, Robert B. "Evolutionary Aspects of Command." *Naval War College Review,* September 1963, pp. 1-15.

_____. "The Grey Areas of Command and Decision." *Naval War College Review,* September 1961, pp. 1-16.

Clark, Harold F. *Classrooms in the Military.* New York: Columbia University Press, 1964.

Coates, Charles H., and Pellegrin, Roland J. *Military Sociology: A Study of American Military*

Institutions and Military Life. University Park, Md.: Social Science Press, 1965. 424 pp.

Collins, Gen. J. Lawton. "Our Modern Military Establishment." *Military Review*, September 1962, pp. 17-30.

Conally, Richard L. "Exercise of Command." *Naval War College Review*, November 1955, pp. 1-24.

Davis, Paul C. "The Negro in the Armed Services." *Virginia Quarterly* 24 (1948):499-520.

Duscha, Julius. "Power on the Potomac: How the War College Polished Our Brass." *Washingtonian*, February 1971, pp. 33-38.

Eccles, Rear Adm. Henry E. "Military Theory and Education: The Need for and Nature of." *Naval War College Review*, February 1969, pp. 70-79.

Finn, James, ed. *Conscience and Command: Justice and Discipline in the Military*. New York: Vintage Books, 1971. 300 pp.

Freeman, Douglas S. "Leadership." *Naval War College Review*, September 1949, pp. 1-14.

Garvey, Capt. Gerald. "The Changing Management Role of the Military Departments Reconsidered." *Air University Review*, March-April 1964, pp. 38-48; May-June 1964, pp. 35-46.

Getlein, Frank. *Playing Soldier: A Diatribe*. New York: Holt, Rinehart & Winston, 1971.

Ginsburgh, Col. Robert N. "The Challenge to Military Professionalism." *Foreign Affairs* 42 (1964):255-68.

Greenfield, Kent R., ed. *Command Decisions*. Washington, D.C.: Government Printing Office, 1959.

Harsch, Joseph C. "The Place of the Armed Forces in the Making of National Strategy." *Naval War College Review,* June 1952, pp. 25-47.

Hays, Samuel H., ed. *Taking Command: The Art and Science of Military Leadership.* Harrisburg, Pa.: Stackpole, 1967. 317 pp.

Heinl, Col. Robert D., Jr. "The Collapse of the Armed Forces." *Armed Forces Journal,* 7 June 1971, pp. 30-38.

Huntington, Samuel P. "Power, Expertise, and the Military Profession." *Daedalus* 92 (1963):785-808.

Janowitz, Morris. *The New Military: Changing Patterns of Organization.* New York: Russell Sage Foundation, 1964.

_____. *The Professional Soldier: A Social and Political Portrait.* Rev. ed. New York: Free Press, 1971.

_____. *The Professional Soldier and Political Power: A Theoretical Orientation and Selected Hypotheses.* Ann Arbor: University of Michigan Bureau of Government, Institute of Public Administration, 1953.

_____. *Sociology and the Military Establishment.* New York: Russell Sage Foundation, 1959.

Kluckhohn, Clyde. *American Culture and Military Life.* Washington, D.C.: Department of Defense Research and Development Board, 1951.

Leach, W. Barton. "The Job of an American Service Secretary." *Revue Militaire Générale,* March 1958, pp. 359-86.

Little, Roger W., ed. *Handbook of Military Institutions.* Beverly Hills, Calif.: Sage, 1971. 607 pp.

Little, Roger W., ed. *Social Research and Military Management: A Survey of Military Institutions.* 2 vols. Arlington, Va.: U.S. Air Force Office of Scientific Research, 1969.

Lyons, Gene M. "The Military Mind." *Bulletin of the Atomic Scientists,* November 1963, pp. 19-22.

McDonald, William G. "The Changing Management Role of the Military Departments." *Air University Quarterly Review,* Summer 1962, pp. 45-55.

Marshal, S. L. A. *Men against Fire.* New York: William Morrow, 1947.

Mendez, Louis G., Jr. "The Soldier and National Security Policy." *Army Information Digest,* January 1959, pp. 32-39.

Millis, Walter. "Place of the Armed Forces in the Making of National Security." *Naval War College Review,* June 1953, pp. 1-22.

_____. "The Puzzle of the 'Military Mind.'" *New York Times Magazine,* 18 November 1962, pp. 33ff.

Moskos, Charles C., Jr., ed. *Public Opinion and the Military Establishment.* Beverly Hills, Calif.: Sage, 1971. 294 pp.

_____. "Racial Integration in the Armed Forces." *American Journal of Sociology* 72 (1966):132-48.

Murray, Roger F. "The Finletter Report." *Air Affairs* 2 (1948):393-403.

Ney, Virgil. "High Military Command: A Historical Overview." *Military Review,* July 1968, pp. 17-28.

Sapin, Burton M., and Snyder, Richard C. *The Role of the Military in American Foreign Policy.* Garden City, N.Y.: Doubleday, 1954.

Simons, William E. *Military Professionals as Policy Advisers.* Santa Monica, Calif.: RAND Corporation, 1968. 21 pp.

_____. "Military Professionals as Policy Makers." *Air University Review,* March–April 1969, pp. 3–10.

Stillman, R. J., III. *Integration of the Negro in the U.S. Armed Forces.* New York: Frederick A. Praeger, 1968.

Taylor, Gen. Maxwell D. "Post-Vietnam Role of the Military in Foreign Policy." *Air University Review,* July–August 1968, pp. 50–58.

U.S. Congress, House Committee on Armed Services, Special Subcommittee on Service Academies. 90th Cong., 1st and 2nd Sess. *Administration of the Service Academies, Report and Hearings.* Washington, D.C.: Government Printing Office, 1968. 932 pp.

U.S. Congress, Senate Committee on Government Operations, Subcommittee on National Security and International Operations. 91st Cong., 1st Sess. *The State-Defense Officer Exchange Program: Analysis and Assessment.* Washington, D.C.: Government Printing Office, 1969. 16 pp.

U.S. Congress, Senate Committee on Military Affairs. 79th Cong., 1st Sess. *Department of Armed Forces, Department of Military Security. Hearings . . . .* Washington, D.C.: Government Printing Office, 1945.

U.S. Department of Defense. *The Armed Forces Officer.* Washington, D.C.: Government Printing Office, 1961. 251 pp.

U.S. Department of the Air Force, Office of the Chief of Staff. *A Study in Officer Motivation.* 2 vols. Washington, D.C., 1966.

Vagts, Alfred. *The Military Attaché*. Princeton, N.J.: Princeton University Press, 1967.

Van Riper, Paul P., and Unwalla, Darah B. "Military Careers at the Executive Level." *Administrative Science Quarterly* 9 (1964):421-36.

_____. "Voting Patterns among the High Ranking Military Officers." *Political Science Quarterly* 80 (1965):48-61.

Walker, Robert M. "The Military Mind." *Military Review*, August 1969, pp. 55-62.

Williams, Richard H., ed. *Human Factors in Military Operations*. TORO-T-259. Chevy Chase, Md.: Johns Hopkins University Operations Research Office, 1954.

Wolfe, J. N., and Erickson, John, eds. *The Armed Services and Society: Alienation, Management and Integration*. Edinburgh: Edinburgh University Press, 1970.

Wool, Harold. *The Military Specialist*. Baltimore: Johns Hopkins Press, 1968.

Zuckert, Eugene M. "The Service Secretary: Has He a Useful Role?" *Foreign Affairs* 44 (1966):458-79.

      b. U.S. Army

Bidwell, Charles E. "The Young Professional in the Army: A Study of Occupational Identity." *American Sociological Review*, June 1961, pp. 360-72.

Collins, Gen. J. Lawton. "The War Department Spreads the News." *Military Review*, September 1947, pp. 9-18.

Crosthwait, M. L. "Financial Management in the United

States Army." *Royal United Service Institution Journal,* February 1956, pp. 48–55.

Davies, Paul L. "A Business Look at the Army." *Harvard Business Review,* July-August 1954, pp. 55–66.

Dupuy, Col. R. E. *The Compact History of the United States Army.* New York: Hawthorn Books, 1956.

Fleming, Thomas J. *West Point: The Men and Times of the United States Military Academy.* New York: William Morrow, 1969. 402 pp.

Forman, Sidney. *West Point: A History of the United States Military Academy.* New York: Columbia University Press, 1951.

Just, Ward. *Military Men.* New York: Alfred A. Knopf, 1970. 256 pp.

Kleinman, Forrest K. *The Modern United States Army.* Princeton, N.J.: Van Nostrand Reinhold, 1965.

Long, William F. "Four Characteristics of the U.S. Army." *Naval War College Review,* January 1966, pp. 42–46.

Mosher, Frederick C. *Program Budgeting: Theory and Practice with Particular Reference to the U.S. Department of the Army.* Washington, D.C.: Public Administration Service, 1954.

Moskos, Charles C., Jr. *The American Enlisted Man.* New York: Russell Sage Foundation, 1970. 274 pp.

Nelson, Maj. Gen. Otto L., Jr. *National Security and the General Staff: A Study in Organization and Administration.* Washington, D.C.: Combat Forces Press, 1946.

Page, Thornton. "National Policy and the Army." *Army,* June 1956, pp. 30–33.

Pappas, Col. George S. *Prudens Future: The U.S. Army War College, 1901-1967*. Carlisle Barracks, Pa.: U.S. Army War College Alumni Association, 1967. 337 pp.

Phillips, Helen C. *United States Army Signal School, 1919-1967*. Fort Monmouth, N.Y.: U.S. Army Signal Center and School, 1967.

Pizer, Vernon. *The United States Army*. New York: Frederick A. Praeger, 1967. 190 pp.

Reichel, Lt. Col. Michael J. "The Hoover Commission and the Army." *Military Review*, March 1954, pp. 24-32.

Ridgway, Gen. Matthew B. *Soldier: The Memoirs of Matthew B. Ridgway*, as told to Harold H. Martin. New York: Harper & Bros., 1956.

U.S. Congress, House Committee on Armed Services. 81st Cong., 2d Sess. *Army Organization Bill, 1950: Hearings* . . . . Washington, D.C.: Government Printing Office, 1950.

U.S. Congress, House Committee on Government Operations. *Investigation of Participation of Federal Officials of the Department of the Army in Publicity and Propaganda, As It Relates to Universal Military Training*. Forrest A. Harness Report. Supplemental report to the fourth report of the Committee on Expenditures. Washington, D.C.: Government Printing Office, 1948.

U.S. Congress, Senate Committee on Armed Services. 80th Cong., 1st Sess. *Army Organization Act of 1950. Report* . . . . Washington, D.C.: Government Printing Office, 1950.

U.S. Department of the Army. *Secretary of the Army's Plan for Army Organization, June 14, 1954*. Mimeographed. Washington, D.C., 1954.

U.S. Department of the Army, Advisory Committee on Army Organization. *Organization of the Army.* Paul L. Davies Report. Washington, D.C., 1953.

U.S. Department of the Army, Army Civil Affairs School. *Civil Affairs Organization, 1965-70.* Fort Gordon, Ga.: Provost Marshal General's School, 1971.

_____. *History of Civil Affairs.* ST-41-170. Fort Gordon, Ga.: The Provost Marshal General's School, 1959.

U.S. Department of the Army, Combat Development Command, Combat Operations Research Group. *Evolution of Military Unit Control, 500 BC to AD 1964.* Fort Belvoir, Va., 1965.

_____. *Evolution of a Theater of Operations Headquarters, 1941-1966.* Fort Belvoir, Va., 1967. 127 pp.

_____. *Evolution of the United States Army Field Manual: Valley Forge to Vietnam.* Fort Belvoir, Va., 1966.

Wallace, Col. Lee. "Keeping Pace with the Future--The Department of the Infantry Division." *Military Review,* September 1958, pp. 65-74.

Weigley, Russell F. *History of the United States Army.* New York: Macmillan, 1967. 688 pp.

_____. *Toward an American Army: Military Thought from Washington to Marshall.* New York: Columbia University Press, 1962.

c. U.S. Navy

Albion, Robert G., and Connery, Robert H. *Forrestal*

and the Navy.   New York: Columbia University
Press, 1962.

Albion, Robert G., and Read, S. H. P., Jr.   *The Navy
at Sea and Ashore.*   NAVEXOS P-472.   Washington,
D.C.:   U.S. Department of the Navy, 1947.

Baldwin, Hanson W.   *The New Navy.*   New York: E. P.
Dutton, 1964.   191 pp.

Banning, Kendall.   *Annapolis Today.*   6th ed., rev. by
A. S. Pitt.   Annapolis: U.S. Naval Institute,
1963.

Beary, Donald B.   "The Naval War College."   *Naval War
College Review,*   February 1949, pp. 1-4.

Beers, Henry P.   "The Development of the Office of the
Chief of Naval Operations."   *Military Affairs,*
Spring 1946, pp. 40-68; Fall 1946, pp. 10-38; and
Winter 1947, pp. 229-37.

Carney, Adm. Robert B.   "The Foundations of Future Naval Planning."   *Naval War College Review,*   October
1949, pp. 1-12.

Carrison, Capt. Daniel J.   *The United States Navy.*
New York: Frederick A. Praeger, 1968.

Davis, Vincent.   *The Admirals Lobby.*   Chapel Hill:
The University of North Carolina Press, 1967.   329
pp.

_____.   *Postwar Defense Policy and the U.S. Navy,
1943-1946.*   Chapel Hill: University of North Carolina Press, 1966.   392 pp.

Dingfelder, Frank A.   "Naval Staff Organization and
Functioning."   *Naval War College Review,*   January
1952, pp. 25-49.

Furer, Julius Augustus.   *Administration of the Navy*

Department in World War II. Washington, D.C.: Government Printing Office, 1959.

Johnson, A. W. *A Brief History of the Organization of the Navy Department.* Washington, D.C.: Army Industrial College, 1933.

Noble, Albert G. "New Ordnance Developments and Their Influence on Naval Operations." *Naval War College Review,* January 1949, pp. 17-20.

Pratt, Fletcher. *The Compact History of the United States Navy.* New ed., rev. by Comdr. Hartley E. Howe. New York: Hawthorn Books, 1967. 384 pp.

Rappaport, Armin. "The Navy League of the United States." *South Atlantic Quarterly* 53 (1954):203-12.

U.S. Congress, House Committee on Armed Services. 80th Cong., 2d Sess. *Making Certain Changes in Organization of Navy Department, and for Other Purposes: Hearings . . . .* Washington, D.C.: Government Printing Office, 1947.

U.S. Congress, Senate Committee on Armed Services, Preparedness Investigating Subcommittee. 84th Cong., 2d Sess. *Eighth Report, Navy Aircraft Procurement Program: Final Report on F3H-1 Development and Procurement.* Washington, D.C.: Government Printing Office, 1956.

U.S. Department of the Navy. *Administration of the Navy Department in World War II.* Washington, D.C.: Government Printing Office, 1960. 1042 pp.

_____. *Department of the Navy: A Description of Its Functional Organization.* Washington, D.C.: Government Printing Office, 1962. 80 pp.

_____. *Management of International Security Affairs of the Department of the Navy Including Mutual*

Assistance Program and International Facilities.
Prepared for Committee on Organization of the De-
partment of the Navy. Mimeographed. Washington,
D.C., 1954.

U.S. Department of the Navy. *Recommendations Concerning the Executive Administration of the Naval Establishment.* Mimeographed. Washington, D.C.,
1945.

_____. *Report of the Committee on Organization of
the Navy Department, April 16, 1954.* Washington,
D.C., 1954.

U.S. Department of the Navy, Bureau of Naval Weapons,
Special Projects Office. *PERT: Summary Report,
Phase 1, and PERT: Summary Report, Phase 2.* Wash-
ington, D.C.: Government Printing Office, 1958.

U.S. Department of the Navy, Naval History Division.
History of the United States Navy. Washington,
D.C.: Government Printing Office, 1969.

U.S. Department of the Navy, Office of the Management
Engineer. *Report on the Survey of the Office of
the Chief of Naval Operations.* OpNAV-2. Washington, D.C., 1947.

_____. *The United States Navy: A Description of Its
Functional Organization.* Washington, D.C., 1947.

U.S. Naval Weapons Laboratory. *Technical Memorandum
No. K-19/59 Mechanization of the PERT System on
NORC.* Compiled by R. A. Niemann and R. N. Learn.
Rev. ed. Dahlgren, Va., 1960. 22 pp.

d. U.S. Air Force

Glines, Carroll V. *The Compact History of the United
States Air Force.* New York: Hawthorn, 1963.

Glines, Carroll V. *The Modern United States Air Force.* Princeton, N.J.: Van Nostrand Reinhold, 1963. 200 pp.

Goldberg, Alfred, ed. *A History of the United States Air Force, 1907-1957.* Princeton, N.J.: Van Nostrand Reinhold, 1957. 277 pp.

Hall, G. R., and Johnson, R. *A Review of Air Force Procurement, 1962-64.* RAND Report RM-4500-PR. Santa Monica, Calif.: RAND Corporation, 1965.

Hildreth, Charles H., and Nalty, Bernard C. *1001 Questions Answered about Aviation History.* New York: Dodd, 1969. 419 pp.

Komons, Nick A. *Science and the Air Force: A History of the Air Force Office of Scientific Research.* Arlington, Va.: Office of Aerospace Research, 1966. 175 pp.

Lamback, Charles H. *Highlights of Air Transportation in the United States Air Force.* Pittsburgh, 1954.

LeMay, Curtis E., with Kantor, MacKinley. *Mission with LeMay: My Story.* Garden City, N.Y.: Doubleday, 1965. 581 pp.

Loosbrock, John F., and Skinner, Richard M., eds. *The Wild Blue: The Story of American Airpower.* New York: G. P. Putnam's Sons, 1961. 620 pp.

McClendon, R. Earl. *Autonomy of the Air Arm.* Maxwell Air Force Base, Ala.: U.S. Air University, Documentary Research Division, 1954.

_____. *The Question of Autonomy for the United States Air Arm 1906-1946.* Montgomery, Ala.: U.S. Air University, Documentary Research Division, 1948.

MacCloskey, Brig. Gen. Munro. *The United States Air*

Force. New York: Frederick A. Praeger, 1967.   244 pp.

McConnell, Gen. John P. "Some Reflections on a Tour of Duty." *Air University Review,* September–October 1969, pp. 2–11.

McDonald, John. "General LeMay's Management Problem." *Fortune,* May 1954, pp. 102–106, 200–206.

McLaughlin, John J. "Organization of the Air Force: A Revolution in Management." *Air University Quarterly Review,* Spring 1963, pp. 2–13.

"Post-War Program: Mobilizing Air Industry." *Army and Navy Journal,* 3 November 1945, pp. 329–60.

Scholin, Allan R. "When an Air Base Closes." *Air Force and Space Digest,* February 1964, pp. 43–47.

Smith, Perry McCoy. *The Air Force Plans for Peace, 1943–1945.* Baltimore: Johns Hopkins Press, 1970. 132 pp.

Stratemeyer, George E. "Administrative History of the U.S. Army Air Forces." *Air Affairs* 1 (1947):510– 25.

Tarr, Curtis W. "The Air Force as a National Resource." *Air University Review,* May–June 1970, pp. 32–40.

U.S. Army Air Force. *Organization of Military Aeronautics, 1935–1945.* AAF Historical Study, no. 46. Washington, D.C., 1946.

_____. *The Army Air Forces in World War II.* Edited by Wesley F. Cravan and James L. Cate. 7 vols. Chicago: University of Chicago Press, 1948–58.

U.S. Congress, House Committee on Armed Services. 82d Cong., 1st Sess. *To Provide for Organization of*

Air Force and Department of Air Force and for Other Purposes. Hearings . . . . Washington, D.C.: Government Printing Office, 1951.

U.S. Congress, Senate Committee on Armed Services. 82d Cong., 1st Sess. *Air Force Organization Act of 1951. Hearings* . . . . Washington, D.C.: Government Printing Office, 1951. 62 pp.

_____. 82d Cong., 1st Sess. *Air Force Reorganization Act of 1951. Report* . . . . Washington, D.C.: Government Printing Office, 1951. 18 pp.

U.S. Department of the Air Force. *Report of General Carl Spaatz, the Chief of Staff, United States Air Force, to the Secretary of the Air Force. 30 June 1948.* Washington, D.C.: Government Printing Office, 1948. 112 pp.

U.S. Department of the Air Force, Air Training Command. *History of the United States Air Force.* ATC Pamphlet 190-1. Randolph Air Force Base, Tex., 1961.

U.S. Department of the Air Force, Historical Division. *Demobilization Planning for the United States Air Force.* USAF Historical Study, no. 59. Maxwell Air Force Base, Ala., 1954.

U.S. Department of the Air Force, Strategic Air Command, Office of the Historian. *The Progressive Development of the Strategic Air Command, 1946-1970.* Offutt Air Force Base, Nebr., 1970.

"USAF—The Momentous Quarter Century since World War II." *Air Force and Space Digest,* September 1970, pp. 47-127.

"U.S. Air Force Systems Command." *Aviation Week,* 25 September 1961, pp. 67-349.

Williams, Edwin L., Jr. "Legislative History of the

Air Arm." *Military Affairs,* Summer 1956, pp. 81-93.

     e. U.S. Marine Corps

DeChant, John A. *The Modern United States Marine Corps.* Princeton, N.J.: D. Van Nostrand, 1966. 230 pp.

Donovan, Col. James A., Jr. *The United States Marine Corps.* New York: Frederick A. Praeger, 1967. 232 pp.

Eliot, George Fielding. "The Hilt of the Sword." *Marine Corps Gazette,* January 1969, pp. 20-27.

Heinl, Col. Robert D., Jr. *Soldiers of the Sea: The United States Marine Corps, 1775-1962.* Annapolis: United States Naval Institute, 1962. 692 pp.

Hyman, M. H. "When Congress Considered Abolishing the Marine Corps." *Marine Corps Gazette,* April 1959, pp. 54-56.

Jeffers, H. Paul, and Levitan, Dick. *See Parris and Die: Brutality in the U.S. Marines.* New York: Hawthorn, 1971. 242 pp.

Lindsay, Robert. *This High Name: Public Relations and the U.S. Marine Corps.* Madison: University of Wisconsin Press, 1956.

Montross, Lynn. *The United States Marines.* New York: Rinehart, 1959.

Pierce, Philip N., and Hough, Frank O. *The Compact History of the United States Marine Corps.* New York: Hawthorn Books, 1960. 326 pp.

Schuon, Karl. *U.S. Marine Corps Biographical Dictionary: The Corps' Fighting Men, What They Did, Where*

They Served. New York: Franklin Watts, 1963. 278 pp.

Sherrod, Robert L. *History of Marine Corps Aviation in World War II.* Washington, D.C.: Combat Forces Press, 1952.

U.S. Marine Corps. *A Concise History of the United States Marine Corps, 1775-1969.* Washington, D.C.: Government Printing Office, 1971. 143 pp.

f. Reserve and National Guard Forces

Adler, Renata. "A Reporter at Large: The National Guard." *New Yorker,* 30 October 1970, pp. 40-64.

"The Air National Guard." *Air Reservist,* February 1966, pp. 2-13.

Derthick, Martha. *The National Guard in Politics.* Cambridge, Mass.: Harvard University Press, 1965.

Galloway, Eilene. *History of the United States Military Policy on Reserve Forces, 1775-1957.* Prepared for the House Committee on Armed Services by U.S. Library of Congress, Legislative Reference Service. Washington, D.C.: Government Printing Office, 1957.

Hill, Jim Dan. *The Minute Man in Peace and War: A History of the National Guard.* Harrisburg, Pa.: Stackpole, 1964.

Jacobs, Bruce. "The National Guard--Policy-Makers and Policy Problems." *Army,* September 1956, pp. 49-55.

Kennedy, Maj. W. V. *State Military Establishments.* Washington, D.C.: National Guard Bureau, 1966. 132 pp.

Levantrosser, William F. "The Army Reserve Merger

Proposal." *Military Affairs*, Fall 1966, pp. 135-47.

Lyons, Gene M., and Masland, John W. *Education and Military Leadership: A Study of the ROTC.* Princeton, N.J.: Princeton University Press, 1959.

MacCloskey, Munro. *Reserve Officers Training Corps.* New York: Richards Rosen Press, 1965.

McGowan, Maj. Gen. Donal W. "Army National Guard Today." *Army Information Digest*, March 1960, pp. 10-21.

McWilliams, Brig. Gen. K. E. "Divisions of Brigades for the Army National Guard." *Military Review*, January 1971, pp. 35-42.

National Guard Association of the United States. *The Nation's National Guard.* Washington, D.C., 1955. 119 pp.

Trainor, James L. "Is Reserve/Guard Merger a Prudent Move?" *Armed Forces Management*, May 1965, pp. 52-57.

U.S. Congress, House Committee on Armed Services. 84th Cong., 1st Sess. *A Legislative History of the Reserve Forces Act of 1955.* Report no. 82. Washington, D.C.: Government Printing Office, 1956.

U.S. Congress, Senate Committee on Armed Services. 84th Cong., 1st Sess. *Hearings: A National Reserve Plan.* Washington, D.C.: Government Printing Office, 1955.

U.S. Department of Defense, Committee on Civilian Components. *Reserve Forces for National Security.* Washington, D.C.: Government Printing Office, 1948.

U.S. National Security Training Commission. *Twentieth*

Century Minutemen: A Report to the President on a Reserve Forces Program. Washington, D.C.: Government Printing Office, 1953. 159 pp.

U.S. Naval Reserve Evaluation Board. *Naval Reserve.* Washington, D.C., 1954.

Worsnop, Richard L. "Reserve Forces and the Draft." *Editorial Research Reports,* 20 January 1965, pp. 43–60.

Young, D. M. "ROTC: Required or Elective?" *Military Review,* February 1962, pp. 21–32.

Zwicker, Maj. Gen. Ralph W. "The United States Army Reserve." *Military Review,* June 1959, pp. 3–13.

4. Budgeting, Planning, Systems Analysis, Operations Research

Archibald, K. A. *Three Views of the Expert's Role in Policy-Making: Systems Analysis, Incrementalism and the Clinical Approach.* RAND Paper 4292. Santa Monica: RAND Corporation, 1970.

Berg, Lt. Col. Robert S. "Cost-Effectiveness as an Aid to Weapon System Selection." *Air University Review,* March–April 1966, pp. 49–56.

Bobrow, Davis B., ed. *Weapons Systems Decisions: Political and Psychological Perspectives on Continental Defense.* New York: Frederick A. Praeger, 1969. 301 pp.

Boldyreff, A. W., ed. "A Decade of Military Operations Research in Perspective: A Symposium." *Operations Research,* November–December 1960, pp. 798–860.

Breckner, Norman V. "Government Efficiency and the Military 'Buyer-Seller' Device." *Journal of*

Political Economy 68 (1960):469-86.

Brown, Harold. "Planning Our Military Forces." *Foreign Affairs* 45 (1967):277-90.

Clark, John J. "Defense and Systems Analysis." *Survival,* March-April 1965, pp. 68-78.

_____. "The Economics of Systems Analysis." *Military Review,* April 1964, pp. 25-31.

Cohen, Bernard C. "Military Policy Analysis and the Art of the Possible." *Journal of Conflict Resolution* 6 (1962):154-59.

Cooper, Parker C. "The U.S. Navy Planning and Budget Process." *Naval War College Review,* December 1965, pp. 59-69.

Crecine, J. P. *Defense Budgeting: Organizational Adaption to External Constraints.* RAND Memorandum RM-6121-PR. Santa Monica, Calif.: RAND Corporation, 1970.

Danhof, Clarence H. *Government Contracting and Technological Change.* Washington, D.C.: Brookings Institution, 1968. 472 pp.

Drake, Hudson B. "Weapon Systems Management: Has the Potential Been Realized?" *Armed Forces Management,* May 1967, pp. 66-74.

Enke, Stephen. *Defense Management.* Englewood Cliffs, N.J.: Prentice-Hall, 1967.

Enthoven, Alain C. "Choosing Strategies and Selecting Weapon Systems." *U.S. Naval Institute Proceedings,* January 1964, pp. 151-58.

_____. "Economic Analysis in the Department of Defense." *American Economic Review* 53 (1963):413-23.

Enthoven, Alain C. "Systems Analysis and Decision-Making." *Military Review,* January 1963, pp. 7-17.

Enthoven, Alain, and Rowen, Henry S. *Defense Planning and Organization.* RAND Paper P-1640. Santa Monica, Calif.: RAND Corporation, 1959.

Enthoven, Alain C., and Smith, K. Wayne. *How Much Is Enough? Shaping the Defense Program, 1961-1969.* New York: Harper & Row, 1971. 364 pp.

Ernst, Martin L. "Operations Research and the Large Strategic Problems." *Operations Research,* July-August 1961, pp. 437-45.

Evans, Stuart J.; Margulis, Harold J.; and Yoshpe, Harry B. *Procurement.* Washington, D.C.: Industrial College of the Armed Forces, 1968.

Fisher, G. H. "Weapon System Cost Analysis." *Operations Research,* October 1956, pp. 558-71.

Foldes, Lucien. "Military Budgeting and Financial Control." *Public Administration Review* 17 (1957): 36-43.

Galper, H., and Gramlich, E. "A Technique for Forecasting Defense Expenditures." *Review of Economics and Statistics* 50 (1968):143-55.

Gilman, Col. Seymour I. "Operations Research in the Army." *Military Review,* July 1956, pp. 54-64.

Glennan, Thomas K. *Innovation and Product Quality under the Total Package Procurement Concept.* RAND Memorandum 5097-PR. Santa Monica, Calif.: RAND Corporation, 1966.

Gordon, Bernard W. "Conflicts in Military Procurement." *Current History* 38 (1960):234-39.

Hall, G. R. *Interaction of Procurement Decisions in*

Weapons Systems Acquisition Projects. RAND Paper
P-4105. Santa Monica, Calif.: RAND Corporation,
1969.

Henderson, Thomas. "Plans, Programs, and Budgets in
the Department of Defense." *Operations Research,*
January-February 1963, pp. 1-17.

Hitch, Charles J. *Decision-Making for Defense.*
Berkeley: University of California Press, 1965.
83 pp.

_____. "Economics and Military Operations Research."
Review of Economics and Statistics 40 (1958):199-
209.

_____. "National Security Policy as a Field for Eco-
nomics Research." *World Politics* 12 (1960):434-52.

Hitch, Charles J., and McKean, Roland N. *The Economics of Defense in the Nuclear Age.* Cambridge,
Mass.: Harvard University Press, 1960. 422 pp.

_____. *Elements of Defense Economics.* Washington,
D.C.: Industrial College of the Armed Forces,
1967.

Hoag, Malcolm W. *Defense Economics in Action in America.* RAND Paper P-3811. Santa Monica, Calif.:
RAND Corporation, 1968.

Hoffman, F. S. "The Economic Analysis of Defense:
Choice Without Markets." *American Economic Review*
49 (1959):368-76.

"How Defense Intends to Streamline Procurement."
Armed Forces Management, November 1962, pp. 78-85.

Johnson, Ellis A. "The Long-Range Future of Operational Research." *Operations Research,* January-
February 1960, pp. 1-23.

Kermisch, J. J., and Tenger, A. J. *On the Role of the Cost Analyst in a Weapons System Study.* RAND Paper 3360. Santa Monica, Calif.: RAND Corporation, 1966.

Knorr, Klaus. "On the Cost-Effectiveness Approach to Military Research and Development." *Bulletin of the Atomic Scientists* 22 (1966):11-14.

Knorr, Klaus, and Morgenstern, Oskar. *Political Conjecture in Military Planning.* Policy Memorandum, no. 35. Princeton: Princeton University Center of International Studies, 1968.

Livingston, J. Sterling. "Decision Making in Weapons Development." *Harvard Business Review,* January-February 1958, pp. 127-36.

McCullough, Hugh. "New Concepts in Defense Planning, Programming and Budgeting." *Federal Accountant,* September 1962, pp. 70-84.

McGarrah, R. E. "Let's Internationalize Defense Marketing." *Harvard Business Review,* May-June 1969, pp. 146-55.

McKean, Roland N. *Economics of Defense.* RAND Paper P-2926. Santa Monica, Calif.: RAND Corporation, 1964.

_____. *Efficiency in Government through Systems Analysis.* New York: John Wiley & Sons, 1958.

_____, ed. *Issues in Defense Economics.* New York: National Bureau of Economic Research, Columbia University, 1967.

Marshall, A. W. *Problems of Estimating Military Power.* RAND Paper 3417. Santa Monica: RAND Corporation, 1966.

Massey, Robert J. "Program Packages and the Program

Budget in the Department of Defense." *Public Administration Review* 23 (1963):30-34.

Miller, John Perry. "Military Procurement Policies: World War II and Today." *American Economic Review* 42 (1952):453-75.

_____. *Pricing Military Procurement*. New Haven: Yale University Press, 1949.

Moore, F. "Efficiency and Public Policy in Defense Procurement." *Law and Contemporary Problems* 29 (1964):3-18.

Murphy, Charles J. V. "Defense: The Converging Decisions: How Much for Which Weapons for Which Services for Which Wars?" *Fortune,* October 1958, pp. 118-20.

National Security Industrial Association. *Defense Acquisition Study*. Washington, D.C., 1970. 103 pp.

NATO Conference on Operational Research, Paris, 1957. *Operational Research in Practice: Report of a NATO Conference*. New York: Pergamon Press, 1958.

Nelson, Richard R. *The Economics of Parallel R and D Efforts: A Sequential Decision Analysis*. RAND Paper RM-2482. Santa Monica, Calif.: RAND Corporation, 1959.

Novick, David. *Costing Tomorrow's Weapon Systems*. RAND Report RM-3170-PR. Santa Monica, Calif.: RAND Corporation, 1962.

_____. *A New Approach to the Military Budget*. RAND Memorandum RM-1759. Santa Monica, Calif.: RAND Corporation, 1956.

_____, ed. *Program Budgeting: Program Analysis and the Federal Government*. Cambridge, Mass.: Harvard University Press, 1965.

Novick, David. *System and Total Force Cost Analysis.*
RAND Report RM-2695-PR. Santa Monica, Calif.:
RAND Corporation, 1961.

_____. *Weapon-System Cost Methodology.* RAND Report
287. Santa Monica, Calif.: RAND Corporation,
1956.

Novick, David, and Springer, J. Y. "Economics of Defense Procurement." *Law and Contemporary Problems*
24 (1959):118-31.

Peck, Merton J., and Scherer, Frederic M. *The Weapons
Acquisition Process: An Economic Analysis.* Boston: Harvard University Graduate School of Business Administration, Division of Research, 1962.
736 pp.

Powell, Craig. "Have the Armed Services Learned to
Live with the Office of Systems Analysis?" *Armed
Forces Management,* October 1965, pp. 73-76.

Prince, Kimball. "Sandia Corporation: A Science-
Industry-Government Approach to Management of a
Special Project." *Federal Bar Journal,* October-
December 1957, pp. 432-43.

Quade, E. S., ed. *Analysis for Military Decisions.*
Santa Monica, Calif.: RAND Corporation, 1964. 382
pp.

_____. *Cost-Effectiveness: An Introduction and
Overview.* RAND Paper 3134. Santa Monica, Calif.:
RAND Corporation, 1965.

Quade, E. S., and Boucher, W. I., eds. *Systems Analysis and Policy Planning: Applications in Defense.*
New York: American Elsevier, 1968.

Rosen, Harris N. "Control of the Army Budgetary
Process." *Military Review,* February 1955, pp. 14-
23.

Scherer, Frederic M. *The Weapons Acquisition Process: Economic Incentives.* Boston: Harvard University Graduate School of Business Administration, Division of Research, 1964. 447 pp.

Schlesinger, James R. *Analysis and Defense in the Sixties.* RAND Paper P-3050. Santa Monica, Calif.: RAND Corporation, 1965. 6 pp.

_____. *Defense Planning and Budgeting: The Issue of Centralized Control.* RAND Paper P-3813. Santa Monica, Calif.: RAND Corporation, 1968.

_____. *On Relating Non-Technical Elements to System Studies.* RAND Paper 2545. Santa Monica, Calif.: RAND Corporation, 1967.

_____. "Organizational Structures and Planning." In *Issues in Defense Economics,* edited by Roland N. McKean, pp. 185-216. New York: National Bureau of Economic Research, Columbia University, 1967.

_____. "Quantitative Analysis and National Security." *World Politics* 15 (1963):295-315.

_____. "The 'Soft' Factors in Systems Studies." *Bulletin of the Atomic Scientists,* November 1968, pp. 12-17.

_____. *Systems Analysis and the Political Process.* RAND Paper R-3464. Santa Monica, Calif.: RAND Corporation, 1967.

_____. "Uses and Abuses of Analysis." *Survival,* October 1968, pp. 334-42.

Smith, T. Arthur, ed. *Economic Analysis and Military Resource Allocation.* Department of the Army Cost Reference Publication. Washington, D.C.: Comptroller of the Army, 1968.

Snyder, William P. *Case Studies in Military Systems*

Analysis. Washington, D.C.: Industrial College of the Armed Forces, 1967.

Sturm, Paul J. "Problem Mongers, Solution Mongers and Weapon Systems Effectiveness." *Defense Industry Bulletin,* July 1966, pp. 1-4, 16-18, 21.

Tucker, Capt. Ralph M. "Cost Effectiveness: Fact and Fancy." *U.S. Naval Institute Proceedings,* September 1964, pp. 74-81.

U.S. Commission on Organization of the Executive Branch of the Government, Task Force on Procurement. *Defense Procurement: The Vital Roles of the National Security Council and the Joint Chiefs of Staff.* Mimeographed. Washington, D.C., 1955.

_____. *Task Force Report on Military Procurement.* Washington, D.C., 1955.

U.S. Congress, House Committee on Armed Services, Subcommittee for Special Investigations. 86th Cong., 1st Sess. *Weapons System Management and Team System Concept in Government Contracting. Hearings* . . . . Washington, D.C.: Government Printing Office, 1959.

U.S. Congress, House Committee on Government Operations. 87th Cong., 2d Sess. *Hearings on Systems Development and Management.* 5 vols. Washington, D.C.: Government Printing Office, 1962.

_____. 90th Cong., 2d Sess. *Military Procurement of Airborne Rocket Launchers, Hearings* . . . . Washington, D.C.: Government Printing Office, 1968. 158 pp.

_____. 91st Cong., 2d Sess. *Policy Changes in Weapon System Procurement* . . . . *Hearings.* Washington, D.C.: Government Printing Office, 1970.

_____. 91st Cong., 2d Sess. *Policy Changes in*

Weapon System Procurement. Report . . . . Washington, D.C.: Government Printing Office, 1970. 37 pp.

U.S. Congress, Joint Economic Committee. 86th Cong., 2d Sess. *Background Material on Economic Aspects of Military Procurement and Supply.* Washington, D.C.: Government Printing Office, 1960.

_____. 90th Cong., 2d Sess. *Economics of Military Procurement, Hearings* . . . . 2 pts. Washington, D.C.: Government Printing Office, 1968. 347, 244 pp.

U.S. Congress, Joint Economic Committee, Subcommittee on Economy in Government. 90th Cong., 1st Sess. *The Analysis and Evaluation of Public Expenditures: The PPB System.* 3 vols. Washington, D.C.: Government Printing Office, 1969.

_____. 91st Cong., 1st Sess. *The Acquisition of Weapons Systems. Hearings* . . . . Washington, D.C.: Government Printing Office, 1970.

_____. 91st Cong., 1st Sess. *The Economics of Military Procurement.* Washington, D.C.: Government Printing Office, 1969.

_____. 91st Cong., 1st Sess. *The Military Budget and National Economic Priorities: Hearings.* 3 pts. Washington, D.C.: Government Printing Office, 1969. 992 pp.

U.S. Congress, Senate Committee on Government Operations, Subcommittee on National Security and International Operations. 86th Cong., 2d Sess. *Planning-Programming-Budgeting: Hearings.* Washington, D.C.: Government Printing Office, 1967. 1960 pp.

_____. 90th Cong., 1st Sess. *Planning-Programming-Budgeting, Selected Comment* . . . . Washington,

D.C.: Government Printing Office, 1967.

U.S. Congress, Senate Committee on Government Opera-
   tions, Subcommittee on National Security and Inter-
   national Operations. 91st Cong., 1st Sess.
   *Planning-Programming-Budgeting, Defense Analysis:
   Two Examples* . . . . Washington, D.C.: Government
   Printing Office, 1969.

U.S. Congress, Senate Committee on the Judiciary, Subcommittee on Anti-trust and Monopoly. 90th Cong.,
   2d Sess. *Competition in Defense Procurement, Hearings* . . . . Washington, D.C.: Government Printing Office, 1969.

U.S. Department of Defense. *The Changing Patterns of
   Defense Procurement.* Washington, D.C.: Government
   Printing Office, 1962.

_____. *Department of Defense Comments on the Hoover
   Commission Report on Military Procurement.* Mimeographed. Washington, D.C., 1955.

_____. *Department of Defense Views on Implementation
   of Report on Budget and Accounting by Commission on
   Organization of the Executive Branch of the Government.* Mimeographed. Washington, D.C., 1955.

_____. *Five Year Trends in Defense Procurement, FY
   1958-FY 1962.* Washington, D.C.: Government Printing Office, 1963.

_____. *Study Report--Programming System for the Of-
   fice of Secretary of Defense.* Washington, D.C.:
   Government Printing Office, 1962.

Whitehead, Clay Thomas. *Uses and Limitations of Systems Analysis.* RAND Paper 3683. Santa Monica,
   Calif.: RAND Corporation, 1967.

Wilson, Andrew. *The Bomb and the Computer: A Crucial*

History of War Games. New York: Delcorte, 1969.
218 pp.

Wood, Marshall; Leach, W. B.; and Ransom, H. H. *The
Budgetary Process and Defense Policy.* Harvard De-
fense Policy Seminar Serial, no. 122. Cambridge,
Mass., 1957.

Wool, Harold. *The Military Specialist.* Baltimore:
Johns Hopkins Press, 1968.

Yosphe, Harry B., ed. *Requirements: Matching Needs
with Resources.* Washington, D.C.: Industrial College of the Armed Forces, 1964.

Yuill, Stuart J. "Quantitative Information for Strategic Decisions." *Naval War College Review,* November 1970, pp. 16-29.

C. THE PRESIDENT AND OTHER EXECUTIVE AGENCIES

1. The Presidential Office

Anderson, Dillon. "The President and National Security." *Atlantic,* January 1956, pp. 42-46.

Anderson, Patrick. *The President's Men.* Garden City,
N.Y.: Doubleday, 1968. 420 pp.

Austin, Anthony. *The President's War.* Philadelphia:
J. B. Lippincott, 1971.

Clark, Keith C., and Legere, Laurence J. *The President and the Management of National Security.* New
York: Frederick A. Praeger, 1969. 274 pp.

Davis, James W., and Ripley, Randall B. "The Bureau
of the Budget and Executive Branch Agencies: Note
on Their Interaction." *Journal of Politics* 29
(1967):749-69.

Fairman, Charles. "The President as Commander-in-Chief." *Journal of Politics* 11 (1949):145-70.

George, Alexander L. *Presidential Control of Force: The Korean War and the Cuban Missile Crisis.* RAND Paper P-3627. Santa Monica, Calif.: RAND Corporation, 1967.

Graff, Henry Franklin. *The Tuesday Cabinet: Deliberation and Decision on Peace and War under Lyndon B. Johnson.* Englewood Cliffs, N.J.: Prentice-Hall, 1970. 200 pp.

Gumz, Donald G. "The Bureau of the Budget and Defense Fiscal Policy." *U.S. Naval Institute Proceedings,* April 1959, pp. 80-89.

Heinlein, J. C. *Presidential Staff and National Security Policy.* Cincinnati: University of Cincinnati, 1963. 65 pp.

Heller, F. H. "The President as Commander-in-Chief." *Military Review,* September 1962, pp. 5-16.

Hewlett, Richard G., and Anderson, Oscar E., Jr. *The New World, 1939-1946.* Vol. 1: *A History of the United States Atomic Energy Commission.* University Park: Pennsylvania State University Press, 1962. 766 pp.

Katzenbach, Edward L., Jr. "Bubud's Defense Policy." *Reporter,* 23 June 1960, pp. 25-30.

Kennedy, Robert F. *Thirteen Days: A Memoir of the Cuban Missile Crisis.* New York: W. W. Norton, 1969. 224 pp.

May, Ernest R. *The Ultimate Decision: The President as Commander-in-Chief.* New York: George Braziller, 1960. 290 pp.

Norman, Floyd. "The Commander in Chief and National

Security Policy." *Army,* February 1962, pp. 46-49.

Paige, Glenn D. *The Korean Decision: June 24-30, 1950.* Introduction by Richard C. Snyder. New York: Free Press, 1968. 394 pp.

Paolucci, Henry. *War, Peace, and the Presidency.* New York: McGraw-Hill, 1968. 241 pp.

Pusey, Merlo J. *The Way We Go to War.* Boston: Houghton Mifflin, 1969. 202 pp.

Rossiter, Clinton L. *The Supreme Court and the Commander in Chief.* Ithaca, N.Y.: Cornell University Press, 1951.

Sorenson, Theodore A. *Decision-Making in the White House: The Olive Branch or the Arrows.* New York: Columbia University Press, 1963.

U.S. Congress, Senate Committee on Foreign Relations. 91st Cong., 2d Sess. *Documents Relating to the War Power of Congress, the President's Authority as Commander-in-Chief, and the War in Indochina.* Washington, D.C.: Government Printing Office, 1970. 252 pp.

2. National Security Council

Bresica, Peter F. "The National Security Council: Integration of American Foreign Policy." *Columbia Journal of International Affairs,* Spring 1950, pp. 74-77.

Cutler, Robert. "The Development of the National Security Council." *Foreign Affairs* 34 (1956):441-58.

Falk, Stanley L. "The National Security Council under Truman, Eisenhower, and Kennedy." *Political Science Quarterly* 79 (1964):403-34.

Hammond, Paul Y. "The National Security Council as a
    Device for Interdepartmental Coordination: An In-
    terpretation and Appraisal." *American Political
    Science Review* 54 (1960):899-910.

Jackson, Henry M., ed. *The National Security Council:
    Jackson Subcommittee Papers on Policy-Making at the
    Presidential Level.* New York: Frederick A. Prae-
    ger, 1965. 352 pp.

Johnson, Robert H. "The National Security Council:
    The Relevance of Its Past to Its Future." *Orbis*
    13 (1969):709-35.

Kirkpatrick, H. P. "Advisers or Policymakers: The
    National Security Council." *American Perspectives,*
    February 1949, pp. 443-50.

Kolodziej, Edward A. "The National Security Council:
    Innovations and Implications." *Public Administra-
    tion Review* 29 (1969):573-85.

Lay, James S., Jr. "National Security Council's Role
    in the U.S. Security and Peace Program." *World Af-
    fairs,* Summer 1952, pp. 37-39.

Nihart, Brooke. "NSC: New Staff System after One
    Year." *Armed Forces Journal,* April 1970, pp. 25-
    29.

Souers, Sidney. "Policy Formation and the National
    Security Council." *American Political Science Re-
    view,* June 1949, pp. 534-43.

U.S. Commission on Organization of the Executive
    Branch of the Government, Task Force on Procure-
    ment. *Defense Procurement: The Vital Roles of the
    National Security Council and the Joint Chiefs of
    Staff.* Mimeographed. Washington, D.C., 1955.

U.S. Congress, Senate Committee on Government Opera-
    tions. 91st Cong., 1st Sess. *The National*

Security Council: New Role and Structure, February 7, 1969. Washington, D.C.: Government Printing Office, 1969. 6 pp.

U.S. Congress, Senate Committee on Government Operations, Subcommittee on National Policy Machinery. 86th Cong., 2d Sess. *Organizational History of the National Security Council.* Prepared by James S. Lay, Jr., and Robert H. Johnson. Washington, D.C.: Government Printing Office, 1960. 52 pp.

_____. 86th Cong., 2d Sess.–87th Cong., 1st Sess. *Organizing for National Security.* 3 vols. Washington, D.C.: Government Printing Office, 1960–61.

U.S. Congress, Senate Committee on Government Operations, Subcommittee on National Security Staffing and Operations. 87th Cong., 2d Sess. *Administration of National Security: Selected Papers.* Washington, D.C.: Government Printing Office, 1962. 203 pp.

_____. 88th Cong., 1st Sess. *Administration of National Security. Basic Issues.* Washington, D.C.: Government Printing Office, 1963. 20 pp.

_____. 88th Cong., 1st Sess. *Administration of National Security, Hearings . . . . Part I.* Washington, D.C.: Government Printing Office, 1963. 128 pp.

Wyeth, George A., Jr. "The National Security Council: Concept of Operation; Organization; Actual Operations." *Journal of International Affairs* 8 (1954): 185–95.

D. CONGRESS AND EXECUTIVE-LEGISLATIVE RELATIONS

Barondes, Lt. Col. Arthur D. "The Congress and

R&D." *Air University Review*, March-April 1967, pp. 55-60.

Batten, James K. "Why the Pentagon Pays Homage to John Cornelius Stennis." *New York Times Magazine*, 23 November 1969, pp. 44ff.

Brown, Richard E. *The GAO: Untapped Source of Congressional Power*. Knoxville: University of Tennessee Press, 1970. 127 pp.

Carroll, Holbert. *The House of Representatives and Foreign Affairs*. Pittsburgh: Pittsburgh University Press, 1958.

Cheever, Daniel S., and Haviland, H. Field, Jr. *American Foreign Policy and the Separation of Powers*. Cambridge, Mass.: Harvard University Press, 1952.

Cobb, Stephen A. "Defense Spending and Foreign Policy in the House of Representatives." *Journal of Conflict Resolution* 13 (1969):358-69.

Dawson, Raymond H. "Congressional Innovation and Intervention in Defense Policy: Legislative Authorization of Weapon Systems." *American Political Science Review* 56 (1962):42-57.

Derthick, Martha. *The National Guard in Politics*. Cambridge, Mass.: Harvard University Press, 1965.

Dvorin, Eugene P., ed. *The Senate's War Powers: Debate on Cambodia from the Congressional Record*. Chicago: Markham, 1971. 244 pp.

Fenno, Richard F. "The Military Budget: Congressional Phase." *Journal of Politics* 23 (1961):689-710.

_____. *The Power of the Purse: Appropriations Politics in Congress*. Boston: Little, Brown, 1966. 704 pp.

Francis, Michael J. "Military Aid to Latin America in
    the U.S. Congress." *Journal of Inter-American
    Studies*, July 1964, pp. 389-404.

Galloway, John. *The Gulf of Tonkin Resolution*.
    Rutherford, N.J.: Fairleigh Dickenson University
    Press, 1970. 578 pp.

Green, Harold, and Rosenthal, Alan. *The Joint Com-
    mittee on Atomic Energy: A Study in the Fusion of
    Governmental Powers*. Washington, D.C.: National
    Law Center of the George Washington University,
    1961. 338 pp.

Halperin, Morton. "The Gaither Committee and the Pol-
    icy Process." *World Politics* 13 (1961):360-87.

Henderson, Thomas. *Congressional Oversight of Execu-
    tive Agencies: A Study of the House Committee on
    Government Operations*. Gainesville: University of
    Florida Press, 1970. 72 pp.

Hersh, Seymour. "The Military Committees." *Washing-
    ton Monthly*, April 1969.

Hilsman, Roger. "Congressional-Executive Relations
    and the Foreign Policy Consensus." *American Polit-
    ical Science Review* 52 (1958):725-44.

Horn, Stephen. *Unused Power: The Work of the Senate
    Committee on Appropriations*. Washington, D.C.:
    Brookings Institution, 1970. 285 pp.

Hyman, M. H. "When Congress Considered Abolishing the
    Marine Corps." *Marine Corps Gazette*, April 1959.

Katzenbach, Edward L., Jr. "How Congress Strains at
    Gnats, Then Swallows Military Budgets." *Reporter*,
    20 July 1954, pp. 31-35.

Kolodziej, Edward A. *The Uncommon Defense and*

Congress, 1945-1963. Columbus: Ohio State University Press, 1966. 630 pp.

Levantrosser, William F. *Congress and the Citizen-Soldier: Legislative Policy-Making for the Federal Armed Forces Reserve.* Columbus: Ohio State University Press, 1967. 267 pp.

McConaughy, James L., Jr. "Congressmen and the Pentagon." *Fortune,* April 1958, pp. 156ff.

"The 'Military Lobby' Its Impact on Congress, Nation." *Congressional Quarterly Weekly Report,* 24 March 1961, pp. 463-78.

Oberdorfer, Don. "Rivers Delivers." *New York Times Magazine,* 29 August 1965, pp. 30ff.

Roback, Herbert. "Congressional Interest in Weapons Acquisition." *Armed Forces Management,* February 1963, pp. 40-44.

Robinson, James A. *Congress and Foreign Policy-Making: A Study in Legislative Influence and Initiative.* Rev. ed. Homewood, Ill.: Dorsey Press, 1967. 254 pp.

U.S. Congress, House Committee on Armed Forces. 91st Cong., 1st Sess. *Report of the Activities of the House Committee on Armed Forces.* Washington, D.C.: Government Printing Office, 1970.

U.S. Congress, Senate Committee on Foreign Relations. 91st Cong., 2d Sess. *Documents Relating to the War Power of Congress, the President's Authority as Commander-in-Chief, and the War in Indochina.* Washington, D.C.: Government Printing Office, 1970. 252 pp.

U.S. Congress, Senate Library. *Domestic Stability, National Defense and World War II: Legislative and Executive Background, 1933-1946.* Washington, D.C.:

Government Printing Office, 1947.

Wallace, Robert A. "Congressional Control of the Budget." *Midwest Journal of Political Science* 3 (1959):160-62.

Williams, Edwin L., Jr. "Legislative History of the Air Arm." *Military Affairs,* Summer 1956, pp. 81-93.

E. NON-GOVERNMENTAL INPUTS INTO POLICY MAKING

1. Defense Industries, the "Military-Industrial Complex"

Adams, Walter. "The Military-Industrial Complex and the New Industrial State." *American Economic Review* 58 (1968):652-65.

Agapos, A. M., and Galloway, Lowell E. "Defense Profits and the Renegotiation Board in the Aerospace Industry." *Journal of Political Economy* 78 (1970): 1093-1105.

Anderson, R. M. "Handling Risk in Defense Contracting." *Harvard Business Review* 47 (1969):90-98.

Baldwin, William L. *The Structure of the Defense Market, 1955-1964.* Durham, N.C.: Duke University Press, 1967.

Barnet, Richard J. *The Economy of Death.* New York: Atheneum, 1969. 201 pp.

Baumgartner, John Stanley. *The Lonely Warriors: Case for the Military-Industrial Complex.* Los Angeles: Nash, 1970. 237 pp.

Benoit, Emile. "Will Defense Cuts Hurt Business?" *Michigan Business Review,* March 1957, pp. 1-6.

Bickner, Robert E. *The Changing Relationship between the Air Force and the Aerospace Industry.* RAND Memorandum RM—4101—PR. Santa Monica, Calif.: RAND Corporation, 1964.

Bosch, Juan. *Pentagonism: A Substitute for Imperialism.* Translated by H. R. Lane. New York: Grove Press, 1969. 141 pp.

Boulding, Kenneth, ed. *Peace and the War Industry.* Chicago: Aldine, 1970. 159 pp.

_____. "The Role of the War Industry in International Conflict." *Journal of Social Issues* 23 (1967): 47—61.

Carey, Omer L., ed. *The Military—Industrial Complex and United States Foreign Policy.* Pullman: Washington State University Press, 1969.

Charles, Robert H. "The So—Called Military—Industrial Complex." *Air Force and Space Digest,* October 1964, pp. 45—47.

Cook, Fred J. *The Warfare State.* New York: Macmillan, 1962. 376 pp.

Demaree, Allan T. "Defense Profits: The Hidden Issue." *Fortune,* August 1969, pp. 82ff.

Dupre, J. Stefan, and Gustafson, Eric. "Contracting for Defense: Private Firms and the Public Interest." *Political Science Quarterly* 77 (1961):161—77.

Duscha, Julius. *Arms, Money and Politics.* New York: Washburn, Ives, 1965.

Galper, H., and Granlich, E. "A Technique for Forecasting Defense Expenditures." *Review of Economics and Statistics* 50 (1968):143—55.

Greenberg, Edward. "Employment Impacts of Defense Expenditures and Obligations." *Review of Economics and Statistics* 49 (1967):186-97.

Gross, John G. "A Reappraisal of Cost Incentives in Defense Contracts." *Western Economic Journal*, June 1968, pp. 205-25.

Gubin, E. K. "Financing Defense Contracts." *Law and Contemporary Problems* 29 (1964):438-52.

Hall, G. R., and Johnson, R. *Competition in Procurement of Military Hard Goods*. RAND Paper P-3769-1. Santa Monica, Calif.: RAND Corporation, 1968.

Herzog, Arthur. *The War-Peace Establishment*. New York: Harper & Row, 1963. 271 pp.

Holman, Mary A. "The Dependence of Business Firms on Government Employment." *Quarterly Review of Economics and Business*, Winter 1968, pp. 73-79.

Horowitz, David, ed. *Corporations and the Cold War*. New York: Monthly Review Press, 1971.

Koistinen, Paul A. C. "The 'Industrial-Military Complex' in Historical Perspective: The Interwar Years." *Journal of American History* 46 (1970):819-39.

Lapp, Ralph E. *The Weapons Culture*. New York: W. W. Norton, 1968. 230 pp.

Lens, Sidney. *The Military-Industrial Complex*. Philadelphia: Pilgrim Press, 1970. 183 pp.

Livingston, J. S. "Weapon System Contracting." *Harvard Business Review*, July-August 1959, pp. 83-92.

Lowry, Ritchie P. "To Arms: Changing Military Roles and the Military-Industrial Complex." *Social Problems* 18 (1970):3-16.

Mansfield, Harold. *Vision: A Saga of the Sky.* New York: Duell, Sloan & Pearce, 1956. 196 pp.

Melman, Seymour, ed. *The War Economy of the United States: Readings in Military Industry and Economy.* New York: St. Martin's Press, 1971. 247 pp.

"Military Industrial Complex." *Congressional Quarterly Weekly Review,* May 24, 1968. Special Issue.

Miller, Arthur S. "The Rise of the Techno-Corporate State in America." *Bulletin of the Atomic Scientists,* January 1969, pp. 14-20.

Mills, C. Wright. *The Power Elite.* New York: Oxford University Press, 1959. 423 pp.

Novick, David. *Are Cost Overruns a Military-Industrial Complex Specialty?* RAND Research Paper RP-4311. Santa Monica, Calif.: RAND Corporation, 1970.

O'Neill, Lt. Gen. John W. "Space and Missile Systems Organization--Working Partner with Industry." *Defense Industry Bulletin,* October 1969, pp. 1-5.

Pilisuk, M., and Hayden, T. "Is There a Military-Industrial Complex which Prevents Peace? Consensus and Countervailing Power in Pluralistic Systems." *Journal of Social Issues* 21 (1965):67-117.

Proxmire, William. *Report from the Wasteland: America's Military Industrial Complex.* New York: Frederick A. Praeger, 1970. 248 pp.

Rice, Berkeley. *The C-5A Scandal: A $5 Billion Boondoggle by the Military-Industrial Complex.* Boston: Houghton Mifflin, 1971.

Schiller, Herbert I., and Phillips, Joseph. *Super-State: Readings in the Military Industrial Complex.* Urbana: University of Illinois Press, 1970.

Shapiro, Albert, and Vollner, Howard M. *The Industry-Government Aerospace Relationship*. 2 vols. Menlo Park, Calif.: Stanford Research Institute, 1963.

Shulman, Stephen N. "Labor Policy and Defense Contracts: A Matter of Mission." *Law and Contemporary Problems* 29 (1964):238-65.

Simonson, G. R. "Missiles and Creative Destruction in the American Aircraft Industry, 1956-1961." *Business History Review* 38 (1964):302-14.

Steiner, George A. *National Defense and Southern California, 1961-1970*. Los Angeles: Southern California Committee for Economic Development Associates, Committee for Economic Development, 1971.

Stekler, Herman O. *The Structure and Performance of the Aerospace Industry*. Berkeley: University of California Press, 1965.

Stockfisch, Jacob A., ed. *Planning and Forecasting in the Defense Industries*. Belmont, Calif.: Wadsworth, 1962.

Tyrrell, C. Merton. *Pentagon Partners: The New Nobility*. New York: Grossman, 1970.

U.S. Arms Control and Disarmament Agency. *Defense Systems Resources in the Civil Sector: Evolving Approach, Uncertain Market*. Washington, D.C., 1967. 201 pp.

U.S. Congress, House Committee on Armed Services, Subcommittee for Special Investigations. 86th Cong., 1st Sess. *Employment of Retired Commissioned Officers by Defense Department Contractors*. Washington, D.C.: Government Printing Office, 1960.

_____. 86th Cong., 1st Sess. *Employment of Retired Military and Civilian Personnel by Defense*

Industries . . . *Hearings.* Washington, D.C.: Government Printing Office, 1959.

U.S. Congress, Senate Committee on Government Operations, Permanent Subcommittee on Investigations. 87th Cong., 2d Sess. *Pyramiding of Profits and Costs in the Missile Procurement Program* . . . *Hearings.* 3 pts. Washington, D.C.: Government Printing Office, 1962.

_____. 88th Cong., 2d Sess. *Pyramiding of Profits and Costs in the Missile Procurement Program* . . . *Report.* Washington, D.C.: Government Printing Office, 1964.

U.S. Congress, Senate Committee on Small Business. 82d Cong., 1st Sess. *Concentration of Defense Contracts, Report No. 551.* Washington, D.C.: Government Printing Office, 1951.

_____. 85th Cong., 2d Sess. *Eighth Annual Report, Small Business and Defense Subcontracts.* Washington, D.C.: Government Printing Office, 1958.

_____. 85th Cong., 2d Sess. *The Role of Small Business in Defense Missile Procurement. Report.* Washington, D.C.: Government Printing Office, 1958.

_____. 86th Cong., 2d Sess. *Case Study in Subcontracting by Weapon-System Contractor, Hearings.* Washington, D.C.: Government Printing Office, 1960.

_____. 86th Cong., 2d Sess. *Case Study in Subcontracting by Weapon-System Contractor, Report.* Washington, D.C.: Government Printing Office, 1960.

Watzman, Sanford. *Conflict of Interest: Politics and the Money Game.* New York: Cowles, 1971.

Weidenbaum, Murray L. "Arms and the American Economy: A Domestic Convergence Hypothesis." *American Economic Review* 58 (1968):428-37.

_____. "Concentration and Competition in the Military Market." *Quarterly Review of Economics and Business,* Spring 1968, pp. 7-18.

_____. "The Defense Business: A Far Cry From Adam Smith." *Challenge,* May-June 1966, pp. 35-44.

_____. "The Defense-Space Complex: Impact on Whom?" *Challenge,* April 1965, pp. 43-46.

Witze, Claude. "Declining Defense Profits. Government Economy or a National Security Risk?" *Air Force and Space Digest,* April 1968, pp. 129-31, 135-36, 140.

Yosphe, Harry B.; and Franke, Charles F.; *et al. Production for Defense.* Washington, D.C.: Industrial College of the Armed Forces, 1968.

2. Private Interest Groups, Public Opinion, Defense Research Organizations

Almond, Gabriel A. "Public Opinion and National Security Policy." *Public Opinion Quarterly* 20 (1956): 371-78.

Aronson, James. *The Press and the Cold War.* New York: Bobbs-Merrill, 1970. 308 pp.

Barrett, Raymond J. "The Role of Consultation in American Defense Policy." *Air University Review,* May-June 1969, pp. 25-32.

Bobrow, Davis R. "Organization of American National Security Opinions." *Public Opinion Quarterly,* Summer 1969, pp. 223-29.

Bull, Hedley. "Strategic Studies and Its Critics."
   World Politics, July 1968, pp. 593-605.

Campbell, J. T., and Cain, L. S. "Public Opinion and
   the Outbreak of War." *Journal of Conflict Resolution* 9 (1965):318-29.

Dickson, Paul. *Think Tanks: America's Newest and
   Most Ambitious Industry.* New York: Atheneum,
   1971.

Dougherty, James E. "The Catholic Church, War, and
   Nuclear Weapons." *Orbis* 9 (1966):845-97.

Erskine, Hazel G. "The Polls, Atomic Weapons and Nuclear Energy." *Public Opinion Quarterly,* Summer
   1963, pp. 155-90.

Gilpin, Robert, and Wright, Christopher, eds. *Scientists and National Policy Making.* New York: Columbia University Press, 1964. 302 pp.

Grodzins, Morton; Rabinowitch, Eugene; *et al. The
   Atomic Age: Scientists in National and World Affairs.* New York: Basic Books, 1963. 616 pp.

Horowitz, Irving Louis. "Noneconomic Factors in the
   Institutionalization of the Cold War." *Annals of
   the American Academy* 351 (1964):110-20.

Inglis, David R. "Conservative Judgments and Missile
   Madness." *Bulletin of the Atomic Scientists,* May
   1968, pp. 6-11.

Kaplan, Morton A. *Dissent and the State in Peace and
   War: An Essai on the Grounds of Public Morality.*
   New York: Dunellen, 1970.

Kraft, Joseph. "RAND: Arsenal for Ideas." *Harper's,*
   July 1960, pp. 69-76.

Leavitt, William. "MITRE, USAF's Think Tank Partner

for Space Age Command and Control." *Air Force and Space Digest,* July 1967, pp. 60-63.

Leavitt, William. "RAND, AF's Original Think Tank." *Air Force and Space Digest,* May 1967, pp. 105-9.

Lincoln, Col. G. A., and Stilwell, Col. R. G. "Scholars Debauch into Strategy." *Military Review,* July 1960, pp. 18-30.

Lyons, Gene M. "The Growth of National Security Research." *Journal of Politics* 25 (1963):489-503.

Rosenberg, Milton J.; Berba, Sidney; and Converse, Philip E. *Vietnam and the Silent Majority.* New York: Harper & Row, 1970. 162 pp.

Smith, Bruce L. R. *The Rand Corporation: Case Study of a Nonprofit Advisory Corporation.* Cambridge, Mass.: Harvard University Press, 1966.

Verba, Sidney, *et al.* "Public Opinion and the War in Vietnam." *American Political Science Review* 61 (1967):317-33.

Wohlstetter, Albert. "Scientists, Seers, and Strategy." *Foreign Affairs* 41 (1963):466-78.

V

Defense Policy Output, Weapons Systems, and Military Programs

A. General Literature
B. Offensive Strategic Nuclear Forces
   1. General Issues
   2. Land Based Missile Systems
   3. Sea Based Missile Systems
   4. Manned Aircraft
   5. Communications and Command Control
   6. Basing Requirements and Deployment
C. Defensive Strategic Forces
   1. General Issues
   2. Continental Defense against Air Attack
   3. Ballistic Missile Defense
      a. General Issues
      b. Specific Programs
   4. Civil Defense
D. General Purpose Forces: Non-Nuclear
   1. General Issues
   2. Combat Ground Forces, Army
      a. Infantry
      b. Armor
      c. Air Cavalry
      d. Support
   3. Combat Ground Forces, Marines
   4. Theater Air Power, Air Force and Army
   5. General Naval Forces, Including Naval and Marine Air Power
   6. Submarines and Anti-Submarine Warfare

       7.   Amphibious Forces
       8.   Chemical and Biological Warfare
  E.   Tactical Nuclear Forces
  F.   Air and Sea Lift
  G.   Guard and Reserve Forces
  H.   Military Intelligence and Communications
  I.   Science, Technology, Research and
       Development
       1.   General Issues
       2.   Weapons Systems
       3.   Military Space Programs
  J.   Manpower, General Support, Supply and
       Logistics
       1.   General Manpower Requirements
       2.   Draft, Volunteer Army
       3.   Supply and Logistics
  K.   Regional Defense Policies, Including
       Military Assistance
       1.   General Issues
       2.   North America, Western Europe,
           Mediterranean
       3.   Middle East, North Africa
       4.   South Asia, Indian Ocean
       5.   Southeast Asia, Vietnam War
       6.   North Asia and Pacific, Korean War
       7.   Latin America and Caribbean
       8.   Africa

In this section will be found materials analyzing specific defense programs since 1945 as well as general works on defense policy. These are arranged under the types of program package usually used to construct the Department of Defense budget.

Part K of this section lists materials that deal with U.S. defense policy and military programs in various geographic areas. Military operations in Korea and Vietnam will be found in K-5 and K-6, respectively. The researcher looking for materials in other subsections--especially D: General Purpose Forces--should also check K-5 and K-6. Part K-1 includes materials on the theory of alliance systems and general literature on military assistance programs. Items dealing with specific alliances or military assistance in specific countries will be found in the appropriate parts from K-2 through K-6.

A. GENERAL LITERATURE

Allison, Graham T. *Essence of Decision: Explaining the Cuban Missile Crisis.* Boston: Little, Brown, 1971.

Bailey, Stephen K., *et al. Agenda for the Nation: Papers on Domestic and Foreign Policy Issues.* Edited by Kermit Gordon. Washington, D.C.: Brookings Institution, 1968. 620 pp.

Baldwin, Hanson W. "Current U.S. Military Strategy." *Naval War College Review,* April 1960, pp. 1-21.

Bauer, Theodore W. *Requirements for National Defense.* Washington, D.C.: Industrial College of the Armed Forces, 1970.

Berkner, Lloyd A., *et al.* "United States Military Policy." *Current History* 26 (1954):257-301.

Bernardo, C. Joseph, and Bacon, Eugene H. *American Military Policy: Its Development since 1775.* Harrisburg, Pa.: Military Service Publishing, 1955.

Brodie, Bernard. "United States Strategic Policies." *Revue Militaire Générale,* November 1970, pp. 519-29.

Davis, Vincent. "American Military Policy." *Naval War College Review,* May 1970, pp. 4-23.

Finletter, Thomas K. *Power and Policy: U.S. Foreign*

Policy and Military Power in the Hydrogen Age. New York: Harcourt, Brace, 1954.

Furniss, Edgar S., Jr. *American Military Policy: Strategic Aspects of World Political Geography.* New York: Rinehart, 1957. 494 pp.

Gilpatric, Roswell L. "Our Defense Needs: The Long View." *Foreign Affairs* 42 (1964):366-78.

Green, Murray. *A Response to Professor Melman and "Overkill."* Washington, D.C.: U.S. Air Force, 1964. 69 pp.

Greene, Fred. "The Military View of American National Policy, 1904-1940." *American Historical Review* 66 (1961):354-77.

Hilsman, Roger. "American Military Policy: The Next Phase." *Current History* 33 (1957):208-15.

Hoag, Malcolm W. "Some Complexities in Military Planning." *World Politics* 11 (1959):553-76.

_____. "What New Look in Defense?" *World Politics* 22 (1969):1-28.

Horowitz, Irving Louis. "United States Policy and the Military Establishment." *Correspondent,* no. 32 (1964), pp. 45-60.

Hughlin, Brig. Gen. Henry C. "Our Strategic Superiority--Why We Must Continue to Have It." *Air University Review,* September-October 1967, pp. 43-49.

Kaufman, William W. "The Crisis in Military Affairs." *World Politics* 10 (1958):579-603.

_____. *The McNamara Strategy.* New York: Harper & Row, 1964.

Kissinger, Henry A. "Military Policy and Defense of

the 'Grey Areas.'" *Foreign Affairs* 33 (1955):416-28.

Knorr, Klaus. *Is the American Defense Effort Enough?* Policy Memorandum, no. 14. Princeton, N.J.: Princeton University Center of International Studies, 1957.

Knorr, Klaus, and Morgenstern, Oskar. *Political Conjecture in Military Planning.* Policy Memorandum, no. 35. Princeton, N.J.: Princeton University Center of International Studies, 1968.

Kuzmack, Arnold M. *Naval Force Levels and Modernization: An Analysis of Shipbuilding Requirements.* Washington, D.C.: Brookings Institution, 1971. 47 pp.

Levine, Robert A. *"Overkill" and the Military Budget: A Review of A Strategy for American Security--An Alternative to the 1964 Military Budget.* Santa Monica, Calif.: RAND Corporation, 1964. 16 pp.

McNamara, Robert S. *The Essence of Security: Reflections in Office.* New York: Harper & Row, 1968. 176 pp.

Melman, Seymour, *et al.* *A Strategy for American Security: An Alternative to the 1964 Military Budget.* New York: Lee, 1963.

Millis, Walter, ed. *American Military Thought.* Indianapolis: Bobbs-Merrill, 1966.

_____. "Military Problems of the New Administration." *Foreign Affairs* 31 (1953):215-24.

Morton, Louis. "National Policy and Military Strategy." *Virginia Quarterly Review* 36 (1960):1-17.

_____. "The Origins of American Military Policy." *Military Affairs,* Summer 1958, pp. 75-82.

Murphy, Charles J. V. "Defense: The Converging Decisions: How Much for Which Weapons for Which Services for Which Wars?" *Fortune,* October 1958, pp. 118-20.

O'Connor, Raymond G., ed. *American Defense Policy in Perspective: From Colonial Times to the Present.* New York: Wiley & Sons, 1965.

Osgood, Charles E. "Questioning Some Unquestioned Assumptions about National Security." *Social Problems* 11 (1963):6-12.

Quester, George H. *Nuclear Diplomacy: The First Twenty-Five Years.* New York: Dunellen, 1971. 327 pp.

Read, Thornton. *Military Policy in a Changing Political Context.* Princeton, N.J.: Princeton University Center of International Studies, 1964.

Roberts, Chalmers M. *The Nuclear Years: The Arms Race and Arms Control, 1945-70.* New York: Frederick A. Praeger, 1970. 159 pp.

Sapin, Burton M. *Contemporary American Foreign and Military Policy.* Glenview, Ill.: Scott, Foresman, 1969.

Schlesinger, James R. *The Political Economy of National Security.* New York: Frederick A. Praeger, 1960.

Schultze, Charles L. "Re-examining the Military Budget." *Public Interest,* Winter 1970, pp. 3-24.

Schultze, Charles L.; Fried, Edward R.; Rivlin, Alice M.; and Teeters, Nancy H. *Setting National Priorities: The 1972 Budget.* Washington, D.C.: Brookings Institution, 1971. 336 pp.

Schultze, Charles L.; Hamilton, Edward K.; and Schick,

Allen. *Setting National Priorities: The 1971 Budget.* Washington, D.C.: Brookings Institution, 1970. 192 pp.

Tarr, David W. *American Strategy in the Nuclear Age.* New York: Macmillan, 1966.

Taylor, Gen. Maxwell D. *Responsibility and Response.* New York: Harper & Row, 1967.

_____. "Security Will Not Wait." *Foreign Affairs* 39 (1961):174-84.

Twining, Nathan F. *Neither Liberty nor Safety.* New York: Holt, Rinehart & Winston, 1966.

U.S. Congress, House. 78th Cong., 2d Sess. *Report on Post-War Military Policy.* House Report, no. 1645. Washington, D.C.: Government Printing Office, 1944.

U.S. Congress, House Committee on Foreign Affairs. 91st Cong., 1st Sess. *Strategy and Science: Toward a National Security Policy for the 1970's. Hearings* . . . . Washington, D.C.: Government Printing Office, 1969. 283 pp.

U.S. Congress, Senate Committee on Armed Services, Preparedness Investigating Subcommittee. 86th Cong., 1st Sess. *Major Defense Matters.* 2 pts. Washington, D.C.: Government Printing Office, 1959.

_____. 90th Cong., 2d Sess. *Investigation of the Preparedness Program, Report by the Preparedness Investigating Subcommittee of the Committee of Armed Services . . . on Status of U.S. Strategic Power.* Washington, D.C.: Government Printing Office, 1968.

U.S. Department of the Air Force, Air University, Air Command and Staff College. *The New Look.* Prepared by W. Barton Leach. Maxwell Air Force Base, Ala., 1954.

U.S. Department of the Air Force, Office of the Administrative Assistant of the Secretary of the Air Force, Research and Analysis Division. *Selected Statements of President Kennedy on Defense Topics, December 1957-August 1, 1962.* Washington, D.C., 1962. 261 pp.

"U.S. Military Policy and World Security: A Symposium." *Current History* 38 (1960):193-239.

U.S. President's Air Policy Commission. *Survival in the Air Age: A Report.* Thomas K. Finletter Report. Washington, D.C.: Government Printing Office, 1948.

Warnke, Paul C., and Gelb, Leslie H. "Security or Confrontation: The Case for a Defense Policy." *Foreign Policy* 1 (1971):6-30.

York, Herbert. "ABM, MIRV, and the Arms Race." *Science,* 17 July 1970, pp. 257-60.

Yudkin, Gen. Richard A. "American Armed Strength and Its Influence." *Annals of the American Academy* 384 (1969):1-13.

B. OFFENSIVE STRATEGIC NUCLEAR FORCES

1. General Issues

Amster, Warren. *A Theory for the Design of a Deterrent Air Weapon System.* Report OR-P-29. San Diego, Calif.: Convair, 1955. 65 pp.

Baar, J., and Howard, W. E. *Combat Missilemen.* New York: Harcourt, Brace & World, 1961. 244 pp.

Beary, Donald B. "Strategic Employment of the Navy:
    Past, Present and Future." *Naval War College Re-
    view*, April 1950, pp. 1-21.

Bottome, Edgar M. *The Missile Gap: A Study of the
    Formulation of Military and Political Policy.*
    Cranbury, N.Y.: Fairleigh Dickinson University
    Press, 1970. 264 pp.

Brodie, Bernard. "Navy Department Thinking on the
    Atomic Bomb." *Bulletin of the Atomic Scientists*
    3 (1947):177-80, 198-99.

_____. "War Department Thinking on the Atomic Bomb."
    Bulletin of the Atomic Scientists 3 (1947):150-55.

Brower, Michael. "Nuclear Strategy of the Kennedy Ad-
    ministration." *Bulletin of the Atomic Scientists*,
    October 1962, pp. 34-41.

Coffey, Joseph I. "Strategic Superiority, Deterrence
    and Arms Control." *Orbis* 13 (1970):991-1007.

Cohen, Paul. *The Realm of the Submarine.* London:
    Macmillan, 1969. 274 pp.

Gallois, Pierre M. "Ballistic Missiles Will Be Polit-
    ical Weapons." *Interavia*, December 1957, pp. 1251-
    52.

Gardner, Trevor. "How We Fell Behind in Guided Mis-
    siles." *Air Power Historian*, January 1958, pp. 3-
    13.

Gibney, Frank. "The Missile Mess." *Harper's*, January
    1960, pp. 38-45.

Hubler, Richard G. *SAC: The Strategic Air Command.*
    New York: Duell, Sloan & Pearce, 1958. 280 pp.

Hunter, Mel. *The Missilemen: A Stirring Story of a*

New Breed of Men. Garden City, N.Y.: Doubleday, 1960.

Hunter, Mel. *Strategic Air Command.* Garden City, N.Y.: Doubleday, 1961. 192 pp.

Kuzmack, Arnold M. "Technological Change and Stable Deterrence." *Journal of Conflict Resolution* 9 (1965):304-17.

Licklider, Roy E. "The Missile Gap Controversy." *Political Science Quarterly* 85 (1970):600-15.

McClelland, Charles A., ed. *Nuclear Weapons, Missiles, and Future War: Problem for the Sixties.* San Francisco: Chandler, 1960. 235 pp.

McGuire, Martin C. *Secrecy and the Arms Race: A Theory of the Accumulation of Strategic Weapons and How Secrecy Affects It.* Cambridge, Mass.: Harvard University Press, 1965. 249 pp.

Martin, Col. Donald F. "View on Aerospace Power." *Air University Review,* March-April 1968, pp. 30-39.

Medaris, Maj. Gen. John B. *Countdown for Decision.* New York: G. P. Putnam's Sons, 1960. 303 pp.

Murphy, Charles J. V. "The Case for Resuming Nuclear Tests." *Fortune,* April 1960, pp. 148-50, 178-90.

_____. "The Case for Resuming Nuclear Tests." *World Affairs,* Spring 1961, pp. 17-20.

Perry, Robert L. *The Ballistic Missile Decisions.* RAND Paper 3686. Santa Monica: RAND Corporation, 1967.

Phillips, Thomas R. "The Growing Missile Gap." *Reporter,* 8 January 1959, pp. 10-16.

Platig, E. Raymond. "The 'New Look' Raises Old

Problems." *Review of Politics,* January 1955, pp. 111-35.

Rathjens, George W. "The Dynamics of the Arms Race." *Scientific American,* April 1969, pp. 15-25.

_____. *The Future of the Strategic Arms Race: Options for the 1970's.* New York: Taplinger, 1969.

Reinhardt, George C., and Kintner, William R. *Atomic Weapons in Land Combat.* Harrisburg, Pa.: Military Service Publishing, 1953. 182 pp.

Scoville, Herbert, Jr. "The Limitations of Offensive Weapons." *Scientific American,* January 1971, pp. 15-25.

Shepley, James R., and Blair, Clay, Jr. *The Hydrogen Bomb: The Men, the Menace, the Mechanism.* New York: David McKay, 1954. 244 pp.

U.S. Congress, House Committee on Appropriations. 87th Cong., 1st Sess. *Report, Air Force Intercontinental Ballistic Missile Construction Program.* Washington, D.C.: Government Printing Office, 1961.

U.S. Congress, House Committee on Armed Services, Subcommittee on National Security Policy and Scientific Development. 91st Cong., 1st Sess. *Diplomatic and Strategic Impact of Multiple Warhead Missiles: Hearings* . . . . Washington, D.C.: Government Printing Office, 1970.

U.S. Congress, House Committee on Government Operations. 86th Cong., 1st Sess. *Organization and Management of Missile Programs* . . . . Hyde Gillette Report. Washington, D.C.: Government Printing Office, 1959.

_____. 86th Cong., 2d Sess. *Organization and Management of Missile Programs. Hearings* . . . .

Clark B. Millikan Report. Washington, D.C.: Government Printing Office, 1960.

U.S. Congress, Senate Committee on Armed Services. 84th Cong., 2d Sess. *Airpower. Hearings* . . . . 2 vols. Washington, D.C.: Government Printing Office, 1956.

_____. 85th Cong., 1st Sess. *Airpower. Report* . . . . Washington, D.C.: Government Printing Office, 1957. 128 pp.

_____. 91st Cong., 1st Sess. *Military Implications of the Treaty on the Non-Proliferation of Nuclear Weapons: Hearings* . . . . Washington, D.C.: Government Printing Office, 1969.

U.S. Congress, Senate Committee on Armed Services, Preparedness Investigating Subcommittee. 85th Cong. *Hearings, Inquiry into Satellite and Missile Programs*. Washington, D.C.: Government Printing Office, 1958.

_____. 88th Cong., 1st Sess. *Hearings on Military Aspects and Implications of Nuclear Test Ban Proposals and Related Matters*. Washington, D.C.: Government Printing Office, 1963.

_____. 88th Cong., 1st Sess. *Interim Report on the Military Implications of the Proposed Limited Nuclear Test Ban Treaty*. Washington, D.C.: Government Printing Office, 1963.

_____. 90th Cong., 2d Sess. *Status of U.S. Strategic Power: Hearings* . . . , *April 1968*. Washington, D.C.: Government Printing Office, 1968.

U.S. Congress, Senate Committee on Armed Services, Subcommittee on Strategic Arms Limitation Talks. 91st Cong., 2d Sess. *The Limitations of Strategic Arms Hearings* . . . . 2 pts. Washington, D.C.: Government Printing Office, 1970. 50, 117 pp.

U.S. Congress, Senate Committee on Foreign Relations. 91st Cong., 2d Sess. *ABM, MIRV, SALT, and Nuclear Arms Race* . . . . *Hearings*. Washington, D.C.: Government Printing Office, 1970.

U.S. Department of the Air Force. *Aerospace Systems Security, System Security Engineering*. Washington, D.C.: Government Printing Office, 1967. 94 pp.

Wilson, Eugene E. *Air Power for Peace*. New York: McGraw-Hill, 1945. 184 pp.

2. Land Based Missile Systems

Armacost, Michael H. *The Politics of Weapons Innovation: The Thor-Jupiter Controversy*. New York: Columbia University Press, 1969. 304 pp.

Bothwell, Frank E. "Is the ICBM Obsolete?" *Bulletin of the Atomic Scientists*, October 1969, pp. 21-22.

Chapman, John L. *Atlas: The Story of a Missile*. New York: Harper & Bros., 1960.

Donnelly, Charles H. *The United States Guided Missile Program*. Washington, D.C.: Government Printing Office, 1959. 130 pp.

Gantz, Lt. Col. Kenneth F. *The United States Air Force Report on the Ballistic Missile, Its Technology, Logistics and Strategy*. Garden City, N.Y.: Doubleday, 1958.

Hart, J. *The Mighty Thor: Missile in Readiness*. New York: Duell, Sloan & Pearce, 1961. 271 pp.

Neal, Roy. *Ace in the Hole: The Story of a Minuteman Missile*. Garden City, N.Y.: Doubleday, 1962.

Schwiebert, Ernest G. *A History of the United States*

Air Force Ballistic Missiles. New York: Frederick A. Praeger, 1965.

U.S. Congress, House Committee on Armed Services. 85th Cong., 2d Sess. *Investigation of National Defense Missiles: Hearings . . . .* Washington, D.C.: Government Printing Office, 1958.

U.S. Congress, House Committee on Government Operations. 86th Cong., 1st Sess. *Eleventh Report, Organization and Management of Missile Programs.* Washington, D.C.: Government Printing Office, 1959.

_____. 86th Cong., 1st Sess. *Organization and Management of Missile Programs: Hearings . . . .* Washington, D.C.: Government Printing Office, 1959.

_____. 86th Cong., 2d Sess. *Organization and Management of Missile Programs. Hearings . . . .* Washington, D.C.: Government Printing Office, 1960. 228 pp.

3. Sea Based Missile Systems

Baar, James, and Howard, William. *Polaris.* New York: Harcourt, Brace, 1960.

Blair, Clay, Jr. *The Atomic Submarine and Admiral Rickover.* New York: Holt, 1954.

Liell, William J. "The Polaris Missile System." *An Cosantoir: The Irish Defense Journal* 25 (1965): 275-77.

U.S. Department of the Navy, Special Projects Office. *Polaris Management; Fleet Ballistic Missile Program.* Rev. ed. Washington, D.C.: Government Printing Office, 1962. 32 pp.

4. Manned Aircraft

Alexander, Tom. "McNamara's Expensive Economy Plane."
  Fortune, June 1967, pp. 89-91, 184-87.

Art, Robert J. *The TFX Decision: McNamara and the
  Military.* Boston: Little, Brown, 1968.

Boeing Airplane Company, Military Airplane Systems Division. *Strategic Air Command Bomber Operations
  and Maintenance.* Seattle, Wash., 1970.

Bollinger, Lynn L.; Lilley, Tom; and Lombard,
  Albert E., Jr. "Preserving American Air Power."
  Harvard Business Review, Spring 1945, pp. 372-92.

Bowers, Peter M. *Boeing Aircraft Since 1916.* London:
  Putnam, 1966. 444 pp.

Bryan, Stanley E. "TFX--A Case in Policy Level
  Decision-Making." *Academy of Management Journal* 7
  (1964):54-70.

_____. "The TFX F-111 Aircraft: A Perspective in
  Military Command and Defense Management." *Naval
  War College Review,* April 1971, pp. 66-87.

Goodie, Maj. Clifford B. *Strategic Air Command: A
  Portrait.* New York: Simon & Schuster, 1965. 191
  pp.

Hammond, Paul Y. "Super Carriers and B-36 Bombers:
  Appropriations, Strategy and Politics." In *American Civil-Military Relations: A Book of Case Studies,* edited by Harold Stein, pp. 465-567. Birmingham: University of Alabama Press, 1963.

Jacobsen, Meyers K. "Design Development of the
  RB-36." *American Aviation Historical Society Journal,* Winter 1970, pp. 224-35.

Jones, Lloyd S. *U.S. Bombers: B-1 to B-70.* Los An-
    geles: Aero, 1962. 237 pp.

King, James E. "Airpower in the Missile Gap." *World
    Politics* 12 (1960):628-39.

Leach, W. Barton. "Obstacles to the Development of
    American Air Power." *Annals of the American Acade-
    my of Political and Social Science,* May 1955, pp.
    67-75.

Lee, Asher. *Air Power.* New York: Frederick A. Prae-
    ger, 1958.

Possony, Stefan T. *Strategic Air Power: The Pattern
    of Dynamic Security.* Washington, D.C.: Infantry
    Journal Press, 1949. 313 pp.

Power, Gen. Thomas S. "Strategic Air Command." *Mili-
    tary Review,* September 1947, pp. 3-8.

Rees, Ed. *Manned Missile: The Story of the B-70.*
    New York: Duell, Sloan & Pearce, 1960. 182 pp.

Robinson, Douglas H. *The B-58 Hustler.* New York:
    Arco, 1967. 64 pp.

Saundby, Robert H. M. S. *Air Bombardment: The Story
    of Its Development.* New York: Harper & Row, 1961.
    259 pp.

"The Strategic Air Command--A Special Report." *Air
    Force,* April 1956, pp. 39-138.

"Ten Years of Global Guard Duty." *Air Force,* April
    1956, entire issue.

U.S. Congress, House Committee on Armed Services.
    81st Cong., 1st Sess. *Investigation of the B-36
    Bomber Program.* 2 pts. Washington, D.C.: Govern-
    ment Printing Office, 1949.

U.S. Congress, House Committee on Armed Services.
89th Cong., 2d Sess. *Hearings before Subcommittee
no. 2 on the Department of Defense Decision to Reduce the Number and Types of Manned Bombers in the
Strategic Air Command.* Washington, D.C.: Government Printing Office, 1966.

_____. 89th Cong., 2d Sess. *Report of Subcommittee
no. 2 on the Department of Defense Decision to Reduce the Number and Types of Manned Bombers in the
Strategic Air Command.* Washington, D.C.: Government Printing Office, 1966.

U.S. Congress, Senate Committee on Armed Services,
Preparedness Investigating Subcommittee. 86th
Cong., 2d Sess. *Report: The B-58 Program.* Wash-
ington, D.C.: Government Printing Office, 1960.

_____. 86th Cong., 2d Sess. *Report: The B-70 Pro-
gram.* Washington, D.C.: Government Printing Office, 1960.

U.S. Congress, Senate Committee on Armed Services,
Subcommittee on the Air Force. 84th Cong., 2d
Sess. *Study of Airpower, Hearings . . . .* 23 pts.
Washington, D.C.: Government Printing Office,
1956.

U.S. Congress, Senate Committee on Government Operations, Permanent Subcommittee on Investigations.
88th Cong., 1st Sess. *Hearings on the TFX Contract
Investigation.* 10 vols. Washington, D.C.: Government Printing Office, 1963-64.

_____. 91st Cong., 2d Sess. *TFX Contract Investiga-
tion . . . Report.* Washington, D.C.: Government
Printing Office, 1970. 97 pp.

U.S. Department of the Air Force, Strategic Air Command, Directorate of Information. *SAC 20: The
Story of the United States Air Force's Strategic*

Air Command.   Offutt Air Force Base, Nebr., 1966.
51 pp.

U.S. Department of the Air Force, Strategic Air Command, Office of the Historian. *The Progressive Development of the Strategic Air Command, 1946-1970.* Offutt Air Force Base, Nebr., 1970.

5. Communications and Command Control

Larus, Joel. *Nuclear Weapons Safety and the Common Defense.* Columbus: Ohio State University Press, 1967. 171 pp.

Shepley, James R., and Blair, Clay, Jr. *The Hydrogen Bomb: The Men, the Menace, the Mechanism.* New York: David McKay, 1954. 244 pp.

6. Basing Requirements and Deployment

Dessette, Capt. Edward F. "Overseas Bases--How Long for This World." *U.S. Naval Institute Proceedings,* July 1960, pp. 23-30.

Goldman, Roy E. "U.S. Spanish Base Rights Agreement and the Atlantic Alliance." *U.S. Naval Institute Proceedings,* February 1969, pp. 102-4.

Hoopes, Townsend. "Overseas Bases in American Strategy." *Foreign Affairs* 37 (1958):69-82.

Lowi, Theodore J. "Bases in Spain." In *American Civil-Military Decisions: A Book of Case Studies,* edited by Harold Stein, pp. 667-705. University, Ala.: University of Alabama Press, 1963.

Packman, Martin. "Future Overseas Bases." *Editorial Research Reports,* 30 January 1957, pp. 65-81.

Rood, Harold W. *The Possible Utility of the U.S.*

Overseas Base Structure. Menlo Park, Calif.:
Stanford Research Institute, 1962. 80 pp.

Rowse, Arthur E. "Foreign Bases: Declining Asset."
Editorial Research Reports, 14 September 1960, pp.
665-82.

Wohlstetter, Albert. "Another Look at the Importance
of Overseas Bases. *Air Force,* May 1960, pp. 73-80.

_____. *On the Value of Overseas Bases.* RAND Paper
P-1877. Santa Monica, Calif.: RAND Corporation,
1960. 16 pp.

Wohlstetter, Albert, *et al. Selection and Use of
Strategic Air Bases.* RAND Report R-266. Santa
Monica, Calif.: RAND Corporation, 1954.

C. DEFENSIVE STRATEGIC FORCES

1. General Issues

Coale, Ansley J. *The Problem of Reducing Vulnerability to Atomic Bombs.* Princeton, N.J.: Princeton
University Press, 1947.

Latter, A. L., and Martinelli, E. A. *Active and Passive Defense.* RAND Paper 3165-1. Santa Monica,
Calif.: RAND Corporation, 1968. 13 pp.

Witze, Claude. "Can an Airborne Alert Prevent a
Space-Age Pearl Harbor?" *Air Force,* March 1960,
pp. 33-37.

2. Continental Defense against Air Attack

Associated Universities, Inc. *Report of the Project
East River.* New York, 1952.

Berkner, Lloyd B. "Continental Defense." *Current History* 26 (1954):257-62.

Conant, Melvin. *The Long Polar Watch: Canada and the Defense of North America.* New York: Harper & Bros., 1962. 204 pp.

Killian, James R., Jr., and Hill, A. G. "For a Continental Defense." *Atlantic,* November 1953, pp. 37-41.

Morenus, Richard. *DEW Line: Distant Early Warning, The Miracle of America's First Line of Defense.* New York: Rand McNally, 1957. 184 pp.

Watson-Watt, Sir Robert. "Radar Defense—Today and Tomorrow." *Foreign Affairs* 32 (1954):230-43.

3. Ballistic Missile Defense

    a. General Issues

Adams, Benson D. *Ballistic Missile Defense.* New York: American Elsevier, 1971. 274 pp.

_____. "McNamara's ABM Policy." *Orbis* 12 (1968): 200-25.

American Security Council, National Strategy Committee. *The ABM and the Changed Strategic Military Balance U.S.A. vs. U.S.S.R.* Washington, D.C., 1969. 60 pp.

Baldwin, Hanson W. "Race for the Anti-Missile Missile." *New York Times Magazine,* 15 April 1962, pp. 21-23, 96-108.

Barnaby, C. F., and Boserup, A., eds. *Implication of Anti-Ballistic Missile Systems.* New York: Humanities Press, 1969. 246 pp.

Bethe, Hans A. "Hard Point vs. City Defense." *Bulletin of the Atomic Scientists*, June 1969, pp. 25-26.

Brennan, Donald G. "The Case for Missile Defense." *Foreign Affairs* 47 (1969):433-48.

_____. "Missile Defense and Arms Control." *Disarmament* 14 (1967):1-4.

_____. "New Thoughts on Missile Defense." *Bulletin of the Atomic Scientists*, June 1967, pp. 10-15.

Center for the Study of Democratic Institutions. *Anti-Ballistic Missile: Yes or No?* New York: Hill & Wang, 1969. 147 pp.

Chayes, Abram, and Wiesner, Jerome B., eds. *ABM: An Evaluation of the Decision to Deploy an Anti-Ballistic Missile System*. New York: Signet Books, 1969.

Coffey, Joseph I. "The Anti-Ballistic Missile Debate." *Foreign Affairs* 45 (1967):403-13.

_____. "The Chinese and Ballistic Missile Defense." *Bulletin of the Atomic Scientists*, December 1965, pp. 17-20.

_____. "Soviet ABM Policy: The Implications for the West." *International Affairs* 43 (1969):205-22.

Dyson, Freeman J. "A Case for Missile Defense." *Bulletin of the Atomic Scientists*, April 1969, pp. 31-34.

_____. "Defense Against Ballistic Missiles." *Bulletin of the Atomic Scientists*, June 1964, pp. 12-18.

Erickson, John. "The Fly in Outer Space: The Soviet Union and the Anti-Ballistic Missile." *World Today* 23 (1967):106-14.

Foster, Richard B. *The Impact of Ballistic Missile Defense on Arms Control Prospects.* Menlo Park, Calif.: Stanford Research Institute, 1966.

Fulbright, J. W. "Foreign Policy Implications of the ABM Debate." *Bulletin of the Atomic Scientists,* June 1969, pp. 20-23.

Garwin, Richard L., and Bethe, Hans A. "Anti-Ballistic Missile Systems." *Scientific American,* March 1968, pp. 21-31.

Hahn, Walter F., and Cottrell, Alvin J. "Ballistic Missile Defense and Soviet Strategy." *Orbis* 9 (1965):316-37.

Hersh, Seymour M. "The Great ABM Pork Barrel." *War-Peace Report,* January 1968, pp. 3-9, 19.

Holst, Johan J., and Schneider, William, Jr., eds. *Why ABM? Policy Issues in the Missile Defense Controversy.* New York: Pergamon Press, 1969.

Inglis, David R. "The Anti-Ballistic Missile: A Dangerous Folly." *Saturday Review,* 7 September 1968, pp. 26-27, 55-56.

Long, Franklin A. "Strategic Balance and the ABM." *Bulletin of the Atomic Scientists,* December 1968, pp. 2-5.

McMahan, Richard H., Jr. "Rationales for Ballistic Missile Defense Policy." *Bulletin of the Atomic Scientists,* March 1965, pp. 37-40.

Martin, Laurence W. "Ballistic Missile Defense and Arms Control." *Arms Control and Disarmament* 1 (1968):61-67.

_____. *Ballistic Missile Defense and the Alliance.* Boulogne-sur-Seine, France: Atlantic Institute, 1969. 51 pp.

Martin, Laurence W. "Ballistic Missile Defense and
   the Strategic Balance." In *Year Book of World Affairs 1967*, pp. 37-54. New York: Frederick A.
   Praeger, 1967.

Morton, Louis. "The Anti-Ballistic Missile: Some Political and Strategic Considerations." *Virginia
   Quarterly Review* 42 (1966):28-40.

Phillips, David C. *Ballistic Missile Defense: Evolution of the Decision-Making Process*. SP-3462.
   Santa Monica, Calif.: Systems Development Corporation, 1969. 63 pp.

Pickus, Robert. *The ABM and a World Without War*.
   Berkeley, Calif.: World Without War Publication,
   1969.

Rabinowitch, Eugene, and Adams, Ruth, eds. *Debate:
   The Anti-ballistic Missile*. Chicago: Educational
   Foundation for Nuclear Science, 1967. 172 pp.

Rothstein, Robert L. "The ABM, Proliferation and International Stability." *Foreign Affairs* 46 (1968):
   487-502.

Russett, Bruce. "The Complexities of Ballistic Missile Defense." *Yale Review* 56 (1967):354-67.

Stone, Jeremy J. "Beginning of the Next Round?" *Bulletin of the Atomic Scientists*, December 1967, pp.
   20-25.

_____. *The Case against Missile Defences*. Adelphi
   Papers, no. 47. London: Institute for Strategic
   Studies, 1968.

Tedeschi, James T. "Civil Defense: Some Literature
   and an Example of Needed Research." *Background*,
   November 1963, pp. 155-62.

Thomas, John. "The Role of Missile Defense in Soviet

Strategy." *Military Review*, May 1964, pp. 46-58.

U.S. Congress, Joint Committee on Atomic Energy, Subcommittee on Military Applications. 90th Cong.,
1st Sess. *Scope, Magnitude and Implications of the
United States ABM Programs: Hearings . . . . November 1967.* Washington, D.C.: Government Printing Office, 1968.

U.S. Congress, Senate Committee on Foreign Relations.
91st Cong., 1st Sess. *Intelligence and the ABM:
Hearings . . . . with Melvin Laird, Secretary of
Defense, and Richard Helms, Director, Central Intelligence Agency, Together With an Exchange of
Letters Between J.W. Fulbright Chairman, Committee
on Foreign Relations, and Secretary Laird, June 23,
1969.* Washington, D.C.: Government Printing Office, 1969.

_____. 91st Cong., 2d Sess. *ABM, MIRV, SALT, and
Nuclear Arms Race . . . . Hearings.* Washington,
D.C.: Government Printing Office, 1970.

U.S. Congress, Senate Committee on Foreign Relations,
Subcommittee on Disarmament. 90th Cong., 1st Sess.
*Status of the Development of the Antiballistic Sys-
tems in the United States.* Washington, D.C.: Government Printing Office, 1967.

U.S. Congress, Senate Committee on Foreign Relations,
Subcommittee on International Organizations and
Disarmament Affairs. 91st Cong., 1st Sess. *Stra-
tegic and Foreign Policy Implications of ABM Sys-
tems: Hearings . . . .* 3 pts. Washington, D.C.:
Government Printing Office, 1969.

Wiesner, Jerome B. "The Case Against an Anti-
Ballistic Missile System." *Look*, 28 November 1967,
pp. 17-25.

Willrich, Mason. "ABM and Arms Control." *International Affairs* 44 (1968):228-39.

Young, Elizabeth. "ABM: No Alternative to Politics." *Bulletin of the Atomic Scientists*, June 1967, pp. 47-49.

_____. "Prospects for SALT and ABM Debate." *World Today*, August 1969, pp. 323-38.

Young, Oran R. "Active Defense and International Order." *Bulletin of the Atomic Scientists*, May 1967, pp. 35-42.

_____. "The Political Consequences of Active Defense." *Bulletin of the Atomic Scientists*, February 1968, pp. 16-20.

b. Specific Programs

Boehm, George A. "Countdown for Nike-X." *Fortune*, May 1965, pp. 133-37, 192-200.

Davis, Paul C. "The Coming Chinese Threat and United States Sea-Based ABM Options." *Orbis* 11 (1967):45-66.

_____. "Sentinel and the Future of SABMIS." *Military Review*, March 1968, pp. 56-66.

Forbes, Allen. *ABM: Point of No Return? A Critique of the Nike-X Anti-Ballistic Missile System.* Washington, D.C.: Council for a Livable World, 1967. 28 pp.

"Is There a Defense Against the ICBM? Nike-Zeus: Suspended Sentence Before Trial." *Interavia* 17 (1962):1016-21.

Kintner, William R., ed. *The Prudent Case for Safeguard.* New York: National Strategy Information Center, 1969. 28 pp.

_____, ed. *Safeguard: Why the ABM Makes Sense.*

New York: Hawthorn, 1969.   413 pp.

Lapp, Ralph E. "From Nike to Safeguard: A Biography
    of ABM." *New York Times Magazine,* 4 May 1969, pp.
    29-30ff.

Ubell, Earl, and Loary, Stuart H. "The Death of the
    Nike-Zeus." *Saturday Evening Post,* 1 June 1963,
    pp. 15-19.

U.S. Congress, House Committee on Appropriations.
    91st Cong., 1st Sess. *Safeguard Antiballistic Mis-
    sile System: Hearings* . . . . Washington, D.C.:
    Government Printing Office, 1969.

_____. 91st Cong., 1st Sess. *Sentinel Antiballistic
    Missile Systems: Briefing* . . . . Washington,
    D.C.: Government Printing Office, 1969.

            4. Civil Defense

American Management Association. *Survival and Recov-
    ery: Industrial Preparedness in the Nuclear Age.*
    AMA Management Bulletin, no. 19. New York, 1962.

Barrett, Kenneth D. *The Deception of Civil Defense,
    and a Plan for a Nuclear War Protection System.*
    Orlando, Fla.: Independence Press, 1964.   215 pp.

Bleicken, G. D. "The Role of Non-Military Defense in
    American Foreign and Defense Policy." *Political
    Science Quarterly* 74 (1959):555-63.

Brynes, A., and Underhill, G. "Shelters and Survival:
    A Report on the Civil Defense Muddle." *New Repub-
    lic,* 15 January 1962, pp. 3-40.

Bullis, Andrew S., and Williams, Lawrence A. *Organiz-
    ing Municipal Governments for Civil Defense.* Wash-
    ington, D.C.: American Municipal Association,
    1963.   318 pp.

Chapman, Seville. "Do We Want Fallout Shelters?" *Bulletin of the Atomic Scientists,* February 1963, pp. 24-26.

Colmery, Benjamin H., Jr. "Civil Defense: An Operational Evaluation." *U.S. Naval Institute Proceedings,* September 1963, pp. 66-73.

Cooling, B. Franklin. "U.S. Army Support of Civil Defense: The Formative Years." *Military Affairs,* February 1971, pp. 7-11.

Cornell, Rogers. "The Active Role of Passive Defense." *Stanford Research Institute Journal* 3 (1959):179-86.

Durkee, William P. "Civil Defense--The Military Support Role." *Army Information Digest,* November 1964, pp. 20-66.

Harvard University Graduate School of Business Administration. *Effective Civil Defense.* Cambridge, Mass., 1962. 323 pp.

Kahn, Herman. "How Many Can Be Saved?" *Bulletin of the Atomic Scientists* 15 (1959):30-34.

_____. *Some Specific Suggestions for Obtaining Early Non-Military Defense Capabilities and Initiating Long-Range Programs.* RAND Memorandum RM-2206-RC. Santa Monica, Calif.: RAND Corporation, 1958.

Kahn, Herman, *et al. A Report on a Study of Non-Military Defense.* RAND Report R-332-RC. Santa Monica, Calif.: RAND Corporation, 1958.

Kahn, Herman; Fromm, Erich; and Maccoby, Michael. "A Debate on the Question of Civil Defense." *Commentary,* January 1962, pp. 1-23.

Lanson, Robert. "The Army and Civil Defense." *Military Review,* December 1964, pp. 3-12.

Lapp, Ralph E. "The Strategy of Civil Defense." *Bulletin of the Atomic Scientists* 6 (1950):241-43.

Melman, Seymour, ed. *No Place to Hide: Fact and Fiction about Fallout Shelters*. New York: Grove Press, 1962. 205 pp.

Mitchell, Donald W. *Civil Defense: Planning for Survival and Recovery*. Washington, D.C.: Industrial College of the Armed Forces, 1966. 217 pp.

Modell, John. *The Politics of Safety: American Civil Defense*. New York: Columbia University Bureau of Applied Social Research, 1963. 40 pp.

National Academy of Science. *The Adequacy of Government Research Programs in Non-Military Defense*. Washington, D.C., 1958.

Nehnevajsa, Jiri. *Americans' Views on Civil Defense in the Cold War Context: 1966*. Pittsburgh: University of Pittsburgh, 1966. 142 pp.

Piel, Gerald. "The Illusion of Civil Defense." *Bulletin of the Atomic Scientists,* February 1962, pp. 2-8.

Systems Development Corporation. *Civil Defense Requirements*. Santa Monica, Calif., 1963. 319 pp.

Tedeschi, James. "Civil Defense: Some Literature and an Example of Needed Research." *Background,* November 1963, pp. 155-62.

U.S. Atomic Energy Commission. *Atomic Warfare Defense.* Washington, D.C., 1955. 182 pp.

U.S. Commission on Intergovernmental Relations. *A Staff Report on Civil Defense and Urban Vulnerability . . . .* Meyer Kestnbaum Commission. Washington, D.C.: Government Printing Office, 1955.

U.S. Congress, House Committee on Agriculture. *Food for Civilian Survival in War.* Interim Report of the Consumers Study Subcommittee. Victor L. Anfuso Report. Washington, D.C.: Government Printing Office, 1957.

U.S. Congress, House Committee on Government Operations. 84th Cong., 2d Sess. *Civil Defense for National Security, Hearings* . . . . 7 vols. Washington, D.C.: Government Printing Office, 1956.

_____. 86th Cong., 2d Sess. *Civil Defense, Hearings* . . . . 3 pts. Washington, D.C.: Government Printing Office, 1960.

U.S. Congress, Senate Committee on Armed Services, Subcommittee on Civil Defense. 84th Cong., 1st Sess. *Civil Defense Program, Hearings* . . . . Washington, D.C.: Government Printing Office, 1955. 377 pp.

U.S. Department of Defense, Office of Civil Defense. *Civil Defense 1965.* Washington, D.C., 1965. 114 pp.

U.S. Department of the Army, Office of the Secretary of the Army. *Organization and Functions Office of Civil Defense.* Washington, D.C., 1967. 109 pp.

U.S. President's Air Policy Commission. *Survival in the Air Age.* Washington, D.C.: Government Printing Office, 1948. 166 pp.

U.S. Superintendent of Documents. *Atomic Energy and Civil Defense.* Price List 84. Washington, D.C.: Government Printing Office, current issue.

Wigner, Eugene P., ed. *Survival and the Bomb: Methods of Civil Defense.* Bloomington: University of Indiana Press, 1969. 307 pp.

_____, ed. *Who Speaks for Civil Defense?* New York:

Charles Scribner's Sons, 1968. 127 pp.

Williams, Lawrence A., *et al.* *Intergovernmental Civil Defense Organization and Programs.* Washington, D.C.: National League of Cities, 1965. 304 pp.

Winter, Sidney S., Jr. *Economic Viability after Thermonuclear War: The Limits of Feasible Production.* RAND Memorandum RM-3426-PR. Santa Monica, Calif.: RAND Corporation, 1963.

Yosphe, Harry B., ed. *Emergency Economic Stabilization.* Washington, D.C.: Industrial College of the Armed Forces, 1964.

D. GENERAL PURPOSE FORCES: NON-NUCLEAR

1. General Issues

Eliot, George F. "The Army and Strategic Mobility." *Military Review,* August 1957, pp. 3-10.

Harvey, Frank. *Strike Command.* New York: Duell, Sloan & Pearce, 1962.

Lemnitzer, Lyman L. "The Most Formidable Conventional Armed Forces in the World Today." *Atlantic Community* 6 (1969):501-7.

"Readiness for the Little War: A Strategic Security Force." *Military Review,* May 1957, pp. 14-21.

"Readiness for the Little War: Optimum 'Integrated Strategy.'" *Military Review,* April 1957, pp. 14-26.

Tompkins, John S. *The Weapons of World War III: The Road Back from the Bomb.* New York: Doubleday, 1966.

Wheeler, Gen. Earle G. "Strategic Mobility." *Army Information Digest,* January 1957, pp. 3-12.

2. Combat Ground Forces, Army

    a. Infantry

Dodson, C. A. "Special Forces." *Army,* June 1961, pp. 44-52.

Eliot, George Fielding. "The Army and Strategic Mobility." *Military Review,* August 1957, pp. 3-10.

Garland, Lt. Col. Albert N., ed. *Infantry in Vietnam.* Fort Benning, Ga.: Infantry Magazine, 1967. 409 pp.

Hamlett, Lt. Gen. B. "Special Forces: Training for Peace and War." *Army Information Digest,* June 1961, pp. 2-9.

Ortner, E. H. "U.S. Special Forces--The Faceless Army." *Popular Science,* August 1961, pp. 56-59ff.

Rowny, Edward L. "Ground Tactics in an Atomic War." *Army Combat Forces Journal,* August 1954, pp. 18-22.

Stillman, Richard J. *The U.S. Infantry: Queen of Battle.* New York: Franklin Watts, 1965.

U.S. Army Command and General Staff College. *Organizational Data for the Army in the Field.* Fort Leavenworth, Kan., April 1967.

U.S. Army Infantry School. *Infantry Reference Data.* Fort Benning, Ga., July 1964.

U.S. Department of the Army, Combat Development Command, Combat Organization Research Group. *Evolution of the U.S. Army Division, 1939-1968.* CORG-M-365. Fort Belvoir, Va., 1969.

U.S. Department of the Army, Combat Development Command, Combat Organization Research Group. *Evolution of the U.S. Army Infantry Battalion, 1939-1968*. CORG-M-343. Fort Belvoir, Va., 1968.

_____. *Evolution of the U.S. Army Infantry Mortar Squad: The Argonne to Pleiku*. Fort Belvoir, Va., 1966.

_____. *Organization . . . Infantry Rifle Squad: From Valley Forge to Road*. CORG-M-194. Fort Belvoir, Va., 1965.

_____. *The United States Soldier in a Nonviolent Role: A Historical Overview*. Fort Belvoir, Va., 1967.

    b. Armor

Cossey, Gerald R. "Tank vs. Tank." *Armor*, September-October 1970, pp. 16-19.

Mackeey, Kenneth. *The History of Armoured Vehicles and Tanks*. London: MacDonald, 1970.

Ogorkiewicz, Richard M. *Armor: A History of Mechanized Forces*. New York: Frederick A. Praeger, 1960.

_____. "Armor in the Nuclear Age." *Military Review*, September 1958, pp. 3-9.

_____. *Armoured Forces: A History of Armoured Forces and Their Vehicles*. New York: Arco, 1970. 475 pp.

_____. *Design and Development of Fighting Vehicles*. London: MacDonald, 1969.

U.S. Army Armor School. *Armor Reference Data*. Fort Knox, Ky., May 1967.

U.S. Congress, House Committee on Armed Services. 91st Cong., 1st Sess. *Review of Army Tanks Program: Report of the Armed Services Investigating Subcommittee . . . .* Washington, D.C.: Government Printing Office, 1969. 39 pp.

U.S. Department of the Army, Combat Development Command, Combat Organization Research Group. *Evolution of the Armored Infantry Squad.* CORG-M-198. Fort Belvoir, Va., 1965.

    c. Air Cavalry

Galvin, John R. *Air Assault: The Development of Airmobile Warfare.* New York: Hawthorn Books, 1969. 318 pp.

McMahon, Col. Robert E. "Airmobile Operations." *Military Review,* June 1959, pp. 28-35.

Mertel, Lt. Col. Kenneth D. *Year of the Horse-- Vietnam. 1st Air Cavalry in the Highlands.* New York: Exposition Press, 1968. 380 pp.

Montross, Lynn. *Cavalry in the Sky: The Story of the U.S. Marine Combat Helicopters.* New York: Harper & Bros., 1954. 270 pp.

    d. Support

Burke, Lt. Col. Robert L. "Corps Logistics Planning in Vietnam." *Military Review,* August 1969, pp. 2-11.

Downey, Fairfax. *Sound of the Guns: The Story of American Artillery.* New York: David McKay, 1956.

Hickey, G. C. *The American Military Advisor and His Foreign Counterpart: The Case of Vietnam.* RAND

Memorandum RM-4482-ARPA. Santa Monica, Calif.:
RAND Corporation, 1969. 105 pp.

U.S. Army Artillery and Missile School. *Field Artillery Data*. Fort Sill, Okla., July 1967.

Westover, Capt. John G. *Combat Support in Korea*.
Washington, D.C.: Combat Forces Press, 1955. 254
pp.

3. Combat Ground Forces, Marines

Geer, Andrew. *The New Breed: The Story of the U.S.
Marines in Korea*. New York: Harper & Bros., 1952.
395 pp.

Hymoff, Edward. *The First Marine Division in Vietnam*.
New York: M. W. Lads, 1967.

Martin, Russ. *The Last Parallel: A Marine's War
Journal*. New York: Rinehart, 1957. 333 pp.

Montross, Lynn. *Cavalry in the Sky: The Story of the
U.S. Marine Combat Helicopters*. New York: Harper
& Bros., 1954. 270 pp.

_____. "Fleet Marine Force Korea." *U.S. Naval Institute Proceedings*, August 1953, pp. 828-41; and
September 1953, pp. 994-1005.

Montross, Lynn, and Canzona, Capt. Nicholas A. *U.S.
Marine Corps Operations in Korea, 1950-1953*. 3
vols. Washington, D.C.: Government Printing Office, 1954-57.

Montross, Lynn; Kuokka, Maj. Hubard D.; and Hicks,
Maj. Norman W. *U.S. Marine Corps Operations in
Korea, 1950-1953*. Vol. 4. Washington, D.C.: Government Printing Office, 1962. 342 pp.

U.S. Congress, Senate Committee on Armed Services.

82d Cong., 1st Sess. *Marine Corps Strength and Joint Chiefs Representation. Hearings . . . .* Washington, D.C.: Government Printing Office, 1951.   183 pp.

U.S. Marine Corps, Headquarters. *Professional Knowledge Gained from Operational Experiences in Vietnam.* Washington, D.C., 1967.

U.S. Marine Corps, Historical Branch, G-3 Division. *Mobilization of the Marine Corps Reserve in the Korean Conflict, 1950-1951.* Prepared by Ernest H. Guisti. Washington, D.C., 1951; reprinted 1967. 80 pp.

4. Theater Air Power, Air Force and Army

"The Air-Ground Operation in Korea." *Air Force,* March 1951, pp. 19-58.

Broughton, Col. Jack. *Thud Ridge.* Philadelphia: J. B. Lippincott, 1969.   254 pp.

Coble, Donald W.   "Air Support in the Korean War." *Aerospace Historian,* Summer 1969, pp. 26-29.

Curton, Warren D.   *Cost Effectiveness and Mission Suitability of Conventional versus Jet Aircraft for Counter-Insurgency Operations.* Maxwell Air Force Base, Ala.:   Air War College, 1966.

Donovan, Stanley J.   "Tactical Aerospace Forces." *Air University Quarterly Review,* Winter-Spring 1960-61, pp. 74-88.

Harvey, Frank. *Air War: Vietnam.* New York: Bantam, 1967.

Holloway, Gen. Bruce K.   "Air Superiority in Tactical Air Warfare." *Air University Review,* March-April 1968, pp. 2-15.

Holloway, Col. Bruce K. "High Sub-Sonic Speeds for
    Air Warfare." *Air University Quarterly Review,*
    Fall 1947, pp. 42-52.

Jackson, B. R. *Douglas Skyraider.* Fallbrook, Calif.:
    Aero, 1969. 144 pp.

Key, William G. *Air Power in Action: Korea, 1950-51.*
    Baltimore: Pegasus, 1952. 51 pp.

Nichols, Franklin A. "Theater Air Forces." *Naval War
    College Review,* December 1951, pp. 37-55; April
    1953, pp. 45-66.

Quesada, Elwood R. "The Tactical Air Command." *Mili-
    tary Review,* September 1960, pp. 62-72.

Reid, William R. "Tactical Air in Limited War." *Air
    University Quarterly Review,* Spring 1956, pp. 40-
    48.

Saundby, Robert H. M. S. *Air Bombardment: The Story
    of Its Development.* New York: Harper & Row, 1961.
    259 pp.

Siekman, Philip. "The Big New Whirl in Helicopters."
    Fortune, April 1966, pp. 124ff.

Sleeper, Col. Raymond S. "Korean Targets for Medium
    Bombardment." *Air University Quarterly Review,*
    Spring 1951, pp. 18-31.

Stewart, Col. James T., ed. *Airpower: The Decisive
    Factor in Korea.* Princeton, N.J.: D. Van Nos-
    trand, 1957.

U.S. Army Aviation School. *Army Aviation.* Fort
    Rucker, Ala., 1959. 16 pp.

U.S. Congress, Senate Committee on Armed Services.
    90th Cong., 2d Sess. *U.S. Tactical Air Power Pro-
    gram: Hearings Before the Preparedness*

Investigation Subcommittee . . . . May and June 1968. Washington, D.C.: Government Printing Office, 1968.

U.S. Congress, Senate Committee on Government Operations, Permanent Subcommittee on Investigations. 88th Cong., 1st Sess. *Hearings on the TFX Contract Investigation*. 10 vols. Washington, D.C.: Government Printing Office, 1963-64.

_____. 91st Cong., 2d Sess. *TFX Contract Investigation . . . Report*. Washington, D.C.: Government Printing Office, 1970. 97 pp.

U.S. Department of the Air Force, Far Eastern Air Force Bomber Command. "Headweights over Korea: B-29 Employment in the Korean Air War." *Air University Quarterly Review*, Spring 1954, pp. 99-115.

U.S. Department of the Air Force, Historical Division. *United States Air Force Operations in the Korean Conflict*. 3 vols. Maxwell Air Force Base, Ala., 1952-56.

U.S. Department of the Air Force, Secretary of the Air Force, Office of Information, Internal Information Division. *United States Air Force Fact Sheet on the F-111A*. Washington, D.C., July 1966.

Verrier, Anthony. "Strategic Bombing--The Lessons of World War II and the American Experience in Vietnam." *Royal United Service Institution Journal*, May 1967, pp. 157-61.

Wagner, Roy. *The North American Sabre*. New York: Doubleday, 1963.

Wayland, Otto P. "Air Power in Limited War." *Ordnance*, July-August 1959, pp. 40-43.

_____. "Tactical Air Power." *Ordnance* 42 (1958): 798-801.

Wayland, Otto P. "Tactical Airpower–Worldwide." *Air Force,* July 1955, pp. 38–44.

5. General Naval Forces, Including Naval and
   Marine Air Power

Chatterton, Howard A. *An Analysis and Optimization of a Combination Minesweeper/Fishing Vessel.* Cambridge, Mass.: M.I.T. Department of Naval Architecture and Marine Engineering, 1968.

Coble, Donald W. "Air Support in the Korean War." *Aerospace Historian,* Summer 1969, pp. 26–29.

Harvey, Frank. *Air War: Vietnam.* New York: Bantam, 1967.

Key, William G. *Air Power in Action: Korea, 1950–51.* Baltimore: Pegasus, 1952. 51 pp.

Kuzmack, Arnold M. *Naval Force Levels and Modernization: An Analysis of Shipbuilding Requirements.* Washington, D.C.: Brookings Institution, 1971. 47 pp.

McCutcheon, Lt. Gen. Keith B. "Marine Aviation in Vietnam, 1962–1970." *U.S. Naval Institute Proceedings,* May 1971, pp. 122–55.

MacDonald, Scot. "Evolution of Aircraft Carriers: The Turbulent Post–War Years." *Naval Aviation News,* October 1963, pp. 22–26.

Nichols, Franklin A. "Theater Air Forces." *Naval War College Review,* December 1951, pp. 37–55; April 1953, pp. 45–66.

Polmar, Norman. *Aircraft Carriers: A Graphic History of Carrier Aviation and Its Influence on World Events.* Garden City, N.Y.: Doubleday, 1969. 788 pp.

Stewart, Col. James T., ed. *Airpower: The Decisive Factor in Korea.* Princeton, N.J.: D. Van Nostrand, 1957.

Turnbull, Archibald, and Lord, Clifford L. *History of United States Naval Aviation.* New Haven: Yale University Press, 1949.

U.S. Congress, Joint Committee on Atomic Energy. 88th Cong., 1st Sess. *Hearings on Nuclear Propulsion for Naval Surface Vessels.* Washington, D.C.: Government Printing Office, 1963.

U.S. Congress, Senate Committee on Armed Services. 90th Cong., 2d Sess. *U.S. Tactical Air Power Program: Hearings Before the Preparedness Investigation Subcommittee . . . . May and June 1968.* Washington, D.C.: Government Printing Office, 1968.

U.S. Congress, Senate Committee on Government Operations, Permanent Subcommittee on Investigations. 88th Cong., 1st Sess. *Hearings on the TFX Contract Investigation.* 10 vols. Washington, D.C.: Government Printing Office, 1963-64.

_____. 91st Cong., 2d Sess. *TFX Contract Investigation . . . Report.* Washington, D.C.: Government Printing Office, 1970. 97 pp.

U.S. Department of the Navy. *America's Use of Sea Mines.* Washington, D.C.: Government Printing Office, 1962. 173 pp.

_____. *Naval Airborne Ordnance.* Washington, D.C.: Government Printing Office, 1959. 377 pp.

_____. *Naval Aviation in Review.* Washington, D.C.: Government Printing Office, 1958. 338 pp.

_____. *Navy Wings.* Washington, D.C.: Government Printing Office, 1955. 216 pp.

U.S. Department of the Navy. *United States Naval Avi-ation, 1910-60.* Washington, D.C.: Government Printing Office, 1961. 239 pp.

U.S. Department of the Navy, Naval History Division. *Aviation in the United States Navy.* 3d ed. Washington, D.C.: Government Printing Office, 1968. 32 pp.

_____. *The Battleship in the United States Navy.* Washington, D.C.: Government Printing Office, 1970. 64 pp.

Wayland, Otto P. "Air Power in Limited War." *Ordnance,* July-August 1959, pp. 40-43.

Wheeler, Gerald E. "Naval Aviation in the Korean War." *U.S. Naval Institute Proceedings,* July 1957, pp. 762-77.

Wright, Quincy. *Prevention of the Expansion of Limited Wars and Preservation of International Order with Special Reference to the Role of Seaborne Weapons Systems.* NOTS TP 2668. China Lake, Calif.: U.S. Naval Ordnance Test Station, 1961.

Xydis, Stephen G. "The Genesis of the Sixth Fleet." *U.S. Naval Institute Proceedings,* August 1958, pp. 41-50.

6. Submarines and Anti-Submarine Warfare

Cohen, Paul. *The Realm of the Submarine.* London: Macmillan, 1969. 274 pp.

Rees, Ed. *The Seas and the Subs.* New York: Duell, Sloan & Pearce, 1961.

U.S. Congress, Joint Committee on Atomic Energy. 85th Cong., 2d Sess. *Report of the Underseas Warfare Advisory Panel to the Submarine Committee on*

Military Application. Washington, D.C.: Government Printing Office, 1958.

U.S. Congress, Joint Committee on Atomic Energy. 90th Cong., 1st and 2d Sess. *Naval Nuclear Propulsion Program--1967-68; Hearings, March 16, 1967; February 8, 1968*. Washington, D.C.: Government Printing Office, 1968.

_____. 90th Cong., 2d Sess. *Nuclear Submarines of Advanced Designs. Hearings*. 2 pts. Washington, D.C.: Government Printing Office, 1968.

_____. 91st Cong., 1st Sess. *Hearings before the Joint Committee on Atomic Energy . . . on the Naval Nuclear Propulsion Program, April 23, 1969*. Washington, D.C.: Government Printing Office, 1969. 232 pp.

U.S. Congress, Senate Committee on Armed Services. 90th Cong., 2d Sess. *U.S. Submarine Program: Hearings before the Preparedness Investigating Subcommittee . . . , March 1968*. Washington, D.C.: Government Printing Office, 1968.

U.S. Department of the Navy. *United States Ship Thresher (SSN-593). In Memoriam April 10, 1963*. Washington, D.C.: Government Printing Office, 1964. 146 pp.

U.S. Department of the Navy, Naval History Division. *The Submarine in the United States Navy*. 3d ed. Washington, D.C.: Government Printing Office, 1969. 27 pp.

Weathrup, R. A. "Defense Against Nuclear-Powered Submarines." *U.S. Naval Institute Proceedings*, December 1959, pp. 70-75.

7. Amphibious Forces

Harrigan, Anthony. "Inshore and River Warfare." *Orbis* 10 (1966):940-46.

Heinl, Robert D. "The Inchon Landing: A Case Study in Amphibious Planning." *Naval War College Review*, May 1967, pp. 51-72.

Isley, J. A., and Crowl, P. A. *The U.S. Marines and Amphibious War*. Princeton, N.J.: Princeton University Press, 1951.

Smith, Gen. H. M. "Development of Amphibious Tactics in the U.S. Navy." *Marine Corps Gazette*, June-October 1948.

U.S. Department of the Navy, Naval History Division. *Riverine Warfare: The U.S. Navy's Operations on Inland Waters*. Washington, D.C.: Government Printing Office, 1968. 53 pp.

8. Chemical and Biological Warfare

Alexander, A. S., *et al*. *The Control of Chemical and Biological Weapons*. New York: Carnegie Endowment for International Peace, 1971. 96 pp.

Brown, Frederic J. *Chemical Warfare: A Study in Restraints*. Princeton, N.J.: Princeton University Press, 1968. 355 pp.

Clarke, Robin. *The Silent Weapons*. New York: David McKay, 1968. 270 pp.

Goldblat, Jozef. "Are Tear Gas and Herbicides Permitted Weapons?" *Bulletin of the Atomic Scientists*, April 1970, pp. 13-16.

Hersh, Seymour M. *Chemical and Biological Warfare:*

America's Hidden Arsenal. Indianapolis: Bobbs-
Merrill, 1968. 354 pp.

McCarthy, Richard D. *The Ultimate Folly: War by Pes-
tilence, Asphyxiation, and Defoliation.* New York:
Alfred A. Knopf, 1969. 176 pp.

Meselson, Matthew S. "Behind the Nixon Policy for
Chemical and Biological Warfare." *Bulletin of the
Atomic Scientists,* January 1970, pp. 23-34.

_____. "Chemical and Biological Weapons." *Scientif-
ic American,* May 1970, pp. 15-25.

Miles, Wyndham D. "The Idea of Chemical Warfare in
Modern Times." *Journal of the History of Ideas,*
April-June 1970, pp. 297-304.

O'Brien, William V. "Biological/Chemical Warfare and
the International Law of War." *Georgetown Law
Journal* 51 (1962):1-63.

Rose, Steven, ed. *CBW: Chemical and Biological Warfare.* London: George G. Harrap, 1968. 209 pp.

Rothschild, Jacquard Hirshorn. *Tomorrow's Weapons:
Chemical and Biological.* New York: McGraw-Hill,
1964. 271 pp.

Stockholm International Peace Research Institute.
*Chemical and Biological Warfare--Developments, Dan-
gers and Disarmament Possibilities.* New York:
Humanities Press, 1971.

Thomas, Ann Van Wynen. *Legal Limits on the Use of
Chemical and Biological Weapons.* Dallas: Southern
Methodist University Press, 1970. 332 pp.

U.S. Congress, House Committee on Armed Services.
91st Cong., 1st Sess. *Chemical-Biological Warfare:
U.S. Policies and International Effects: Hearings
. . . . November 18, 20, December 2, 9, 18 and 19,*

1969. Washington, D.C.: Government Printing Office, 1970.

U.S. Congress, House Committee on Foreign Affairs, Subcommittee on National Security Policy and Scientific Developments. 91st Cong., 2d Sess. *Chemical-Biological Warfare: U.S. Policies and International Affairs*. Washington, D.C.: Government Printing Office, 1970.

U.S. Congress, House Committee on Science and Astronautics. 86th Cong., 1st Sess. *Report on Research in Chemical, Biological and Radiological Warfare*. Washington, D.C.: Government Printing Office, 1959.

U.S. Congress, Senate Committee on Foreign Relations. 91st Cong., 1st Sess. *Chemical and Biological Warfare: Hearings . . . , April 30, 1969*. Washington, D.C.: Government Printing Office, 1969.

U.S. Congress, Senate Committee on Foreign Relations, Subcommittee on Disarmament. 86th Cong., 2d Sess. *Chemical-Biological-Radiological Warfare and Its Disarmament Aspects*. Washington, D.C.: Government Printing Office, 1960. 43 pp.

U.S. Department of the Navy. *ABC Warfare Defense*. Washington, D.C.: Government Printing Office, 1960. 161 pp.

E. TACTICAL NUCLEAR FORCES

Inglis, David H., and Cavers, D. F. "Tactical Atomic Weapons and the Problem of Ultimate Control." *Bulletin of the Atomic Scientists* 8 (1952):74-87.

Kissinger, Henry A. "Missiles and the Western Alliance." *Foreign Affairs* 36 (1958):383-400.

Kissinger, Henry A. "NATO's Nuclear Dilemma." *Reporter*, 28 March 1963, pp. 22-37.

Mataxis, Col. T. C., and Goldberg, Lt. Col. S. L. *Nuclear Tactics, Weapons and Firepower in the Pentomic Division, Battle Group and Company.* Harrisburg, Pa.: Stackpole, 1958.

Miksche, Lt. Col. Ferdinand O. *Atomic Weapons and Armies.* London: Faber & Faber, 1955. 222 pp.

Read, Thornton. "Nuclear Tactics for Defending a Border." *World Politics* 15 (1963):390-402.

Reinhardt, George C. "Notes on the Tactical Employment of Atomic Weapons." *Military Review*, September 1952, pp. 28-37.

Reinhardt, George C., and Kintner, William R. *Atomic Weapons in Land Combat.* Harrisburg, Pa.: Military Service Publishing, 1954.

_____. "The Tactical Side of Atomic Warfare." *Bulletin of the Atomic Scientists* 11 (1955):53-58.

F. AIR AND SEA LIFT

"Army Requirements for Strategic Mobility." *Army Information Digest*, June 1958, pp. 31-40.

Bowie, Beverley M. "MATS: America's Long Arm of the Air." *National Geographic*, March 1957, pp. 283-317.

Brown, Neville. *Strategic Mobility.* London: Chatto & Windus, 1963.

Callaghan, William M. "Military Sea Transportation Service." *Naval War College Review*, January 1953, pp. 31-60.

Eliot, George F. "The Army and Strategic Mobility." *Military Review*, August 1957, pp. 3-10.

Gano, Roy A. "MSTS Operations." *Naval War College Review*, May 1957, pp. 25-52.

Kelly, Gen. Joe W. "MATS Looks at the Cuban Crisis." *Air University Review*, September-October 1963, pp. 2-20.

Kennedy, T. B. "Airlift in Southeast Asia." *Air University Review*, January-February 1965, pp. 72-82.

Lawrence, Samuel A. *United States Merchant Shipping Policies and Politics*. Washington, D.C.: Brookings Institution, 1966. 405 pp.

McMahon, Col. Robert E. "Keeping Pace with the Future--Air Mobility for Army Forces." *Military Review*, July 1958, pp. 49-62.

Porter, Rufus C. "American Merchant Shipping: A Recurring National Dilemma." *Naval War College Review*, November 1962, pp. 13-61.

Rice, Berkeley. *The C-5A Scandal: A $5 Billion Boondoggle by the Military-Industrial Complex*. Boston: Houghton Mifflin, 1971.

Synon, George D. "The Relationship of the Merchant Marine in National Power." *Naval War College Review*, November 1949, pp. 1-20.

Thayer, Frederick C., Jr. *Air Transport Policy and National Security: A Political, Economic, and Military Analysis*. Chapel Hill: University of North Carolina Press, 1965. 376 pp.

Thompson, Annis G. *The Greatest Airlift: The Story of Combat Cargo*. Tokyo: Dai-Nippon, 1954. 461 pp.

Ulanoff, Stanley M. *MATS: The Story of the Military Air Transport Service*. New York: Franklin Watts, 1964. 124 pp.

U.S. Army Aviation School. *Air Mobility and the Army*. Fort Rucker, Ala., 1958; rev. ed., 1960. 8 pp.; 10 pp.

U.S. Congress, House Committee on Armed Services, Subcommittee on Military Airlift. 91st Cong., 2d Sess. *Military Airlift . . . Hearings*. Washington, D.C.: Government Printing Office, 1970.

U.S. Congress, House Committee on Government Operations. 88th Cong., 1st Sess. *Military Air Transportation--1963*. Washington, D.C.: Government Printing Office, 1963.

_____. 91st Cong., 2d Sess. *Military Supply System: Lessons from the Vietnam Experience*. Washington, D.C.: Government Printing Office, 1970. 61 pp.

G. GUARD AND RESERVE FORCES

"Armor in the National Guard: A Feature Folio." *Armor*, September-October 1957, pp. 7-41.

"Army Reserve Components: A Special Issue." *Air Reservist*, January 1962, pp. 4-15.

Blumenfeld, Col. Charles H. "The Case for ROTC." *Military Review*, March 1963, pp. 3-13.

Eliot, George Fielding. *Reserve Forces and the Kennedy Strategy*. Harrisburg, Pa.: Stackpole, 1962.

Elliott, J. C. *The Modern Army and Air National Guard*. Princeton, N.J.: Van Nostrand Reinhold, 1965.

Lyons, Gene M., and Masland, John W. "The Origins of the ROTC." *Military Affairs*, Spring 1959, pp. 1-12.

"The Reserves of the Armed Forces: A Historical Symposium." *Military Affairs*, Spring 1953, pp. 1-36.

Riker, William H. *Soldiers and the States: The Role of the National Guard in American Democracy*. Washington, D.C.: Public Affairs Press, 1957.

Schiffman, Lt. Col. Maurice. "Army ROTC." *Military Review*, September 1958, pp. 60-64.

Stern, Frederick Martin. *The Citizen Army: Key to Defense in the Atomic Age*. New York: St. Martin's Press, 1957.

Traupane, Philip E. "The ROTC Officer." *Armor*, March-April 1965, pp. 14-17.

U.S. Department of Defense. *Report of the Special Committee on ROTC to the Secretary of Defense*. Washington, D.C., September 1969. 61 pp.

U.S. Department of Defense, Committee on Civilian Components. *Reserve Forces for National Security*. Washington, D.C.: Government Printing Office, 1948.

U.S. National Security Training Commission. *20th Century Minutemen: A Report to the President on a Reserve Forces Program*. Julius Ochs Adler Report. Washington, D.C.: Government Printing Office, 1953.

H. MILITARY INTELLIGENCE AND COMMUNICATIONS

Andregg, Charles H. *Management of Defense Intelligence*. Washington, D.C.: Industrial College of the Armed Forces, 1968. 52 pp.

Bennett, Edward; Degan, James; and Spiegel, Joseph,
    eds. *Military Information Systems: The Design of
    Computer-Aided Systems for Command.* New York:
    Frederick A. Praeger, 1964.

Brown, S.; Hammond, Paul Y.; Jones, W. M.; and Pat-
    rick, R. L. *An Information System for the National
    Security Community.* RAND Memorandum RM-6054.
    Santa Monica, Calif.: RAND Corporation, 1969. 44
    pp.

Donovan, William J. "Strategic Services in Cold War."
    Naval War College Review, September 1953, pp. 31-
    42.

Heymont, Irving. *Combat Intelligence in Modern War-
    fare.* Harrisburg, Pa.: Stackpole, 1961.

Hilsman, Roger. *Strategic Intelligence and National
    Decisions.* Glencoe, Ill.: Free Press, 1956.

Institute for Defense Analyses. *Computers in Command
    and Control.* TR No. 61-12. Washington, D.C.,
    1961.

Kahn, David. *The Code Breakers: History of Secret
    Communications.* New York: Macmillan, 1967.

Katz, Amrom H. *Hiders and Finders: An Approach to
    Inspection and Evasion Technology.* RAND Paper P-
    2432. Santa Monica, Calif.: RAND Corporation,
    1961.

Kent, Sherman. *Strategic Intelligence for American
    World Policy.* Princeton, N.J.: Princeton Univer-
    sity Press, 1966. 226 pp.

Klass, Philip. *Secret Sentries in Space.* New York:
    Random House, 1971.

Knorr, Klaus. "Failure in National Estimates: The Case of the Cuban Missiles." *World Politics* 16 (1964):455-67.

Platt, Washington. *Strategic Intelligence Production.* New York: Frederick A. Praeger, 1957.

Powers, Francis Gary, with Gentry, Curt. *Operation Overflight.* New York: Holt, Rinehart & Winston, 1970. 370 pp.

Ransom, Harry Howe. *Central Intelligence and National Security.* Cambridge, Mass.: Harvard University Press, 1958.

Read, Thornton. *Command Control.* Policy Memorandum, no. 24. Princeton, N.J.: Princeton University Center of International Studies, 1961.

U.S. Congress, House Committee on Government Operations. 90th Cong., 2d Sess. *Military Communications--1968. Hearings . . . .* Washington, D.C.: Government Printing Office, 1968. 120 pp.

U.S. Congress, Senate Committee on Government Operations, Subcommittee on National Policy Machinery. 86th Cong., 2d Sess. *Intelligence and National Security . . . Report.* Washington, D.C.: Government Printing Office, 1960.

Wohlstetter, Roberta. "Cuba and Pearl Harbor: Hindsight and Foresight." *Foreign Affairs* 43 (1965): 691-707.

Wood, Chester C. "The Military Aspects of the National Estimate." *Naval War College Review,* April 1962, pp. 1-19.

Zlotnick, Jack. *National Intelligence.* Washington, D.C.: Industrial College of the Armed Forces, 1964.

I. SCIENCE, TECHNOLOGY, RESEARCH AND DEVELOPMENT

1. General Issues

Berkowitz, Marvin. *The Conversion of Military-Oriented Research and Development to Civilian Uses.* New York: Frederick A. Praeger, 1970. 649 pp.

Bright, James R. *Research, Development and Technological Innovation.* Homewood, Ill.: R. D. Irwin, 1964. 783 pp.

Buchheim, Robert W. *Problems of Planning and Decision in Military R & D.* RAND Paper 3021. Santa Monica: RAND Corporation, 1964.

Cockroft, John, ed. *The Organization of Research Establishments.* New York: Cambridge University Press, 1965. 281 pp.

Danhoj, Clarence H. *Government Contracting and Technical Change.* Washington, D.C.: Brookings Institution, 1968. 472 pp.

Davita, Sal F. "Selling R & D to the Government." *Harvard Business Review,* September–October 1965, pp. 62–75.

Dedijer, S. "The R & D Depression in the U.S." *Science,* 17 April 1970, pp. 344–45.

Dupre, J. Stefan. "The Efficiency of Military Research and Development: Kaysen, Cherington and the Budget Bureau." *Public Policy* 12 (1963):287–301.

Dupre, J. Stefan, and Lakoff, Sanford A. *Science and the Nation: Policy and Politics.* Englewood Cliffs, N.J.: Prentice-Hall, 1962. 181 pp.

Dyson, Freeman J. "The Future Development of Nuclear Weapons." *Foreign Affairs* 38 (1960):457–64.

Erickson, John; with Crowley, Edward L.; and Galay, Nikolai, eds. *The Military-Technical Revolution: Its Impact on Strategy and Foreign Policy.* New York: Frederick A. Praeger, 1966. 296 pp.

Feld, B. T.; Greenwood, T.; Rathjens, G. W.; and Weinberg, S., eds. *Impact of New Technologies on the Arms Race: A Pugwash Monograph.* Cambridge, Mass.: M.I.T. Press, 1971.

Feldman, Arnold S., and Knorr, Klaus. *American Capability in Basic Science and Technological Invention.* Princeton, N.J.: Princeton University Center of International Studies, 1960.

Foster, John S. "Focus on Research: FY 1971 Defense Research, Development, Test and Evaluation Program." *Defense Industry Bulletin,* May 1970, pp. 18-29.

Fox, William T. R. "Science, Technology and International Politics." *International Studies Quarterly* 12 (1968):1-15.

Gilpin, Robert. *American Scientists and Nuclear Weapons Policy.* Princeton, N.J.: Princeton University Press, 1962. 352 pp.

_____. "Technological Strategies and National Purpose." *Science,* 31 July 1970, pp. 441-48.

Glennan, Thomas K. *Policies for Military Research and Development.* RAND Paper 3253. Santa Monica, Calif.: RAND Corporation, 1965.

Grabowski, Henry G. *The Determinants and Effects of Industrial Research and Development.* Princeton, N.J.: Princeton University Press Research Program, 1966.

Grodzins, Morton, and Rabinowitch, Eugene, eds. *The Atomic Age: Scientists in National and World*

Affairs. New York: Basic Books, 1963. 416 pp.

Hamberg, Daniel. *R and D: Essays on the Economics of Research and Development.* New York: Random House, 1966. 170 pp.

Hodgson, Peter E. *Nuclear Physics in Peace and War.* New York: Hawthorn Books, 1961.

Holzman, Benjamin G. "Basic Research for National Survival." *Air University Quarterly Review,* Spring 1960, pp. 28-52.

Hyde, Margaret O. *From Submarines to Satellites: Science in Our Armed Forces.* New York: Whittlesey House, 1958.

The Implications of Military Technology in the 1970s. Adelphi Papers, no. 46. London: Institute for Strategic Studies, 1968.

Johnson, Ellis A. "The Crisis in Science and Technology and Its Effect on Military Development." *Operations Research,* January-February 1958, pp. 11-34.

Kash, D. E., and Weinstein, M. A. "The R and D Contract and Democratic Theory." *Policy Sciences,* Spring 1970, pp. 113-21.

Kaysen, Carl. "Improving the Efficiency of Military Research and Development." *Public Policy* 12 (1964):219-73.

Klein, Burton H. "The Decision Making Problem in Government R & D." In *The Rule and Direction of Inventive Activity: Economic and Factors.* National Bureau of Economic Conference Report, pp. 477-508. Princeton, N.J.: Princeton University Press, 1962.

Klein, Burton H.; Mackling, William H.; and Mesthene, E. G. *Military Research and Development Policies.*

RAND Report 233.   Santa Monica, Calif.:   RAND Corporation, 1958.

Knorr, Klaus.   "On the Cost-Effectiveness Approach to Military Research and Development."   *Bulletin of the Atomic Scientists,* November 1966, pp. 11-14.

_____.   *Science and Defense: Some Critical Thoughts on Military Research and Development.*   Policy Memorandum, no. 32.   Princeton, N.J.:   Princeton University Center of International Studies, 1965.

Long, Franklin A.   "Growth Characteristics of Military Research and Development."   In *Impact of New Technologies on the Arms Race,* edited by B. T. Feld, *et al.,* pp. 271-301.   Cambridge, Mass.:   M.I.T. Press, 1971.

Mansfield, Edwin, ed.   *Defense, Science, and Public Policy: An Introduction.*   New York: W. W. Norton, 1968.   224 pp.

Marshak, T. A.   *The Role of Project Histories in the Study of R & D.*   RAND Paper 2850.   Santa Monica, Calif.:   RAND Corporation, 1965.

Marshall, A. W., and Mecklin, W. H.   *Predictability of Costs, Time, and Success of Development.*   RAND Paper 1821.   Santa Monica, Calif.:   RAND Corporation, 1960.

Miksche, Ferdinand Otto.   "Technology in Warfare."   *Military Review,* May 1959, pp. 3-8.

National Academy of Sciences.   *The Biological Effects of Atomic Radiation.*   Washington, D.C., 1956-60.

Nelson, Richard R.   *The Economics of Parallel R and D Efforts: A Sequential Decision Analysis.*   RAND Paper RM-2482.   Santa Monica, Calif.:   RAND Corporation, 1959.

Nelson, Richard R. "The Impact of Arms Reduction on Research and Development." *American Economic Review* 53 (1963):435-46.

_____. "Uncertainty, Learning and the Economics of Parallel Research and Development Efforts." *Review of Economics and Statistics* 43 (1961):351-64.

"New Controls Planned for R & D." *Armed Forces Management,* July 1962, pp. 29-34.

Novick, David. *Identifying R & D: A Management Problem.* RAND Paper 2135. Santa Monica, Calif.: RAND Corporation, 1960.

_____. *Separating Research from Research and Development.* RAND Paper 2907. Santa Monica, Calif.: RAND Corporation, 1964.

"Office Overhauls R & D Rules: Tactical Weapons Now Biggest Market." *Missiles and Rockets,* 30 March 1964, pp. 28-31.

Perry, Robert L. *The Mythography of Military R & D.* RAND Paper 3356. Santa Monica, Calif.: RAND Corporation, 1966.

_____. *Variable Sweep: A Case History of Multiple Re-Innovation.* RAND Paper 3459. Santa Monica, Calif.: RAND Corporation, 1966.

Phillips, David C. *Automation: Some Pioneering Military Applications.* SP-3465. Santa Monica, Calif.: Systems Development Corporation, 1970. 39 pp.

Pirie, Antoinette, ed. *Fallout: Radiation Hazards from Nuclear Explosions.* London: MacGibbon & Kee, 1958.

Pokrovsky, G. I. *Science and Technology in Contemporary War.* Translated and annotated by Raymond L.

Garthoff. New York: Frederick A. Praeger, 1959.
    180 pp.

Possony, Stefan T., and Pournelle, J. E. *The Strategy
    of Technology: Winning the Decisive War.* New
    York: Dunellen, 1970.

Rapoport, Anatol. "Classified Military Research and
    the University." *Humanist,* January-February 1969,
    pp. 4-10.

Reid, R. W. *Tongues of Conscience: Weapons Research
    and the Scientists' Dilemma.* New York: Walker,
    1969. 352 pp.

Roberts, Edward B. "Facts and Folklore in R & D Man-
    agement." *Industrial Management Review,* Spring
    1967, pp. 5-18.

_____. "Questioning the Cost Effectiveness of the R
    & D Procurement Process." In *Research Program Ef-
    fectiveness,* by M. C. Yovitz, *et al.* New York:
    Gordon & Breach, 1966.

Sanders, Ralph, ed. *Defense Research and Development.*
    Washington, D.C.: Industrial College of the Armed
    Forces, 1968. 198 pp.

Sanders, Ralph, and Brown, Fred R., eds. *Science and
    Technology: Vital National Assets.* National Secu-
    rity Management Series. Washington, D.C.: Indus-
    trial College of the Armed Forces, 1966. 105 pp.

Scherer, F. "Measuring Benefits from Government Re-
    search and Development Program." In *Measuring Ben-
    efits of Government Investments,* edited by R. Dorf-
    mann. Washington, D.C.: Brookings Institution,
    1965.

Schriever, Gen. Bernard A. "The Role of Management in
    Technological Conflict." *Air University Quarterly
    Review,* Winter-Spring 1962-63, pp. 19-32.

Sherwin, C. W. "Securing Peace through Military Technology." *Bulletin of the Atomic Scientists* 12 (1956):159-64.

Singer, J. David. "Weapons Technology and International Stability." *Centennial Review* 5 (1961): 415-35.

Solo, Robert A. "Gearing Military R and D to Economic Growth." *Harvard Business Review,* November-December 1962, pp. 49-60.

Stanford Research Institute. R & D Study Series for ODDR & E. *The Economic Impact of Defense R & D Expenditures: In Terms of Value Added and Employment Generated.* Menlo Park, Calif., 1966.

_____. *An Exploratory Study of the Structure and Dynamics of the R & D Industry.* Menlo Park, Calif., 1964.

_____. *The Role of the University in Defense R & D.* Menlo Park, Calif., 1966.

_____. *The Structure and Dynamics of Research and Exploratory Development in Defense R & D Industry.* Menlo Park, Calif., 1966.

_____. *The Structure and Dynamics of the Defense R & D Industry: The Los Angeles and Boston Complexes.* Menlo Park, Calif., 1965.

Sternberg, Fritz. *The Military and Industrial Revolution of Our Time.* New York: Frederick A. Praeger, 1959.

Stewart, Irvin. *Organizing Scientific Research for War.* Boston: Little, Brown, 1948. 358 pp.

Tanguy, Col. Robert B. "The Impact on National Security Caused by Restrictions on Defense Research and Development Information." *National War College Forum,* Spring 1971, pp. 33-53.

Trudeau, Arthur G. "R & D--Key to National Security." *Army Information Digest,* May 1960, pp. 38-49.

Tybout, Richard A., ed. *Economics of Research and Development.* Columbus: Ohio State University Press, 1965.

U.S. Bureau of the Budget. *Report to the President on Government Contracting for Research and Development.* David E. Bell Report. Washington, D.C.: Government Printing Office, 1962.

U.S. Commission on Organization of the Executive Branch of the Government. *Subcommittee Report on Research Activities in the Department of Defense and Defense Related Agencies.* Washington, D.C.: Government Printing Office, 1955.

U.S. Congress, House Committee on Armed Services, Subcommittee on Military Operations. 83rd Cong., 2d Sess. *Organization and Administration of the Military Research and Development Programs.* House Report, no. 2618. Washington, D.C.: Government Printing Office, 1954. 72 pp.

U.S. Congress, House Committee on Government Operations. 83rd Cong., 2d Sess. *Organization and Administration of the Military Research and Development Programs: Twenty-fourth Intermediate Report.* R. Walter Riehlman Report. Washington, D.C.: Government Printing Office, 1954.

_____. 84th Cong., 2d Sess. *24th Intermediate Report, Organization and Administration of the Military Research and Development Programs.* Washington, D.C.: Government Printing Office, 1954.

_____. 89th Cong., 2d Sess. *The Federal Research and Development Programs: The Decision-Making*

Process. Washington, D.C.: Government Printing Office, 1966.

U.S. Congress, House Committee on Government Operations. 90th Cong., lst Sess. *Federal Research and Development Programs: The Decision-Making Process, Comments by the National Academy of Sciences and the Bureau of the Budget, Eighth Report.* Washington, D.C.: Government Printing Office, 1967.

U.S. Congress, House Committee on Government Operations, Military Operations Subcommittee. 90th Cong., lst Sess. *The Office of Science and Technology. A Report Prepared by the Science Policy Research Division of the Legislative Reference Services, Library of Congress.* Washington, D.C.: Government Printing Office, 1967.

U.S. Congress, House Committee on Science and Astronautics. 87th Cong., lst Sess. *Science, Astronautics, and Defense: The 1961 Review of Scientific and Astronautic Research and Development in the Department of Defense.* Charles S. Sheldon Report. Washington, D.C.: Government Printing Office, 1961.

U.S. Department of Defense, Defense Supply Agency, Defense Documentation Center. *Defense R & D in the 1960's.* 4 vols. Alexandria, Va., 1970.

_____. *Management of Scientific Research, An ASTIA Report Bibliography.* Compiled by Herman W. Miles. Arlington, Va., 1962.

U.S. Department of the Army. *Effects of Nuclear Weapons.* DD Pamphlet 39-3. Rev. ed. Washington, D.C.: Government Printing Office, 1962.

Ward, J. Carlton, Jr. "Science as Related to National Defense." *Naval War College Review,* October 1956, pp. 1-43; November 1958, pp. 1-50.

"Why R & D Continues to Influence National Policy." *Armed Forces Management,* November 1962, pp. 59-65.

Yarmolinsky, Adam. "Science Policy and National Defense." *American Economic Review* 56 (1966):489-93.

York, Herbert F. "Military Technology and National Security." *Scientific American,* August 1969, pp. 17-29.

Yovitz, M. C., *et al. Research Program Effectiveness.* New York: Gordon & Breach, 1966.

Zuckerman, Sir Solly. *Scientists and War: The Impact of Science on Military and Civil Affairs.* London: Hamish Hamilton, 1966. 177 pp.

2. Weapons Systems

Arnold, James R. "The Hydrogen-Cobalt Bomb." *Bulletin of the Atomic Scientists* 6 (1950):290-92.

Batchelder, Robert C. *The Irreversible Decision, 1939-1950.* Boston: Houghton Mifflin, 1962. 306 pp.

De Volpi, Alexander. "MIRV--Gorgon Medusa of the Nuclear Age." *Bulletin of the Atomic Scientists,* January 1970, pp. 35-38.

Eliot, George Fielding, *et al. The H Bomb.* Introduction by Albert Einstein. New York: Didier, 1950. 175 pp.

Everett, H., and Pugh, G. E. "Distribution and Effects of Fallout in Large Nuclear Weapons Campaigns." *Operations Research,* March-April 1959, pp. 226-48.

Fowler, John M., ed. *Fallout: A Study of Superbombs;*

Strontium 90 and Survival. New York: Basic Books, 1960. 235 pp.

Glennan, Thomas K. *Methodological Problems in Evaluating the Effectiveness of Military Aircraft Development*. RAND Paper 3357. Santa Monica, Calif.: RAND Corporation, 1966.

Groueff, Stéphane. *Manhattan Project: The Untold Story of the Making of the Atomic Bomb*. Boston: Little, Brown, 1967. 238 pp.

Groves, Leslie R. *Now It Can Be Told: The Story of the Manhattan Project*. New York: Harper & Bros., 1962. 464 pp.

Heer, David H. *After Nuclear Attack: A Demographic Inquiry*. New York: Frederick A. Praeger, 1965. 440 pp.

Lambright, W. Henry. *Shooting Down the Nuclear Plane*. Indianapolis: Bobbs-Merrill, 1967.

Lawrence, William Leonard. *The Hell Bomb*. New York: Alfred A. Knopf, 1951.

Lewis, Richard S., and Wilson, Jane, eds. *Almagordo Plus Twenty-Five Years*. New York: Viking, 1970.

Moss, Norman. *Men Who Play God: The Story of the H-Bomb and How the World Came to Live with It*. New York: Harper & Row, 1969. 352 pp.

Murray, Thomas E. "Nuclear Testing and American Security." *Orbis* 4 (1961):405-21.

National Academy of Sciences. *The Biological Effects of Atomic Radiation*. Washington, D.C., 1956-60.

Oppenheimer, J. Robert. "Comments on the Military Value of the Atom." *Bulletin of the Atomic Scientists* 7 (1951):43-45.

Pirie, Antoinette, ed. *Fallout: Radiation Hazards from Nuclear Explosions*. London: MacGibbon & Kee, 1958.

U.S. Congress, Joint Committee on Atomic Energy. 86th Cong., 1st Sess. *Biological and Environmental Effects of Nuclear War*. Washington, D.C.: Government Printing Office, 1959.

_____. 86th Cong., 1st Sess. *Fallout from Nuclear Weapons Tests*. 3 vols. Washington, D.C.: Government Printing Office, 1959.

U.S. Congress, Joint Committee on Atomic Energy. Special Subcommittee on Radiation. *Biological and Environmental Effects of Nuclear War*. Washington, D.C.: Government Printing Office, 1959. 58 pp.

U.S. Congress, Joint Committee on Atomic Energy, Subcommittee on Research and Development. 86th Cong., 1st Sess. *Aircraft Nuclear Propulsion Program*. Washington, D.C.: Government Printing Office, 1959.

U.S. Congress, Senate Committee on Foreign Relations. 91st Cong., 1st Sess. *Underground Weapons Testing: Hearings . . . to Provide for a Study and Evaluation of the International and Other Foreign Policy Aspects of Underground Weapons Testing, September 29, 1969*. Washington, D.C.: Government Printing Office, 1970.

U.S. Defense Atomic Support Agency. *Effects of Nuclear Weapons*. Rev. ed. Edited by Samuel Glasstone. Washington, D.C.: U.S. Atomic Energy Commission, 1962.

U.S. Department of Defense. *Maximum Improvement in Air Weapon Systems in Minimum Time: Summary of Actions Taken to Reduce the Time Required for Research, Development, Procurement, and Production of Manned Aircraft Weapon Systems*. Washington,

D.C.: Government Printing Office, 1957.

U.S. Department of Defense, Office of the Director of
Defense Research and Engineering. *Seventh
Military-Industry Missile and Space Reliability
Symposium, June 1962.* Washington, D.C.: Govern-
ment Printing Office, 1962. 497 pp.

U.S. Department of the Army. *Effects of Nuclear Weapons.* DD Pamphlet 39-3. Rev. ed. Washington,
D.C.: Government Printing Office, 1962.

Van Cleave, William R. "The Nonproliferation Treaty
and Fission-Free Explosive Research." *Orbis* 11
(1968):1055-66.

3. Military Space Programs

Downs, Lt. Col. Eldon W. *The United States Air Force
in Space.* New York: Frederick A. Praeger, 1966.
160 pp.

Emme, Eugene M., comp. *Aeronautics and Astronautics:
An American Chronology of Science and Technology in
the Exploration of Space, 1915-1960.* Washington,
D.C.: National Aeronautics & Space Administration,
1961.

Gantz, Lt. Col. Kenneth F., ed. *Men in Space: The
United States Air Force Program for Developing the
Spacecraft Crew.* New York: Duell, Sloan & Pearce,
1959. 303 pp.

_____, ed. *Nuclear Flight: The United States Air
Force Programs for Atomic Jets, Missiles and Rockets.* New York: Duell, Sloan & Pearce, 1960.

Golovine, Michael N. *Conflict in Space: A Pattern of
War in a New Dimension.* New York: St. Martin's
Press, 1962. 143 pp.

Griffith, Alison. *The National Aeronautics and Space Act*. Washington, D.C.: Public Affairs Press, 1961. 119 pp.

Paine, Thomas O. "Space and National Security in the Modern World." *Air Force and Space Digest,* May 1969, pp. 107-9.

Rigg, Lt. Col. Robert B. "Outer Space and National Defense." *Military Review,* May 1959, pp. 21-26.

Robison, David. "Self Restrictions in the American Military Use of Space." *Orbis* 9 (1965):116-39.

U.S. Congress, House Committee on Science and Astronautics. 87th Cong., 1st Sess. *Defense Space Interests. Hearings* . . . . Washington, D.C.: Government Printing Office, 1961.

_____. 87th Cong., 1st Sess. *Military Astronautics*. House Report, no. 360. Washington, D.C.: Government Printing Office, 1961.

_____. 87th Cong., 1st Sess. *Science, Astronautics, and Defense: The 1961 Review of Scientific and Astronautic Research and Development in the Department of Defense*. Washington, D.C.: Government Printing Office, 1961. 68 pp.

U.S. Congress, Senate Committee on Armed Services, Preparedness Investigating Subcommittee. 85th Cong., 1st and 2d Sess. *Hearings, Inquiry into Satellite and Missile Programs*. Washington, D.C.: Government Printing Office, 1958.

U.S. National Aeronautics & Space Administration, Scientific and Technical Information Division, Office of Technology Utilization. *The New Ocean: A History of Project Mercury*. Prepared by Lloyd S. Swenson, Jr., James M. Grimwood, and Charles C. Alexander. NASA Historical Series. Washington, D.C.: Government Printing Office, 1966. 681 pp.

J. MANPOWER, GENERAL SUPPORT, SUPPLY AND LOGISTICS

1. General Manpower Requirements

Cameron, Juan. "Our Gravest Military Problem Is Manpower." *Fortune,* April 1971, pp. 60-63, 137-40.

Carmichael, Leonard, and Mead, Leonard C., eds. *The Selection of Military Manpower: A Symposium.* Washington, D.C.: National Academy of Sciences National Research Council, 1951. 269 pp.

David, Jay, and Crane, Elaine. *The Black Soldier: From the American Revolution to Vietnam.* New York: William Morrow, 1971.

Devan, S. Arthur. *Universal Military Training and the Problem of Military Manpower.* Public Affairs Bulletin, no. 90. Washington, D.C.: Library of Congress Legislative Reference Service, 1951.

Drath, Col. Francis S. "Manpower for Cold War Forces." *Army,* November 1960, pp. 30-36.

Falk, Stanley L. *Defense Military Manpower.* National Security Management Series. Washington, D.C.: Industrial College of the Armed Forces, 1969. 151 pp.

Fisher, Franklin M., and Morton, Anton S. "Reenlistments in the U.S. Navy: A Cost Effectiveness Study." *American Economic Review,* May 1967, pp. 32-38.

Foot, M. R. D. *Men in Uniform: Military Manpower in Modern Industrial Societies.* New York: Frederick A. Praeger, 1961.

Forsythe, Col. George I. "Personnel Management in the Army and in Business." *Military Review,* June 1950, pp. 54-62.

Gerhardt, James M. *Military Manpower Procurement Policies, 1945-1969*. Columbus: Ohio State University Press, 1970.

Ginzberg, Eli, *et al*. *The Ineffective Soldier*. 3 vols. New York: Columbia University Press, 1959.

Hackel, Erwin. *Military Manpower and Political Purpose*. Adelphi Papers, no. 72. London: Institute for Strategic Studies, 1970.

Hickens, Victor. *The American Fighting Man: An Analysis of the Essential Qualities of American Soldiers, Sailors and Marines from the American Revolution to the War in Vietnam*. New York: Macmillan, 1969. 496 pp.

Howe, Raymond F., ed. *Proceedings: Conference on Military Manpower*. Washington, D.C.: American Council on Education, 1955.

Huntington, Samuel P. "Men at Arms? The Regrettable Story of Our Military Manpower." *Columbia University Forum*, Spring 1959, pp. 42-47.

Johnson, Donald E. "A Quarter-Century of the GI Bill." *School and Society*, April 1970, pp. 226-28.

Katenbrink, Irving G., Jr. *Military Service and Occupation Mobility*. Working Paper, no. 88. Chicago: Center for Social Organization Studies, 1967.

Lecht, Leonard. *Manpower Requirements for National Objectives in the 1970's*. Washington, D.C.: National Planning Association, 1968.

Moskos, Charles C., Jr. *The American Enlisted Man-- The Rank and File in Today's Military*. New York: Russell Sage Foundation, 1970. 274 pp.

_____. "Grace Under Pressure: The U.S. Soldier in

the Dominican Republic." *Army*, September 1966, pp. 41-45.

Moskos, Charles C., Jr.   "Racial Integration in the Armed Forces." *American Journal of Sociology*, September 1966, pp. 132-48.

Nelson, Dennis D.   *The Integration of the Negro into the United States Navy*.   New York: Farrar, Straus & Young, 1951.

Nichols, Leo.   *Breakthrough on the Color Front*.   New York: Random House, 1954.

Poiner, Murray.   *No Victory Parades: The Return of the Vietnam Veteran*.   New York: Holt, Rinehart & Winston, 1971.   169 pp.

Purdon, Eric.   *Black Company*.   New York: Robert Luce, 1970.

Ross, David R. B.   *Preparing for Ulysses: Politics and Veterans during World War II*.   New York: Columbia University Press, 1969.   315 pp.

Shelburne, James C.   *Education in the Armed Forces*. New York: Center for Applied Research in Education, 1965.

Smedberg, William R.   "Leadership and the Military Commander." *Naval War College Review*, June 1963, pp. 26-36.

Sparrow, John C.   *History of Personnel Demobilization in the United States Army*.   Washington, D.C.:   Government Printing Office, 1951.   525 pp.

Spencer, John C.   *Crime and the Services*.   New York: Grove Press, 1955.   306 pp.

Sprung, G. M. C.   *The Soldier in Our Times: An Essay*. Philadelphia: Dorrance, 1960.

Stillman, Richard J., III. *Integration of the Negro in the U.S. Armed Forces*. New York: Frederick A. Praeger, 1968.

Stouffer, Samuel A., *et al*. *The American Soldier*. 2 vols. Princeton, N.J.: Princeton University Press, 1949.

U.S. Advisory Commission on Service Pay. *Career Compensation for the Uniformed Forces: Army, Navy, Air Force, Marine Corps, Coast Guard, Coast and Geodetic Survey, Public Health Service. A Report and Recommendation for the Secretary of Defense*. Charles R. Hook Report. Washington, D.C.: Government Printing Office, 1948.

U.S. Commission on Organization of the Executive Branch of the Government. *Subcommittee Report on Special Personnel Problems in the Department of Defense*. Washington, D.C.: Government Printing Office, 1955.

U.S. Commission on the Organization of the Executive Branch of the Government (1947-1949). Committee on Veterans Affairs. *Report of the Hoover Commission Committee on Veterans Affairs*. Washington, D.C.: Government Printing Office, 1949.

U.S. Congress, Senate Committee on Military Affairs. 79th Cong., 1st Sess. *Hearings on Demobilization of Armed Forces*. Washington, D.C.: Government Printing Office, 1945.

_____. 79th Cong., 2d Sess. *Hearings on Demobilization*. Washington, D.C.: Government Printing Office, 1946.

U.S. Defense Advisory Committee on Professional and Technical Compensation. *A Modern Concept of Manpower Management and Compensation for Personnel of the Uniformed Services*. Washington, D.C.: Government Printing Office, 1957.

U.S. Defense Advisory Committee on Professional and Technical Compensation. *Report and Recommendation of the Secretary of Defense.* Ralph Cordiner Report. Washington, D.C.: Government Printing Office, 1957.

U.S. Department of Defense. *Modernizing Military Pay, Report of the First Quadrennial Review of Military Compensation.* 5 vols. Washington, D.C.: Government Printing Office, 1968-69.

U.S. Department of the Army. *Marginal Man and Military Service.* Washington, D.C.: Government Printing Office, 1966.

U.S. Library of Congress, Legislative Reference Service. *Mobilization Planning and the National Security (1950-1960): Problems and Issues.* Public Bulletin, no. 81. Washington, D.C.: Government Printing Office, 1950. 245 pp.

U.S. Office of Defense Mobilization, Manpower Policy Committee. *A Manpower Program for Full Mobilization.* Rocco C. Siciliano Report. Washington, D.C.: Government Printing Office, 1954.

U.S. President's Committee on Equality of Treatment and Opportunity in the Armed Services. *Freedom to Serve, Equality of Treatment and Opportunity in the Armed Services: A Report.* Charles Falry Report. Washington, D.C.: Government Printing Office, 1950.

U.S. President's Committee on Equal Opportunity in the Armed Forces. *Equality of Treatment and Opportunity for Negro Military Personnel Stationed within the United States: Initial Report.* Washington, D.C.: Government Printing Office, 1963.

U.S. President's Committee on Religion and Welfare in the Armed Forces. *Free Time in the Armed Forces: A Study of the Armed Forces' Services and Recreation*

Programs. Washington, D.C.: Government Printing Office, 1951. 79 pp.

U.S. President's Committee on Veterans' Pensions. *Veterans' Benefits in the United States.* Omar N. Bradley Report. Washington, D.C.: Government Printing Office, 1956.

U.S. War Department. Board on Officer-Enlisted Man Relationships. *Report of Officer-Enlisted Man Relationships . . . 27 May 1946.* James H. Doolittle Report. Washington, D.C.: Government Printing Office, 1946.

Weinstein, Paul A. "Military Manpower Procurement: Comment." *American Economic Review,* May 1967, pp. 66-69.

Williams, Colin J., and Weinberg, Martin S. *Homosexuals and the Military.* New York: Harper & Row, 1971.

Wool, Harold. "Military Manpower Procurement: Comment." *American Economic Review,* May 1967, pp. 69-70.

2. Draft, Volunteer Army

Altman, Stuart H., and Fechter, Alan E. "The Supply of Military Personnel in the Absence of a Draft." *American Economic Review,* May 1967, pp. 19-31.

American Friends Service Committee. *The Draft?* Prepared by Kenneth E. Boulding, *et al.* New York: Hill & Wang, 1968. 112 pp.

Bradford, D. F. "The Enlistment Decision under Draft Uncertainty." *Quarterly Journal of Economics* 82 (1968):621-38.

Carper, Jean. *Bitter Greetings: The Scandal of the*

Military Draft. New York: Grossman, 1967.   205 pp.

Davis, James W., Jr., and Dolbeare, Kenneth M. *Little Groups by Neighbors: The Selective Service System.* Chicago: Markham, 1968.

Duggan, Joseph C. *The Legislative and Statutory Development of the Federal Concept of Conscription for Military Service.* Washington, D.C.: Catholic University of America Press, 1946.

Eberly, Donald J., ed. *A Profile on National Service.* New York: Overseas Educational Service, 1966.

Eisenhower, Dwight D. "The Country Needs Universal Military Training." *Reader's Digest,* September 1966, pp. 49–55.

Friedman, Leon. *The Wise Minority: An Argument for Draft Resistance and Civil Disobedience.* New York: Dial Press, 1970.

Ginzberg, Eli. "The Case for a Lottery." *Public Interest,* Fall 1966, pp. 83–89.

Hansen, W. L., and Weisbrod, B. A. "Economics of the Military Draft." *Quarterly Journal of Economics* 81 (1967):395–421.

Hart, Lt. Col. Irving. *Outline of Historical Background of Selective Service and Chronology.* Washington, D.C.: Selective Service, 1961. 60 pp.

Jacobs, Clyde E., and Gallagher, John F. *The Selective Service Act: A Case Study of the Governmental Process.* New York: Dodd, Mead, 1967.

Leach, Jack Franklin. *Conscription in the United States: Historical Background.* Rutland, Vt.: Charles E. Tuttle, 1952. 501 pp.

Lerwill, Lt. Col. Leonard L. *The Personnel Replacement System in the United States Army.* D.A. Pamphlet 20-211. Washington, D.C.: Government Printing Office, 1954. 492 pp.

Little, Roger W., ed. *Selective Service and American Society.* New York: Russell Sage Foundation, 1969. 220 pp.

Marmion, Harry A. *The Case against a Volunteer Army.* Chicago: Quadrangle Books, 1971. 107 pp.

_____. *Selective Service: Conflict and Compromise.* New York: Wiley & Sons, 1968. 168 pp.

Miller, James C., III, *et al.,* eds. *Why the Draft? The Case for a Volunteer Army.* Baltimore: Penguin Books, 1968. 197 pp.

Oi, Walter Y. "The Economic Cost of the Draft." *American Economic Review,* May 1967, pp. 39-62.

Rankin, Robert H. "A History of Selective Service." *U.S. Naval Institute Proceedings,* October 1951, pp. 1073-81.

Reedy, George E. *Who Will Do Our Fighting for Us?* New York: World, 1969. 126 pp.

Renshaw, Edward F. "The Economics of Conscription." *Southern Economic Journal,* October 1960, pp. 111-17.

Report of the Task Force on the Structure of the Selective Service System: October 16, 1967. Washington, D.C.: Government Printing Office, 1968. 108 pp.

Saunders, Jacquin. *The Draft and the Vietnam War.* New York: Walker, 1966.

Sibley, Mulford, and Jacob, Philip. *Conscription of*

Conscience. Ithaca, N.Y.: Cornell University Press, 1952.

Stafford, Robert T., *et al. How to End the Draft.* Washington, D.C.: National Press, 1967.

Tax, Sol, ed. *The Draft: Facts and Alternatives.* Chicago: University of Chicago Press, 1967.

U.S. Congress, House Committee on Armed Services. 89th Cong., 2d Sess. *Review of the Administration and Operation of the Selective Service System, Hearings . . . . June 22-30, 1966.* Washington, D.C.: Government Printing Office, 1966. 560 pp.

_____. 90th Cong., 1st Sess. *Extension of the Universal Military Training and Service Act, Hearings . . . . May 2-11, 1967.* Washington, D.C.: Government Printing Office, 1967. 806 pp.

U.S. Congress, House Committee on Government Operations, Committee on Expenditures in Executive Departments. 80th Cong., 1st Sess. *War Department Publicity and Propaganda Relating to Universal Military Training.* Washington, D.C.: Government Printing Office, 1947.

U.S. Congress, House Committee on Military Affairs. 79th Cong., 1st Sess. *Hearings on Universal Military Training.* Washington, D.C.: Government Printing Office, 1945.

_____. 79th Cong., 1st Sess. *Report on Universal Military Training.* House Report, no. 857. Washington, D.C.: Government Printing Office, 1945.

_____. 79th Cong., 2d Sess. *Hearings on Universal Military Training.* Washington, D.C.: Government Printing Office, 1946.

U.S. Congress, House Select Committee on Post-War Military Policy. 79th Cong., 1st Sess. *Universal*

Military Training. Hearings. Washington, D.C.:
Government Printing Office, 1945.

U.S. National Security Training Commission. *First Report.* Julius Ochs Adler Report on Compulsory Military Service. Washington, D.C.: Government Printing Office, 1951.

U.S. President's Advisory Commission on Universal Training. *A Program for National Security, May 29, 1947.* Karl Compton Report. Washington, D.C.: Government Printing Office, 1947.

U.S. President's Commission on an All-Volunteer Armed Forces. *Report.* Thomas S. Gates Report. Washington, D.C.: Government Printing Office, 1970.

_____. *Studies Prepared for the President's Commission on an All-Volunteer Armed Forces.* 2 vols. Washington, D.C.: Government Printing Office, 1970.

U.S. Selective Service System. *Annual Report of the Director of Selective Service.* Washington, D.C.: Government Printing Office, 1948-67; semiannual, 1967-date.

_____. *Organization and Functions of Selective Service.* Rev. ed. Washington, D.C., 1951. 109 pp.

_____. *Problems of Selective Service.* Special Monograph, no. 16. Washington, D.C., 1959. 259 pp.

Walton, Col. George. *Let's End the Draft Mess.* New York: David McKay, 1967.

Wamsley, Gary L. *Selective Service and a Changing America: A Study of Organizational-Environmental Relationships.* Columbus, Ohio: Charles E. Merrill, 1969. 259 pp.

Willett, T. D. "Another Cost of Conscription."

Western Economic Journal 6 (1968):425-26.

Worsnop, Richard L.   "Reserve Forces and the Draft."
Editorial Research Reports, 20 January 1965, pp.
43-60.

3. Supply and Logistics

Algire, K. D.   "Major Logistics Lessons of World War
II."   *Naval War College Review*, February 1951, pp.
25-43.

"AMC--The Army's Giant Logistics Command."   *Armed
Forces Journal*, 3 May 1969, pp. 13-17, 20-28.

American Ordnance Association.   *Industrial Conversion
to a National Emergency*.   Washington, D.C., 1967.

_____.   *Industrial Mobilization in a Limited War*.
Washington, D.C., 1966.

Appleton, Diane.   "DSA--The Nation's Military Whole-
saler."   *Armed Forces Journal*, January 1969, pp.
13-19, 22-31.

Badger, Oscar C.   "The Principles of Command and Logistics."   *Naval War College Review*, December 1951,
pp. 21-36.

_____.   "Problems of Command and Logistics."   *Naval
War College Review*, November 1950, pp. 13-27.

Ballantine, Duncan S.   *U.S. Naval Logistics in the
Second World War*.   Princeton, N.J.:   Princeton University Press, 1947.

Barnett, H. J.   "The Changing Relations of Natural Resources to National Security."   *Economic Geography*,
July 1958, pp. 189-201.

Carney, Robert B.   "Logistical Planning for War."

Naval War College Review, October 1948, pp. 3-16.

Chesarek, Gen. Ferdinand J. "Army Material Command: Meeting Today's Logistical Challenge." *Defense Industry Bulletin*, December 1969, pp. 17-24.

Clark, Earl W.; Haddock, Hoyts; and Volens, Stanley. *The U.S. Merchant Marine Today--Sunrise or Sunset?* Washington, D.C.: Labor-Management Maritime Committee, 1970. 243 pp.

Colby, Brig. Gen. Joseph M. "Logistics Problems Today." *Ordnance*, November-December 1966, pp. 277-80.

Conklin, David L., *et al*. *Economics of Nuclear and Conventional Merchant Ships, June 30, 1958*. Washington, D.C.: Government Printing Office, 1959.

Eccles, Rear Adm. Henry E. "Basic Elements of Naval Logistics." *Naval War College Review*, November 1949, pp. 21-34.

_____. "Logistics and Strategy." 2 pts. *Naval War College Review*, January 1958, pp. 17-39; March 1962, pp. 15-31.

_____. *Logistics in the National Defense*. Harrisburg, Pa.: Stackpole, 1959. 347 pp.

_____. *Operational Naval Logistics*. Washington, D.C.: Department of the Navy, 1950.

_____. "Theatre Logistic Planning." *Naval War College Review*, October 1950, pp. 1-21.

Elliott, William Y. *Mobilization Planning and the National Security, 1950-1960: Problems and Issues*. Washington, D.C.: Government Printing Office, 1960.

Enke, Stephen. "An Economist Looks at Air Force

Logistics." *Review of Economics and Statistics* 49 (1958):230-39.

Ferguson, Allen R. "Air Force Logistics." *Aeronautical Engineering Review*, January 1957.

Fieser, Max E. *Economic Policy and War Potential*. Washington, D.C.: Public Affairs Press, 1964.   136 pp.

Harmon, George M., ed. *Transportation: The Nation's Lifelines*. Washington, D.C.: Industrial College of the Armed Forces, 1968.

Hunt, Capt. R. B. *Definitions of Logistics*. Washington, D.C.: George Washington University Logistics Research Project, 1956.

Huston, James A. "Korea and Logistics." *Military Review*, February 1957, pp. 18-32.

_____. *The Sinews of War: Army Logistics, 1775-1953*. U.S. Army Historical Series. Washington, D.C.: Government Printing Office for the Office of the Chief of Military History, 1966.   789 pp.

Kuhlman, Capt. Norman H. G. *Supply Management*. Washington, D.C.: Industrial College of the Armed Forces, 1969.

Mendershausen, Horst. "Economic Problems in Air Force Logistics." *American Economic Review* 58 (1958): 632-48.

Ostrom, Arnold E. *Defense Transportation: The Military Traffic Management and Terminal Service*. Washington, D.C.: Industrial College of the Armed Forces, 1967.

Rawlings, Edwin W. "A New Equation for Jet Age Logistics." *Air University Quarterly Review*, Spring 1955, pp. 8-29.

Shifley, Ralph L. "The Role of the Chief of Naval Material in Logistics Administration." *Naval War College Review*, April 1965, pp. 1-17.

Snyder, Glenn H. *Stockpiling Strategic Materials*. San Francisco: Chandler, 1966.

U.S. Congress, House Committee on Government Operations. 86th Cong., 1st Sess. *Military Supply Management*. House Report, no. 674. Washington, D.C.: Government Printing Office, 1959.

_____. 87th Cong., 2d Sess. *Defense Supply Agency*. *Hearings* . . . . Washington, D.C.: Government Printing Office, 1962.

_____. 87th Cong., 2d Sess. *Defense Supply Agency: Twenty-Fourth Report*. Washington, D.C.: Government Printing Office, 1962. 86 pp.

_____. 90th Cong., 2d Sess. *Military Supply Systems*. *Hearings* . . . . Washington, D.C.: Government Printing Office, 1968. 330 pp.

_____. 91st Cong., 2d Sess. *Military Supply Systems: 1970*. *Hearings* . . . . Washington, D.C.: Government Printing Office, 1970. 239 pp.

U.S. Defense Supply Agency. *An Introduction to the Defense Supply Agency*. Washington, D.C.: Government Printing Office, 1970. 46 pp.

U.S. Department of Defense. *Industrial Mobilization Production Planning Manual: Guidance for Operational Phases of Advanced Planning to Insure Adequate and Timely Production of Military Items during Future Limited War*. DOD 4005.3-M. Washington, D.C.: Government Printing Office, 1968. 209 pp.

U.S. Department of the Navy, Bureau of Supplies and Accounts. *Newsletter*, September 1957, May 1958.

U.S. Department of the Navy, Bureau of Supplies and
    Accounts. *Supply Support of the Navy*. NAVSANDA
    Publication 340. Washington, D.C., 1957.

U.S. Office of War Mobilization. *War and Post-war Ad-
    justment Policy* . . . . Bernard M. Banich Report.
    Washington, D.C.: Government Printing Office,
    1944.

Yosphe, Harry B. *The National Security Resources
    Board, 1947-1953: A Case Study in Peacetime Mobi-
    lization Planning*. Washington, D.C.: Industrial
    College of the Armed Forces, 1953.

K. REGIONAL DEFENSE POLICIES, INCLUDING MILITARY
    ASSISTANCE

1. General Issues

Ahmed, Azia. "American Alliances with Asian Coun-
    tries." *Military Review*, December 1960, pp. 98-
    103.

"Arms Sales and U.S. Foreign Policy." *Current*, August
    1967, pp. 33-41.

Atwater, Elton. *American Regulation of Arms Exports*.
    Washington, D.C.: Carnegie Endowment for Interna-
    tional Peace, 1941. 287 pp.

Barber, Hollis W. "United States Alliance Policy."
    U.S. Naval Institute Proceedings, September 1958,
    pp. 74-82.

Barnet, Richard J. *Intervention and Revolution:
    America's Confrontation with Insurgent Movements
    around the World*. New York: World, 1969. 301 pp.

Bloomfield, Lincoln P., and Leiss, Amelia C. *Regional
    Arms Control Arrangements for Developing Areas:*

Arms and Arms Control in Latin America, the Middle East, and Africa. CIS Document C.64-25. Cambridge, Mass.: M.I.T. Press, 1964.

Browne & Shaw Research Corporation. *The Diffusion of Combat Aircraft, Missiles and Their Supporting Technologies.* Prepared for the Office of the Assistant Secretary of Defense under Contract DA-49-083. Washington, D.C., October 1966.

_____. *International Defense Planning: A Study of Methods for Sharing Skills and Concepts in Defense Policy Planning.* Prepared for the Office of the Assistant Secretary of Defense for International Security Affairs. Washington, D.C., 1967.

Buchan, Alastair. "Problems of an Alliance Policy: An Essay in Hindsight." In *The Theory and Practice of War: Essays Presented to Captain B. H. Liddell Hart,* edited by Michael Howard, pp. 293-310. London: Cassell, 1965.

Clem, Harold J. *Collective Defense and Foreign Assistance.* Washington, D.C.: Industrial College of the Armed Forces, 1968. 152 pp.

Coffey, Joseph I. "Strategy, Alliance Policy and Nuclear Proliferation." *Orbis* 11 (1968):975-95.

Connery, Robert H., and David, Paul T. "The Mutual Defense Assistance Program." *American Political Science Review* 45 (1951):321-47.

Dessette, Capt. Edward F. "Overseas Bases--How Long for This World." *U.S. Naval Institute Proceedings,* July 1960, pp. 23-30.

Duffy, A. E. P. "The Present Viability of NATO, SEATO, AND CENTO." *Annals of the American Academy of Political and Social Science,* July 1967, pp. 33-39.

Eliot, George Fielding. "Influence of Military Alliance on Strategy." *Naval War College Review,* June 1952, pp. 1-24.

Fedder, Edwin H. "The Concept of Alliance." *International Studies Quarterly* 12 (1968):65-86.

Finkelstein, Marina S., and Finkelstein, Lawrence S. *Collective Security.* San Francisco: Chandler, 1966. 278 pp.

Friedrich, Carl J., *et al. American Experience in Military Government in World War II.* New York: Rinehart, 1948.

Froehlich, Dean K. *The Military Advisor as Defined by Counterparts.* Alexandria, Va.: Human Resources Research Organization, 1970.

Fromkin, David. "Entangling Alliances." *Foreign Affairs* 48 (1970):688-700.

Furniss, Edgar S., Jr. "Regional Associations." *Naval War College Review,* January 1959, pp. 21-38.

_____. *Some Perspectives on American Military Assistance.* Policy Memorandum, no. 13. Princeton, N.J.: Princeton University Center of International Studies, 1957.

Gibert, Stephen P. "Soviet-American Military Aid Competition in the Third World." *Orbis* 12 (1970): 1117-37.

Grabb, Robert C. "The Status of Armed Forces Abroad." *Naval War College Review,* January 1956, pp. 85-98.

Heymont, Col. Irving. "U.S. Military Assistance Programs." *Military Review,* January 1968, pp. 89-95.

Hoagland, John H., and Clapp, Priscilla A. *Notes on the Small Arms Traffic.* M.I.T. Publication, no.

C/70-7. Cambridge, Mass.: M.I.T. Press, 1970.

Hogan, Willard N. *International Conflict and Collective Security*. Lexington: University of Kentucky Press, 1955.

Holbron, Hajo. *American Military Government: Its Organization and Policies*. Washington, D.C.: Infantry Journal Press, 1947.

Hovey, Harold A. *United States Military Assistance. A Study of Policies and Practices*. New York: Frederick A. Praeger, 1965. 324 pp.

Jordan, Amos A., Jr. "Military Assistance and National Policy." *Orbis* 2 (1958):241-44.

Katzenbach, Nicholas. "U.S. Arms for the Developing World: Dilemmas of Foreign Policy." *Department of State Bulletin* 57 (1967):794-98.

Kemp, Geoffrey. "Arms Sales and Arms Control in the Developing Countries." *World Today,* September 1966, pp. 386-95.

_____. "Arms Traffic and Third World Conflicts." *International Conciliation,* March 1970, pp. 5-80.

_____. *A Classification of Weapons Systems and Force Designs in Less Developed Country Environments: Implications for Arms Transfer Policies*. M.I.T. Publication, no. C/70-3. Cambridge, Mass.: M.I.T. Press, 1970.

_____. "U.S. Military Policy: Dilemmas of the Arms Traffic." *Foreign Affairs* 48 (1970):274-84.

Kintner, William R. "The Role of Military Assistance." *U.S. Naval Institute Proceedings,* March 1961, pp. 76-84.

Kissinger, Henry A. "Coalition Diplomacy in a Nuclear

Age." *Foreign Affairs* 42 (1964):525-45.

Kyre, Martin, and Kyre, Jean. *Military Occupation and National Security*. Washington, D.C.: Public Affairs Press, 1968. 198 pp.

Leiss, Amelia C. *Past Patterns of Arms Transfers*. M.I.T. Publication, no. C/70-2. Cambridge, Mass.: M.I.T. Press, 1970.

Leiss, Amelia C., *et al*. *Arms Transfers to Less Developed Countries*. M.I.T. Publication, no. C/70-1. Cambridge, Mass.: M.I.T. Press, 1970.

Lincoln, George A. "Factors Determining Arms Aid." *Academy of Political Science Proceedings* 25 (1953): 263-72.

Logan, John A., Jr. *The No-Transfer Principle: A Fundamental American Security Policy*. New Haven: Yale University Press, 1961.

McCarthy, Eugene J. "Arms and the Man Who Sells Them." *Atlantic*, June 1969, pp. 346-51.

Nuechterlein, Donald E. "Small State in Alliances: Iceland, Thailand, Australia." *Orbis* 13 (1969): 600-623.

Olson, M., Jr., and Zeckhauser, R. "An Economic Theory of Alliances." *Review of Economics and Statistics* 48 (1966):266-79.

Palmer, Gen. W. B. "The Military Assistance Program as a Tool for Peace with Honor." *Department of State Bulletin*, 29 February 1960, pp. 329-33.

Ransom, Harry Howe, ed. *Foreign Military Assistance and National Policy: Some Background Materials*. Harvard Defense Policy Serial, no. 114. Cambridge, Mass., 1957.

Refson, Jacob S. *U.S. Military Training and Advice: Implications for Arms Transfers*. M.I.T. Publication, no. C/70-5. Cambridge, Mass.: M.I.T. Press, 1970.

Rothstein, Robert L. *Alliances and Small Powers*. New York: Columbia University Press, 1968.

Roy, Elizabeth C. *U.S. Military Commitments*. Washington, D.C.: Institute for Defense Analyses, 1963. 40 pp.

Stambuk, George. *American Military Forces Abroad: Their Impact on the Western State System*. Columbus: Ohio State University Press, 1963.

Stromberg, Roland N. *Collective Security and American Foreign Policy: From the League of Nations to NATO*. New York: Frederick A. Praeger, 1964. 312 pp.

Sutton, John L., and Kemp, Geoffrey. *Arms to Developing Countries, 1964-65*. Adelphi Papers, no. 28. London: Institute for Strategic Studies, October 1966.

Tarr, David. "The American Military Presence Abroad." *Orbis* 9 (1965):630-54.

_____. "The Military Abroad." *Annals of the American Academy of Political and Social Science,* November 1966, pp. 31-42.

Taylor, Philip H., and Braibanti, Ralph J. D. *Administration of Occupied Areas*. Syracuse, N.Y.: Syracuse University Press, 1948.

Thayer, George. "American Arms Abroad." *Washington Monthly,* January 1970, pp. 62-73.

_____. *The War Business: The International Trade in Armaments*. New York: Simon & Schuster, 1969.

Thomas, John R., and Vreeland, Mildred C. *The Role of Military Aid in National Strategy.* McLean, Va.: Research Analysis Corporation, 1968.

U.S. Committee to Strengthen the Security of the Free World. *The Scope and Distribution of United States Military and Economic Assistance Programs.* Lucius D. Clay Report. Washington, D.C.: Government Printing Office, 1963.

U.S. Committee to Study the United States Military Assistance Program. *Composite Report and Supplement.* 2 vols. Washington, D.C.: Government Printing Office, 1959.

U.S. Congress. *Foreign Assistance Act 1968.* Public Law 90-556; 82 STAT 960. Washington, D.C.: Government Printing Office, 1968.

_____. *Foreign Military Sales Act.* Public Law 90-629; STAT 1320. Washington, D.C.: Government Printing Office, 1968.

U.S. Congress, House Committee on Foreign Affairs. 90th Cong., 2d Sess. *Foreign Military Sales Act: Hearings* . . . . Washington, D.C.: Government Printing Office, 1968.

_____. 90th Cong., 2d Sess. *Foreign Military Sales Act: Report of the Committee on Foreign Affairs.* House Report, no. 1641. Washington, D.C.: Government Printing Office, 1968.

U.S. Congress, Senate. 90th Cong., 2d Sess. *Foreign Military Sales Act: Report no. 1632.* Washington, D.C.: Government Printing Office, 1968.

U.S. Congress, Senate Committee on Armed Services and Committee on Foreign Relations. 81st Cong., 2d Sess. *Mutual Defense Assistance Program: Hearings* . . . . Washington, D.C.: Government Printing Office, 1950.

U.S. Congress, Senate Committee on Armed Services and
    Committee on Foreign Relations. 82d Cong., 1st
    Sess. *Mutual Security Act of 1951, Hearings
    . . . .* Washington, D.C.: Government Printing Of-
    fice, 1951.

U.S. Congress, Senate Committee on Foreign Relations.
    82d Cong., 1st Sess. *Mutual Security Act of 1951.*
    Washington, D.C.: Government Printing Office,
    1951.

_____. 90th Cong., 1st Sess. *Arms Sales and Foreign
    Policy, Staff Study.* Washington, D.C.: Government
    Printing Office, 1967.

_____. 91st Cong., 1st Sess. *Collective Defense
    Treaties . . . .* Washington, D.C.: Government
    Printing Office, 1969.

U.S. Congress, Senate Committee to Study the Foreign
    Aid Programs. 85th Cong., 1st Sess. *The Military
    Assistance Program of the United States: Two Stud-
    ies and a Report.* Washington, D.C.: Government
    Printing Office, 1957.

_____. 85th Cong., 1st Sess. *Personnel for the Mu-
    tual Security Program.* Prepared by Louis J. Kroe-
    ger and Associates. Washington, D.C.: Government
    Printing Office, 1957. 68 pp.

U.S. Department of Defense. *Military Assistance
    Facts.* Published by the Office of the Assistant
    Secretary of Defense for International Security Af-
    fairs, annually, 1964–70.

U.S. Department of State. *Collective Defense Trea-
    ties, with Maps, Texts of Treaties, a Chronology,
    Status of Forces Agreement, and Comparative Chart.*
    Washington, D.C.: Government Printing Office,
    1969. 514 pp.

U.S. Department of the Air Force, Directorate of

Military Assistance and Sales. *Information and Guidance on Military Assistance, Grant Aid, and Foreign Military Sales.* Annually, 1964-68.

U.S. President's Citizen Advisers on the Mutual Security Program. *Report to the President, 1 March 1957.* Washington, D.C.: Government Printing Office, 1957.

U.S. President's Committee to Study the United States Military Assistance Program. *Composite Report* . . . . 2 vols. Washington, D.C.: Government Printing Office, 1959.

_____. *Interim Report.* Washington, D.C.: Government Printing Office, 1959.

Van Alstyne, Richard W. "New Patterns of Military Cooperation." *World Affairs Interpreter,* April 1955, pp. 22-34.

Vandevanter, Brig. Gen. E., Jr. *A Further Inquiry into the Nature of Alliances: NATO and OAS.* RAND Paper P-3832. Santa Monica, Calif.: RAND Corporation, 1968. 77 pp.

Van Ypersele de Strihou, J. "Sharing the Defense Burden among the Allies." *Review of Economics and Statistics* 49 (1967):527-36.

Windle, Charles, and Vallance, T. R. "Optimizing Military Assistance Training." *World Politics* 15 (1962):91-107.

Wolf, Charlotte. *Garrison Community: A Study of an Overseas American Military Colony.* Westport, Conn.: Greenwood Press, 1970. 324 pp.

Wolfers, Arnold O. "Alliances as a Means of Defense." *Naval War College Review,* April 1955, pp. 1-22.

_____. "The American Alliance Strategy in Peace and

War." *Naval War College Review,* April 1956, pp. 1-20.

2. North America, Western Europe, Mediterranean

Amme, Carl H. "NATO Strategy and Flexible Response." *U.S. Naval Institute Proceedings,* May 1967, pp. 58-69.

_____. *NATO without France: A Strategic Appraisal.* Stanford, Calif.: Hoover Institution on War, Revolution and Peace, 1967. 195 pp.

_____. "Nuclear Control and the Multilateral Force." *U.S. Naval Institute Proceedings,* April 1965, pp. 24-35.

Aron, Raymond. "Why Europe Fears U.S." *Atlantic,* December 1964, pp. 47-52.

Ashcroft, Geoffrey. *Military Logistics Systems in NATO: The Goal of Integration. Pt. 1: Economic Aspects.* Adelphi Papers, no. 62. London: Institute for Strategic Studies, 1962. 35 pp.

_____. *Military Logistics Systems in NATO: The Goal of Integration. Pt. 2: Military Aspects.* Adelphi Papers, no. 68. London: Institute for Strategic Studies, 1970. 35 pp.

Barnet, Richard J., and Raskin, Marcus G. *After 20 Years: The Decline of NATO and the Search for a New Policy in Europe.* New York: Random House, 1965.

Battelle Memorial Institute. *Trends in Western European Political, Economic, and Defense Policies, 1969-1985 and Implications for U.S. Security and Strategy.* Columbus, Ohio, 1970.

Beaton, L. *The Western Alliance and the McNamara*

Doctrine. Adelphi Papers, no. 11. London: Institute for Strategic Studies, 1964. 11 pp.

Beaufre, Gen. André. *NATO and Europe.* Translated by Joseph Green. New York: Alfred A. Knopf, 1966.

_____. "Security and Defense in Western Europe." *Orbis* 13 (1969):76-86.

Birrenbach, Kurt. "The Reorganization of NATO." *Orbis* 6 (1962):244-57.

Bowie, Robert R. "Strategy and the Atlantic Alliance." *International Organization* 17 (1963):709-32.

Brodie, Bernard. "What Price Conventional Capabilities in Europe." *Reporter,* 23 May 1963, pp. 25-33.

Buchan, Alastair. "The Control of Western Strategy." *Royal United Service Institution Journal* 108 (1963):303-10.

_____. "The Future of NATO." *International Conciliation,* November 1967, pp. 5-61.

_____. *The Implications of a European System for Defense Technology.* Defense, Technology and the Western Alliance Series, no. 6. London: Institute for Strategic Studies, 1967.

_____. *The Multilateral Force: An Historical Perspective.* Adelphi Papers, no. 13. London: Institute for Strategic Studies, 1964.

_____. "The Multilateral Force: A Study in Alliance Politics." *International Affairs* 40 (1964):619-37.

_____. *NATO in the 1960's: The Implications of Interdependence.* Rev. ed. New York: Frederick A. Praeger, 1963. 179 pp.

Buchan, Alastair. *NATO Series II: Crisis Management.*
Boulogne-sur-Seine, France: Atlantic Institute,
1966.

_____. "The Reform of NATO." *Foreign Affairs* 40
(1962):165-82.

Buchan, Alastair, and Windsor, Philip. *Arms and Stability in Europe.* London: Chatto & Windus, 1963.

Bull, Hedley. *Strategy and the Atlantic Alliance: A
Critique of United States Doctrine.* Policy Memorandum, no. 29. Princeton, N.J.: Princeton University Center of International Studies, 1964. 42
pp.

Calleo, David. *The Atlantic Fantasy: The U.S., NATO,
and Europe.* Baltimore: Johns Hopkins Press, 1970.
182 pp.

Calman, John. *European Co-operation in Defense Technology: The Political Aspect.* Defense, Technology
and the Western Alliance Series, no. 1. London:
Institute for Strategic Studies, 1967.

Cerny, Karl H., and Briefs, Henry W., eds. *NATO in
Quest of Cohesion.* New York: Frederick A. Praeger, 1965. 481 pp.

Coffey, Joseph I. "A NATO Nuclear Deterrent?" *Orbis*
8 (1964):584-94.

_____. "Strategy, Alliance Policy, and Nuclear Pro-
liferation." *Orbis* 11 (1968):975-95.

_____. "The United States and the Defense of Western
Europe." *Revue Militaire Générale,* December 1969,
pp. 628-37; January 1970, pp. 47-61.

Conant, Melvin. *The Long Polar Watch: Canada and the
Defense of North America.* New York: Harper &
Bros., 1962. 204 pp.

Dawson, Raymond H. "What Kind of NATO Nuclear Force?"
  Annals of the American Academy 351 (1964):30-39.

de Rose, François. "Atlantic Relationships and Nuclear Problems." *Foreign Affairs* 41 (1963):479-90.

Dillon, John G. "Spain: Keystone or Millstone of
  NATO?" *Naval War College Review,* September 1960,
  pp. 77-120.

Emmet, Christopher. "The U.S. Plan for a NATO Nuclear
  Deterrent." *Orbis* 7 (1963):265-71.

Enthoven, Alain C. "Arms and Men: The Military Balance in Europe." *Interplay,* May 1969, pp. 11-14.

Enthoven, Alain C., and Smith, K. Wayne. "What Forces
  for NATO? And from Whom?" *Foreign Affairs* 48
  (1969):80-96.

Ford, C., and Perkins, J. "Our Key SAC Bases in Spain
  and How We Got Them." *Reader's Digest,* August
  1958, pp. 23-26.

Foulkes, Gen. Charles. *Canadian Defense Policy in a
  Nuclear Age.* Toronto: Canadian Institute of International Affairs, 1961.

Fox, William T., and Fox, Annette Baker. *NATO and the
  Range of American Choice.* New York: Columbia University Press, 1967. 352 pp.

Furniss, Edgar S., Jr. "Problems Facing NATO." *Naval
  War College Review,* April 1958, pp. 25-41.

_____. "Western Alliance Development and Technologi-
  cal Cooperation." *International Studies Quarterly*
  11 (1967):339-52.

Gallois, Pierre M. "New Teeth for NATO." *Foreign Affairs* 39 (1960):67-80.

Gallois, Pierre M. "U.S. Strategy and the Defense of Europe." *Orbis* 7 (1963):226-49.

Garnett, John C. "The United States and Europe: Defense, Technology, and the Western Alliance." *International Affairs* 44 (1968):282-88.

Gasteyger, Curt. *The American Dilemma: Bipolarity or Alliance Cohesion.* Adelphi Papers, no. 24. London: Institute for Strategic Studies, 1966. 11 pp.

Gellner, John. "Canada in NATO and NORAD." *Air University Review,* March-April 1967, pp. 22-37.

_____. *North America and NATO.* Toronto: Baxter, 1964. 20 pp.

Georgetown University Center for Strategic and International Studies. *NATO after Czechoslovakia.* Special Report Series, no. 9. Washington, D.C., April 1969. 96 pp.

Goldman, Roy E. "U.S. Spanish Bases Rights Agreement and the Atlantic Alliance." *U.S. Naval Institute Proceedings,* February 1969, pp. 102-104.

Goodpaster, Col. Andrew J. "The Development of SHARE: 1950-1953." *International Organization* 9 (1955): 257-62.

Gordon, Bernard K. "NATO's Missing Shield." *Bulletin of the Atomic Scientists* 15 (1959):229-33.

Gruenther, Gen. Alfred M. "The Supreme Commander Surveys the Situation." *Forces Magazine,* June 1955, pp. 6-12.

Harlow, C. J. E. *The European Armaments Base: A Survey.* Defense, Technology and the Western Alliance Series, no. 2. London: Institute for Strategic Studies, 1967.

Harrison, Stanley L. "NATO's Role after Czechoslovakia." *Military Review*, July 1969, pp. 12-23.

_____. "A New Role for NATO: An American View."
Military Review, February 1968, pp. 14-24.

Heilbrunn, Otto. "NATO and the Flexible Response."
Military Review, May 1965, pp. 22-26.

Heymont, Irving. "The NATO Nuclear Bilateral Forces."
Orbis 9 (1966):1025-41.

Hilsman, Roger. "NATO: The Developing Strategic Context." In *NATO and American Security*, edited by
Klaus Knorr, pp. 11-36. Princeton, N.J.: Princeton University Press, 1959.

Hoag, Malcolm W. "NATO: Deterrent or Shield?" *Foreign Affairs* 36 (1958):278-92.

_____. "Nuclear Strategic Options and European Force
Participation." In *The Dispersion of Nuclear Weapons*, edited by R. N. Rosecrance. New York: Columbia University Press, 1964.

_____. *The Place of Limited War in NATO Strategy*.
RAND Paper P-1566. Santa Monica, Calif.: RAND
Corporation, 1958. 48 pp.

_____. "What Interdependence for NATO?" *World Poli-
tics* 12 (1960):369-90.

Hoile, Maj. K. J. T. "Allied Command, Europe's Mobile
Force." *An Cosantoir, The Irish Defense Journal* 25
(1965):301-4.

Hunt, Kenneth. *The Requirements of Military Technology in the 1970's*. Defense, Technology and the
Western Alliance Series, no. 5. London: Institute
for Strategic Studies, 1967.

"Iceland: Reluctant Ally." *World Today* 12 (1956): 321-30.

Institute for Strategic Studies. *The Evolution of NATO.* Adelphi Papers, no. 5. London, 1963.

Jackson, Col. Bennett L. "Nuclear Weapons and NATO." *Military Review,* April 1959, pp. 16-21.

Jackson, Henry M., ed. *The Atlantic Alliance: Jackson Subcommittee Hearings and Findings.* New York: Frederick A. Praeger, 1967. 309 pp.

James, Robert Rhodes. *Standardization and Common Production of Weapons in NATO.* Defense, Technology and the Western Alliance Series, no. 3. London: Institute for Strategic Studies, 1967.

Kaplan, Lawrence A. "The United States and the Origins of NATO, 1946-1949." *Review of Politics* 31 (1969):210-22.

Kintner, W. R., and Possony, S. T. "NATO's Nuclear Crisis." *Orbis* 6 (1962):217-43.

Kissinger, Henry A. "Coalition Diplomacy in a Nuclear Age." *Foreign Affairs* 42 (1964):525-46.

_____. "Missiles and the Western Alliance." *Foreign Affairs* 36 (1958):383-400.

_____. "NATO's Nuclear Dilemma." *Reporter,* 28 March 1963, pp. 22-37.

_____. *Nuclear Weapons and Foreign Policy.* New York: Harper & Row, 1957.

_____. *The Troubled Partnership: A Reappraisal of the Atlantic Alliance.* New York: McGraw-Hill, 1965. 263 pp.

Kissinger, Henry A. "Unresolved Problems of European Defense." *Foreign Affairs* 40 (1962):515-41.

Klein, Lee. "The Western Alliance--More Symbol Than Shield." *Air Force,* February 1956, pp. 53-59.

Knorr, Klaus. "Canada and Western Defense." *International Journal* 13 (1963):1-16.

_____. *NATO: Past, Present, Prospect.* Headline Series, no. 198. New York: Foreign Policy Association, 1969. 62 pp.

_____, ed. *NATO and American Security.* Princeton, N.J.: Princeton University Press, 1959. 342 pp.

_____. *A NATO Nuclear Force: The Problem of Management.* Policy Memorandum, no. 26. Princeton, N.J.: Princeton University Center of International Studies, 1963. 21 pp.

Kotch, John B. "NATO Nuclear Arrangements in the Aftermath of MLF." *Air University Review,* March-April, pp. 78-87.

Kramish, Arnold. *Atlantic Technological Imbalance: An American Perspective.* Defense, Technology and the Western Alliance Series, no. 4. London: Institute for Strategic Studies, 1967.

Lemnitzer, Lyman L. "The Most Formidable Conventional Armed Forces in the World Today." *Atlantic Community* 6 (1969):501-7.

Lerner, Max. "European Attitudes and U.S. Weapon System Characteristics." Cambridge, Mass.: M.I.T. Press, 1961.

Liddell Hart, B. H. "Danger on the Flanks of NATO." *Marine Corps Gazette,* January 1961, pp. 20-28.

Liddell Hart, B. H. *Defense of the West.* New York:
William Morrow, 1950.

_____. *Deterrent or Defense: A Fresh Look at the
West's Military Posture.* New York: Frederick A.
Praeger, 1960. 257 pp.

_____. "Military Strategy vs. Common Sense." *Satur-
day Review,* 3 March 1956, pp. 7ff.

_____. "Western Defense Planning." *Military Review,*
June 1956, pp. 3-10.

Lowenstein, H., and Zuhlsdorff, Volkmar von. *NATO and
the Defense of the West.* New York: Frederick A.
Praeger, 1963. 383 pp.

McNamara, Robert S. "Defense Arrangements of the
North Atlantic Community." *Department of State
Bulletin* 47 (1962):64-69.

Martin, Laurence W. "The American Decision to Rearm
Germany." In *American Civil-Military Relations: A
Book of Case Studies,* edited by Harold Stein, pp.
643-65. University, Ala.: University of Alabama
Press, 1963.

_____. "Ballistic Missile Defense and Europe." *Bul-
letin of the Atomic Scientists,* May 1967, pp. 42-
46.

_____. *Ballistic Missile Defense and the Alliance.*
Paris: Atlantic Institute, 1969.

Mendershausen, Horst. "Fetishes of NATO and the Dollar." *Orbis* 12 (1968):441-54.

_____. *Troop Stationing in Germany: Values and
Cost.* RAND Memorandum RM-5881-PR. Santa Monica,
Calif.: RAND Corporation, 1968. 144 pp.

Middleton, Drew. *The Defense of Western Europe.* New

York: Appleton-Century-Crofts, 1952. 313 pp.

Miksche, Ferdinand Otto. "The Case for Nuclear Sharing." *Orbis* 5 (1961):292-305.

_____. "Defense Organization for Western Europe."
Military Review, January 1961, pp. 52-61.

_____. "The Nuclear Deterrent and Western Strategy."
Orbis 8 (1964):221-37.

Mountbatten of Burma, Earl. "Allied Naval and Air
Commands in the Mediterranean." *Royal United Service Institution Journal,* May 1955, pp. 171-86.

Mulley, Frederick W. "NATO's Nuclear Problems: Control or Consultation." *Orbis* 8 (1964):21-35.

_____. "Nuclear Weapons: Challenge to National Sov-
ereignty." *Orbis* 7 (1963):32-40.

Murphy, Charles J. V. "A New Strategy for NATO."
Fortune, January 1953, pp. 80-85ff.

"NATO and Atomic Strategy." *Interavia,* July 1954, pp.
415-45.

NATO Information Service. *Aspects of NATO: NATO--The
First Twenty Years.* Brussels, 1969. 54 pp.

_____. *The Atlantic Alliance and the Warsaw Pact: A
Comparative Study.* Brussels, 1970. 30 pp.

Neustadt, Richard E. *Alliance Policies.* New York:
Columbia University Press, 1970. 167 pp.

Newhouse, John. "The Multilateral Force: An Appraisal." *Bulletin of the Atomic Scientists,* September
1964, pp. 13-18.

_____, ed. *U.S. Troops in Europe.* Washington,
D.C.: Brookings Institution, 1971.

Osgood, Robert E. *The Case for the MLF: A Critical Evaluation*. Washington, D.C.: Center of Foreign Policy Research, 1964. 57 pp.

_____. *NATO, The Entangling Alliance*. Chicago: University of Chicago Press, 1959. 416 pp.

_____. *NATO's Strategic Troubles*. Chicago: University of Chicago Center for the Study of Foreign and Military Policy, 1959.

_____. "Nuclear Arms for NATO?" *New Republic*, 18 December 1961, pp. 17-20.

_____. *Nuclear Control in NATO*. Washington, D.C.: Center for Foreign Policy Research, 1962. 42 pp.

Owen, Henry. "NATO Strategy: What Is Past Is Prologue." *Foreign Affairs* 43 (1965):682-90.

Pasti, Gen. Nino. "NATO's Defense Strategy." *Military Review*, November 1969, pp. 39-50.

Patterson, Gardner, and Furniss, Edgar S., Jr. *NATO: A Critical Appraisal*. Princeton, N.J.: Princeton University Conference on NATO, 1957.

Pearson, Lester B. "Canada and the North Atlantic Alliance." *Foreign Affairs* 27 (1949):369-76.

Pfaltzgraff, Robert L., Jr. *The Atlantic Community: A Complex Imbalance*. New York: Van Nostrand Reinhold, 1969. 216 pp.

Pincus, John. *Economic Aid and International Cost Sharing*. Baltimore: Johns Hopkins Press, 1965.

Ranger, Robert. "NATO's Reaction to Czechoslovakia: The Strategy of Ambiguous Response." *World Today*, January 1969, pp. 19-29.

Rathjens, George W., Jr. "Notes on the Military

Problems of Europe." *World Politics* 10 (1958):182–201.

Ries, John C. "NATO Reorganization: A Critique." *Western Political Quarterly* 18 (1965):64–72.

Ritchie, Ronald S. *NATO: The Economics of an Alliance.* Toronto: Ryerson, 1956. 147 pp.

Schaetzel, J. Robert. "The Nuclear Problem and Atlantic Interdependence." *Atlantic Community Quarterly,* Winter 1963–64, pp. 561–69.

Schelling, Thomas C. "The Future of NATO." *Air University Review,* March–April 1968, pp. 40–47.

_____. "Nuclear Strategy in Europe." *World Politics* 14 (1962):421–33.

_____. "Nuclears, NATO and the 'New Strategy.'" In *Problems of National Strategy,* edited by Henry A. Kissinger, pp. 170–85. New York: Frederick A. Praeger, 1965.

Schick, Jack M. "The Berlin Crisis of 1961 and U.S. Military Strategy." *Orbis* 8 (1965):816–31.

Schutze, Walter. *European Defense Co-operation and NATO.* Paris: Atlantic Institute, 1969. 60 pp.

Silard, John. "The Case against the Multi-lateral Forces." *Bulletin of the Atomic Scientists,* September 1964, pp. 18–20.

Slessor, Sir John. "Multilateral or Multinational--An Alternative to MLF." *Atlantic Community Quarterly* 2 (1964):285–91.

Smith, Gerard C. "The Nuclear Defense of NATO." *Department of State Bulletin* 50 (1964):783–90.

"Special Issue on NATO and European Security." *Orbis* 13 (1969):9-372.

Stambuk, George. *American Military Forces Abroad: Their Impact on the Western State System.* Columbus: Ohio State University Press, 1963. 252 pp.

Stanley, Timothy W. "Decentralizing Nuclear Control in NATO." *Orbis* 7 (1963):41-48.

_____. *NATO in Transition: The Future of the Atlantic Alliance.* New York: Frederick A. Praeger, 1965. 417 pp.

_____. "A Strategic Doctrine for NATO in the 1970's." *Orbis* 13 (1969):87-99.

Stanley, Timothy W., and Whitt, Darnell M. *Detente Diplomacy: United States and European Security in the 1970's.* New York: Dunellen, 1970. 170 pp.

Steel, Ronald. *The End of Alliance: America and the Future of Europe.* New York: Viking, 1964. 148 pp.

_____. "NATO's Nuclear Crisis." *Commonweal* 74 (1961):301-3.

Stehlin, Gen. Paul. "The Evolution of Western Defense." *Foreign Affairs* 42 (1963):70-83.

Stillman, Edmund, *et al. Alternatives for European Defense in the Next Decade.* Harmond-on-Hudson, N.Y.: Hudson Institute, 1964. 165 pp.

Taylor, Kenneth W., and Corry, J. A. *Canada, the North Atlantic Community and NATO.* Toronto: University of Toronto Press, 1952.

U.S. Congress, House Committee on Foreign Affairs. 85th Cong., 1st Sess. *Expressing the Sense of the Congress that Efforts Should Be Made to Invite*

Spain to Membership in the North Atlantic Treaty Organization. Report no. 206. Washington, D.C.: Government Printing Office, 1957.

U.S. Congress, House Committee on Foreign Affairs. 89th Cong., 2d Sess. *The Crisis in NATO . . . . Hearings.* Washington, D.C.: Government Printing Office, 1966. 366 pp.

U.S. Congress, Senate Combined Subcommittee of Foreign Relations and Armed Services Committees on the Subject of U.S. Troops in Europe. 90th Cong., 2d Sess. *United States Troops in Europe: Report to the Committee on Foreign Relations and Committee on Armed Services, United States Senate, October 15, 1968.* Washington, D.C.: Government Printing Office, 1968.

U.S. Congress, Senate Committee on Foreign Relations. 85th Cong., 1st Sess. *Favoring Admission of Spain as a Member of the North Atlantic Treaty Organization.* Report no. 212. Washington, D.C.: Government Printing Office, 1957.

U.S. Congress, Senate Committee on Foreign Relations and Committee on Armed Services. 82d Cong., 1st Sess. *Hearings on Senate Concurrent Resolution Relative to the Assignment of Ground Forces . . . to the European Area.* Washington, D.C.: Government Printing Office, 1951.

U.S. Congress, Senate Committee on Government Operations. 89th Cong., 2d Sess. *The Atlantic Alliance . . . . Hearings.* Washington, D.C.: Government Printing Office, 1966.

U.S. Congress, Senate Committee on Government Operations, Subcommittee on National Security and International Operations. 90th Cong., 1st Sess. *The Atlantic Alliance, Current Views.* Washington, D.C.: Government Printing Office, 1967.

U.S. Congress, Senate Committee on Government Opera-
     tions, Subcommittee on National Security and Inter-
     national Operations. 90th Cong., 1st Sess. *The
     Atlantic Alliance, Unfinished Business*. Washing-
     ton, D.C.: Government Printing Office, 1967.

U.S. Department of State. *Issues in United States
     Foreign Policy, No. 2: NATO and the Defense of Eu-
     rope*. Publication no. 8476. Washington, D.C.:
     Government Printing Office, 1970. 32 pp.

U.S. Department of State, Office of Public Affairs.
     *North Atlantic Treaty Organization: Its Develop-
     ment and Significance*. Department of State Publi-
     cation 4630, General Foreign Policy Series 75.
     Washington, D.C., 1952. 50 pp.

Vandevanter, Brig. Gen. E., Jr. *Common Funding in
     NATO*. RAND Memorandum RM-5282. Santa Monica,
     Calif.: RAND Corporation, 1967. 137 pp.

_____. *Coordinated Weapons Production in NATO: A
     Study of Alliance Processes*. RAND Report RM-4169-
     PR. Santa Monica, Calif.: RAND Corporation, 1964.
     99 pp.

_____. *How Allies Collaborate: The NATO Training
     Experience*. RAND Memorandum RM-5847-PR. Santa
     Monica, Calif.: RAND Corporation, 1968. 56 pp.

_____. "Nuclear Forces and the Future of NATO." *Air
     University Review*, July-August 1964, pp. 3-8.

_____. *Nuclear Forces and the Future of NATO*. Santa
     Monica, Calif.: RAND Corporation, 1964. 15 pp.

_____. *Some Fundamentals of NATO Organization*. RAND
     Memorandum RM-3359-PR. Santa Monica, Calif.: RAND
     Corporation, 1963. 78 pp.

_____. *Studies on NATO: An Analysis of Integration*.

RAND Memorandum RM-5600-PR. Santa Monica, Calif.: RAND Corporation, 1966. 113 pp.

Van Ypersele de Strihou, Jacques M. "Sharing the Defense Burden among Western Allies." *Yale Economic Essays* 8 (1968):261-320.

Warnock, John W. *Partner to Behemoth: The Military Policy of a Satellite Canada.* Toronto: New Press, 1970. 340 pp.

Whetten, Lawrence L. "The Mediterranean Threat: Has Strategic Parity Been Achieved?" *Survey,* Winter-Spring 1970, pp. 270-81.

Whipple, Sidney B. "AFNORTH, NATO's Left Flank." *NATO's Fifteen Nations,* April-May 1964, pp. 60-68.

Whitaker, Arthur F. "Spain and the Atlantic Alliance." *Orbis* 10 (1966):42-78.

Wiegele, Thomas C. "The Origins of the MLF Concept, 1957-1960." *Orbis* 12 (1968):465-89.

Wilmot, Chester. "If NATO Had to Fight." *Foreign Affairs* 31 (1953):200-214.

Wohlstetter, Albert. "Nuclear Sharing: NATO and the N + 1 Country." *Foreign Affairs* 39 (1961):355-87.

Wolfers, Arnold. "Could a War in Europe Be Limited?" *Yale Review* 45 (1956):214-28.

_____. "Europe and the NATO Shield." *International Organization* 12 (1958):425-39.

Wyman, Lt. Col. Philip A. "SACLANT--NATO's Atlantic Partner." *Military Review,* October 1956, pp. 39-45.

Zink, Harold. *American Military Government in Germany.* New York: Macmillan, 1947.

Zurcher, Arnold J. "Europe's Northern Flank: Its Strategic Economic and Political Significance in the Cold War." *Naval War College Review*, March 1963, pp. 12-28.

3. Middle East, North Africa

Campbell, John C. *Defense of the Middle East: Problems of American Policy*. Rev. ed. New York: Harper & Row, 1960. 400 pp.

Hurewitz, J. C., ed. *Soviet-American Rivalry in the Middle East*. New York: Frederick A. Praeger, 1969.

Levine, Irving R. "Mediterranean: The Sixth Fleet and the Russians." *Atlantic*, February 1970, pp. 4-18.

McArdle, Lt. Col. John F. "CENTO--The Forgotten Barricade." *Military Review*, September 1968, pp. 84-90.

"U.S. Military Commitments in Europe and the Middle East." *Current History*, July 1969, entire issue.

4. South Asia, Indian Ocean

Millar, T. B. *The Indian and Pacific Oceans: Some Strategic Considerations*. Adelphi Papers, no. 57. London: Institute for Strategic Studies, 1969.

"U.S. Military Commitments in Asia." *Current History*, August 1969, entire issue.

5. Southeast Asia, Vietnam War

Adams, Nina S., and McCoy, Alfred W. *Laos: War and Revolution*. New York: Harper & Row, 1971. 482 pp.

Armbruster, Frank E., *et al.* *Can We Win in Vietnam?*
New York: Frederick A. Praeger, 1968. 427 pp.

Austin, Anthony. *The President's War.* Philadelphia:
J. B. Lippincott, 1971.

Bator, Victor. *Vietnam, A Diplomatic Tragedy: The
Origins of the United States Involvement.* New
York: Oceana, 1965.

Black, Eugene R. *Alternatives to Southeast Asia.* New
York: Frederick A. Praeger, 1969. 180 pp.

Blacker, Irwin. *Search and Destroy.* New York: Dell,
1967.

Brandon, Henry. *Anatomy of Error: The Inside Story
of the Asian War on the Potomac, 1954-1969.* Boston: Gambit, 1969.

Bundy, William P. "The Path to Vietnam: Ten Decisions." *Orbis* 11 (1967):637-63.

Burchett, Wilfred G. *The Fugitive War: The United
States in Vietnam and Laos.* New York: International Publishers, 1963. 224 pp.

_____. *The Second Indochina War: Cambodia and Laos.*
New York: International Publishers, 1970. 204 pp.

Chatham House Study Group. *Collective Defense in
Southeast Asia.* London: Royal Institute for International Affairs, 1956.

Chomsky, Noam. *At War with Asia.* New York: Pantheon
Books, 1970. 313 pp.

Clifford, Clark M. "A Viet Nam Reappraisal: The Personal History of One Man's View and How It
Evolved." *Foreign Affairs* 47 (1969):35-49.

Cooper, Chester L. "The Complexities of Negotiation."
    Foreign Affairs 46 (1968):454-66.

_____. *The Lost Crusade: America in Vietnam.* New
    York: Dodd, Mead, 1970.

Drendel, Tom. *The Air War in Vietnam.* New York:
    Aero, 1968. 96 pp.

Ellsberg, Daniel. *Some Lessons from Failure in Viet-
    nam.* RAND Paper P-4036. Santa Monica, Calif.:
    RAND Corporation, 1969. 20 pp.

Fall, Bernard B. *Anatomy of a Crisis: The Laotian
    Crisis of 1960-61,* edited by Roger M. Smith. Gar-
    den City, N.Y.: Doubleday, 1969. 283 pp.

_____. "Indochina--The Last Year of the War." *Mili-
    tary Review,* October 1956, pp. 3-11; December 1956,
    pp. 48-56.

_____. "Indochina--The Seven Year Dilemma." *Mili-
    tary Review,* October 1953, pp. 23-35.

Fishel, Wesley R. *Vietnam: Is Victory Possible?* New
    York: McGraw-Hill, 1970. 480 pp.

Galbraith, John K. *How to Get Out of Vietnam.* New
    York: New American Library, 1967.

Garland, Lt. Col. Albert N. *Combat Notes from Viet-
    nam.* Fort Benning, Ga.: Infantry Magazine, 1968.
    96 pp.

George, Alexander L.; Hall, David K.; and Simons, Wil-
    liam E. *The Limits of Coercive Diplomacy: Laos,
    Cuba, Vietnam.* Boston: Little, Brown, 1970.

Gettleman, Marvin; Gettleman, Susan; Kaplan, Law-
    rence; and Kaplan, Carl, eds. *Conflict in Indo-
    China: A Reader on the Widening War in Laos and*

Cambodia. New York: Vintage Books, 1970. 461 pp.

Gordon, Bernard. *East Asian Regionalism and United States Security.* RAC Paper P-45. McLean, Va.: Research Analysis Corporation, 1968.

Grant, Jonathan S., ed. *Cambodia: The Widening War in Indochina.* New York: Washington Square Press, 1971. 355 pp.

Gurtov, Melvin. *The First Vietnam Crisis: Chinese Communist Strategy and United States Involvement, 1953-1954.* New York: Columbia University Press, 1967. 228 pp.

_____. *Problems and Prospects of United States Policy in Southeast Asia.* RAND Memorandum RM-5910-ISA. Santa Monica, Calif.: RAND Corporation, 1969. 134 pp.

Gurtov, Melvin, and Kellen, K. *Vietnam: Lessons and Mislessons.* RAND Paper P-4084. Santa Monica, Calif.: RAND Corporation, 1969. 22 pp.

Harries, Owen. "Should the U.S. Withdraw from Asia?" *Foreign Affairs* 47 (1968):15-25.

Harrigan, Anthony. *A Guide to the War in Vietnam.* New York: Panther, 1966.

Herman, Edward, and DuBoff, Richard. *America's Vietnam Policy.* Washington, D.C.: Public Affairs Press, 1966.

Hersh, Seymour M. *My Lai 4.* New York: Random House, 1970. 210 pp.

Hickey, G. C. *The American Military Advisor and His Foreign Counterpart: The Case of Vietnam.* RAND Memorandum RM-4482-ARPA. Santa Monica, Calif.: RAND Corporation, 1969. 105 pp.

Higgins, Marguerite. *Our Vietnam Nightmare.* New York: Harper & Row, 1965.

Hilsman, Roger. "Must We Invade the North?" *Foreign Affairs* 46 (1968):425-41.

Hilsman, Roger, *et al. Vietnam: Which Way to Peace?* Chicago: University of Chicago Press, 1970. 27 pp.

Hoopes, Townsend. *The Limits of Intervention.* New York: David McKay, 1969. 245 pp.

_____. "Vietnam: Legacy of the Cold War in Indochina." *Foreign Affairs* 48 (1970):601-16.

Infantry Magazine Staff. *A Distant Challenge: The U.S. Infantryman in Vietnam, 1967-70.* Fort Benning, Ga.: U.S. Army Infantry School, 1971. 400 pp.

Irving, Frederick F. "The Battle of Hue." *Military Review,* January 1969, pp. 56-63.

Isard, Walter, ed. *Vietnam: Some Basic Issues and Alternatives.* Cambridge: Schenkman, 1969. 213 pp.

Jordan, Amos A., Jr. *Foreign Aid and the Defense of Southeast Asia.* New York: Frederick A. Praeger, 1962. 272 pp.

Just, Ward. *To What End: A Report on Vietnam.* New York: Houghton Mifflin, 1968.

Kahin, George McT., and Lewis, John W. "The United States in Vietnam." *Bulletin of the Atomic Scientists,* June 1965, pp. 28-40.

Kennedy, D. E. *The Security of Southern Asia.* New York: Frederick A. Praeger, 1965. 308 pp.

Kleinman, Forrest K. "Report from Vietnam." *Army*, September 1962, pp. 21-36, 90, 92.

Kriegel, Richard C. "Tet Offensive: Victory or Defeat?" *Marine Corps Gazette*, December 1968, pp. 24-28.

Lacouture, Jean. "From the Vietnam War to an Indochina War." *Foreign Affairs* 48 (1970):617-28.

Lane, Gen. Thomas A. *America on Trial: The War for Vietnam*. Arlington, Va., 1970.

Lansdale, Maj. Gen. Edward G. "Viet Nam: Still the Search for Goals." *Foreign Affairs* 47 (1968):92-98.

McCloud, Donald G. "United States Policies toward Regional Organizations in Southeast Asia." *World Affairs*, September 1970, pp. 133-45.

McCoskey, James L. "Horsepower for Vietnam." *Military Review*, May 1969, pp. 85-92.

McMahon, John F., Jr. "Vietnam: Our World War II Legacy." *Air University Review*, July-August 1968, pp. 60-66.

Marshall, S. L. A. *Ambush: The Battle of Dau Tieng. Also Called the Battle Dong Minh Chau, War Zone C, Operation Attlebore, and Other Deadfalls in South Vietnam*. New York, 1968.

_____. *Battles in the Monsoon: Campaign in the Central Highlands, South Vietnam, Summer 1966*. New York: William Morrow, 1970. 408 pp.

_____. *The Field of Bamboo: Dong Tre, Trung Luong, and Hoa Hoi, Three Battles Just Beyond the South China Sea*. New York: Dial Press, 1971. 242 pp.

_____. "Men Facing Death: The Destruction of an

American Platoon." *Harper's*, September 1966, pp. 47-55; December 1966, pp. 16ff.

Marshall, S. L. A. *West to Cambodia*. New York: Cowles Education Corporation, 1968. 253 pp.

Marshall, S. L. A., with Hackworth, Lt. Col. David H. *Bird: The Christmastide Battle*. New York: Cowles Education Corporation, 1968. 206 pp.

Miller, August C., Jr. "SEATO--Segment of Collective Security." *U.S. Naval Institute Proceedings*, January 1960, pp. 50-62.

Modelski, George. *SEATO*. Vancouver: University of British Columbia, 1962.

_____, ed. *SEATO: Six Studies*. Melbourne: F. W. Cheshire, 1962.

Moeser, Robert D. *U.S. Navy: Vietnam*. Annapolis: U.S. Naval Institute, 1969. 256 pp.

Montgomery, John D. *The Politics of Foreign Aid: American Experience in Southeast Asia*. New York: Frederick A. Praeger, 1962. 352 pp.

Pfeffer, Richard M., ed. *No More Vietnams? The War and the Future of American Foreign Policy*. New York: Harper & Row, 1968.

Queenin, Lt. Col. Hugh F. "The Military Implications of SEATO." *Military Review*, February 1956, pp. 25-29.

Ridgway, Gen. Matthew B. "Indochina: Disengaging." *Foreign Affairs* 49 (1971):583-92.

Royal Institute of International Affairs. *Collective Defence in Southeast Asia: The Manila Treaty and Its Implications*. London, 1956.

Russett, Bruce. "Vietnam and Restraints on Aerial Warfare." *Bulletin of the Atomic Scientists*, January 1970, pp. 9-12.

Schell, Jonathan. *The Village of Ben Suc: The American Destruction of a Vietnamese Village*. New York: Alfred A. Knopf, 1969.

Schreadley, Comdr. R. L. "The Naval War in Vietnam, 1950-1970." *U.S. Naval Institute Proceedings*, May 1971, pp. 180-209.

Schurmann, Franz; Scott, Peter Dale; and Zeinik, Reginald. *The Politics of Escalation in Vietnam*. New York: Fawcett, 1966.

Shaplen, Robert. *The Lost Revolution: The Story of 20 Years of Neglected Opportunities in Vietnam*. New York: Harper & Row, 1965.

_____. "Our Involvement in Laos." *Foreign Affairs* 48 (1970):478-93.

_____. *The Road from War*. New York: Harper & Row, 1971.

_____. "Viet Nam: Crisis of Indecision." *Foreign Affairs* 46 (1967):95-110.

Shazo, Thomas E. de. "U.S. Counterinsurgency Assistance to Rural Vietnam in 1964." *Naval War College Review*, March 1967, pp. 40-83.

Sheehan, Neil; Smith, Hedrick; Kenworthy, E. W.; and Butterfield, Fox. *The Pentagon Papers*. New York: Bantam, 1971. 667 pp.

Thompson, Sir Robert G. K. *No Exit from Vietnam*. New York: Frederick A. Praeger, 1969.

_____. "The Vietnam War: On the Way to Victory." *Survival*, February 1970, pp. 54-55.

Trager, Frank N. "A U.S. Program for Southern Asia." *Current History,* March 1961, pp. 129–38.

_____. "Vietnam: The Military Requirements for Victory." *Orbis* 8 (1964):563–83.

_____. "What Is Security in Southeast Asia?" *Air University Review,* November–December 1968, pp. 103–12.

_____. *Why Vietnam?* New York: Frederick A. Praeger, 1966.

U.S. Commander-in-Chief, Pacific, and Commander, U.S. Military Assistance Command, Vietnam. *Report on the War in Vietnam.* As of 30 June 1968. Washington, D.C.: Government Printing Office, 1968. 347 pp.

U.S. Congress, House Committee on Armed Services. 90th Cong., 2d Sess. *Review of the Vietnam Conflict and Its Impact on U.S. Military Commitments Abroad.* Washington, D.C.: Government Printing Office, 1968.

U.S. Congress, House Committee on Foreign Affairs. 91st Cong., 2d Sess. *To Amend the Foreign Assistance Act of 1961 (Supplemental Authorization for Assistance to Cambodia and Other Countries). Hearings . . . .* Washington, D.C.: Government Printing Office, 1970. 227 pp.

U.S. Congress, Senate Committee on Armed Services. Preparedness Investigating Subcommittee. 90th Cong., 1st Sess. *Air War against North Vietnam. Hearings . . . .* 5 pts. Washington, D.C.: Government Printing Office, 1967.

_____. 90th Cong., 1st Sess. *Air War against North Vietnam. Summary Report.* Washington, D.C.: Government Printing Office, 1967.

U.S. Congress, Senate Committee on Foreign Relations.
89th Cong., 2d Sess. *Vietnam Hearings*. New York:
Random House, 1966.

_____. 91st Cong., 1st Sess. *Background Information
Relating to Southeast Asia and Vietnam*. 5th rev.
ed. Washington, D.C.: Government Printing Office,
1969. 272 pp.

_____. 91st Cong., 2d Sess. *Documents Relating to
the War Power by Congress: The President's Authority as Commander-in-Chief, and the War in Indochina*. Washington, D.C.: Government Printing Office, 1970. 252 pp.

U.S. Congress, Senate Republican Policy Committee.
The War in Vietnam. New York: Public Affairs
Press, 1967. 62 pp.

U.S. Department of State. *Southeast Asia Treaty Or-
ganization: First Annual Report of the Council of
Representatives*. Washington, D.C.: Government
Printing Office, 1956. 27 pp.

U.S. Department of the Army, Office of the Chief of
Military History. *Seven Firefights in Vietnam*.
Prepared by John Albright, John A. Cash, and Allen
W. Sandstrum. Washington, D.C.: Government Print-
ing Office, 1970. 154 pp.

U.S. Marine Corps, Historical Branch G-3. *The Battle
for Khe Sanh*. Prepared by Capt. Moyers S. Shore
II. Washington, D.C., 1969. 203 pp.

_____. *Small Unit Action in Vietnam, Summer 1966*.
Prepared by Capt. Francis J. West, Jr. Marine
Corps Historical Reference Pamphlet. Washington,
D.C., 1967. 123 pp.

_____. *U.S. Marine Corps Civic Action Efforts in
Vietnam, March 1965-March 1966*. Prepared by Russell H. Stolfi. Washington, D.C., 1968.

"U.S. Military Commitments in Asia." *Current History*, August 1969, entire issue.

Verrier, Anthony. "Strategic Bombing--The Lessons of World War II and the American Experience in Vietnam." *Royal United Service Institution Journal*, May 1967, pp. 157-61.

Walt, Gen. Lewis W. *Strange War, Strange Strategy: A General's Report on Vietnam.* New York: Funk & Wagnalls, 1970.

Weed, A. C., II. "Army Special Forces and Vietnam." *Military Review*, August 1969, pp. 63-68.

Weil, Charles A. *Curtains over Vietnam: Strategic Appraisal of Suppressed Aspects of U.S. Security Stake in Vietnam.* Jericho, N.Y.: Exposition Press, 1969. 155 pp.

White, Ralph K. "Misperception of Aggression in Vietnam." *Journal of International Affairs* 21 (1967): 123-40.

_____. *Nobody Wanted War: Misperception in Vietnam and Other Wars.* Garden City, N.Y.: Doubleday, 1968. 347 pp.

Windchy, Eugene G. *Tonkin Gulf.* Garden City, N.Y.: Doubleday, 1971.

Wolf, Charles, Jr. *Foreign Aid: Theory and Practice in Southern Asia.* Princeton, N.J.: Princeton University Press, 1960.

_____. *Military Assistance Programs.* Santa Monica, Calif.: RAND Corporation, 1965.

Young, Kenneth. "The Role of American Advisors in Thailand, 1902-1949." *Asia*, Spring 1970, pp. 1-31.

Zinn, Howard. *Vietnam: The Logic of Withdrawal.* Boston: Beacon Press, 1967.

6. North Asia and Pacific, Korean War

Appleman, Roy E. *South to the Naktong, North to the Yalu (June-November 1950).* Washington, D.C.: Office of the Chief of Military History, Department of the Army, 1961. 813 pp.

Barnett, A. Doak. "A Nuclear China and U.S. Arms Policy." *Foreign Affairs* 48 (1970):427-42.

Barr, J. "Ryukyu Islands: A U.S. Bastion in the Pacific." *World Today,* May 1961, pp. 187-97.

Berger, Carl. *The Korean Knot: A Military-Political History.* Philadelphia: University of Pennsylvania Press, 1957.

Bishop, Peter V. "ANZUS: Shield or Shroud?" *International Journal* 16 (1961):405-9.

Cagle, Comm. Malcolm W. "Errors of the Korean War." *U.S. Naval Institute Proceedings,* March 1958, pp. 31-35.

Cagle, Comm. Malcolm W., and Manson, Comm. Frank A. *The Sea War in Korea.* Annapolis, Md.: U.S. Naval Institute, 1957.

Clark, Gen. Mark. *From the Danube to the Yalu.* New York: Harper & Bros., 1954.

Collins, Gen. J. Lawton. *War in Peacetime: The History and Lessons of Korea.* Boston: Houghton Mifflin, 1969. 416 pp.

Crofts, Alfred. "The Start of the Korean War Reconsidered." *Rocky Mountain Social Science Journal,* April 1970, pp. 109-18.

DeWeerd, Harvey A. *The Korean War: Political Limitations*. RAND Paper P-2059. Santa Monica, Calif.: RAND Corporation, 1960.

_____. "Strategic Surprise in the Korean War." *Orbis* 6 (1962):435-52.

_____. *The Triumph of the Limiters: Korea*. RAND Paper 3949. Santa Monica, Calif.: RAND Corporation, 1960. 16 pp.

Fearey, Robert A. *The Occupation of Japan, Second Phase, 1948-1950*. New York: Macmillan, 1950.

Fehrenbach, T. R. *This Kind of War: A Study in Unpreparedness*. New York: Macmillan, 1963. 688 pp.

Field, James A., Jr. *History of United States Naval Operations: Korea*. Washington, D.C.: Government Printing Office, 1962. 499 pp.

Fifield, Russell H. "U.S. Objectives and Treaty Organization in Asia and the Western Pacific." *Naval War College Review*, April 1966, pp. 4-15.

Freymond, Jacques. "Supervising Agreements: The Korean Experience." *Foreign Affairs* 37 (1959):496-503.

Futtrell, R. Frank. *The United States Air Force in Korea, 1950-1953*. New York: Duell, Sloan & Pearce, 1961. 774 pp.

Gelber, Harry G. *The Australian-American Alliance: Costs and Benefits*. Baltimore: Penguin Books, 1968. 160 pp.

_____. "The Impact of Chinese ICBM's on Strategic Deterrence." *Orbis* 13 (1969):407-34.

George, Alexander L. "American Policy-Making and the

North Korean Aggression." *World Politics* 7 (1955):
209-32.

Goodrich, Leland M. *Korea: A Study in U.S. Policy in
the United Nations*. New York: Council on Foreign
Relations, 1959.

Grey, Arthur L., Jr. "The Thirty-Eighth Parallel."
Foreign Affairs 29 (1951):482-87.

Hartmann, Frederick H. "The Issues in Korea." *Yale
Review* 42 (1952):54-66.

Heinl, Robert D. *Victory at High Tide: The Inchon-
Seoul Campaign*. Philadelphia: J. B. Lippincott,
1968. 315 pp.

Hermes, Walter G. *Truce Tent and Fighting Front*.
Washington, D.C.: Office of the Chief of Military
History, Department of the Army, 1966. 571 pp.

Higgins, Marguerite. *War in Korea*. Garden City,
N.Y.: Doubleday, 1951.

Higgins, Trumbull. *Korea and the Fall of MacArthur:
A Précis in Limited War*. New York: Oxford University Press, 1960.

Hittle, J. D. "Korea--Back to the Facts of Life."
U.S. Naval Institute Proceedings, December 1950,
pp. 1289-97.

Jabara, James. "Air War in Korea." *Air Force,* October 1951, pp. 53, 60.

Johns Hopkins University Operations Research Office.
U.N. Partisan Warfare in Korea, 1951-1954. Washington, D.C., 1956. 209 pp.

Kahn, E. J., Jr. *The Peculiar War*. New York: Random
House, 1952.

Karig, Walter; Cagle, Malcolm W.; and Manson, Frank A. *Battle Report: The War in Korea.* New York: Rinehart, 1952. 520 pp.

Kaufmann, W. W. *Policy Objectives and Military Action in the Korean War.* RAND Paper P-886. Santa Monica, Calif.: RAND Corporation, 1956.

Kennan, George F. "Japanese Security and American Policy." *Foreign Affairs* 43 (1964):14-28.

Kim, Sang Mo. "The Implications of the Sea War in Korea from the Standpoint of the Korean War." *Naval War College Review,* Summer 1967, pp. 105-39.

Kinkead, Eugene. *In Every War But One.* New York: W. W. Norton, 1959.

Knight, Charlotte. "Air War in Korea." *Air Force,* August 1950, pp. 21-34.

Leckie, Robert. *Conflict: The History of the Korean War.* New York: G. P. Putnam's Sons, 1963.

Levi, Burna D. "The Japanese-American Treaty of Mutual Cooperation and Security and the United States Navy--1970." *Naval War College Review,* September 1965, pp. 20-62.

Lichterman, Martin. "Korea: Problems in Limited War." In *National Security in the Nuclear Age: Basic Facts and Theories,* edited by Gordon B. Turner and Richard D. Challener, pp. 31-56. New York: Frederick A. Praeger, 1960.

_____. "To the Yalu and Back." In *American Civil-Military Relations: A Book of Case Studies,* edited by Harold Stein, pp. 569-643. Birmingham: University of Alabama Press, 1963.

Lyons, Gene M. *Military Policy and Economic Aid: The*

Korean Case, 1950-1953. Columbus: Ohio State University Press, 1961. 298 pp.

Marshall, S. L. A. *Commentary on Infantry Operations and Weapons Usage in Korea, Winter 1950-51.* Baltimore: Operations Research Office, Johns Hopkins University, 1953. 142 pp.

_____. *The Military History of the Korean War.* New York: Franklin Watts, 1963. 99 pp.

_____. "A New Strategy for Korea." *Reporter,* 3 March 1953, pp. 17-20.

_____. *Operation Punch and the Capture of Hill 440, Suwon, Korea, February 1951.* Baltimore: Operations Research Office, Johns Hopkins University, 1952.

_____. "Our Mistakes in Korea." *Atlantic,* September 1953, pp. 46-49.

_____. *Pork Chop Hill.* New York: William Morrow, 1956.

_____. *The River and the Gauntlet: Defeat of the Eighth Army by the Chinese Communist Forces, November 1950, in the Battle of the Chongchon River, Korea.* New York: William Morrow, 1953. 385 pp.

Martin, Edwin M. *The Allied Occupation of Japan.* Stanford, Calif.: Stanford University Press, 1948.

Meade, E. Grant. *American Military Government in Korea.* New York: King's Crown Press, 1951.

Morris, M. D. *Okinawa: A Tiger by the Tail.* New York: Hawthorn, 1968. 238 pp.

Norman, John. "MacArthur's Blockade Proposals against Red China." *Pacific Historical Review,* May 1957, pp. 161-74.

O'Balance, Edgar. *Korea: 1950-1953.* Hamden, Conn.: Archon Books, 1969. 171 pp.

Oggloblin, Peter. *The Korean War.* Cambridge, Mass.: M.I.T. Center for International Studies, 1958.

Oliver, Robert T. *Verdict in Korea.* State College, Pa.: Bald Eagle Press, 1952.

_____. *Why War Came to Korea.* New York: Fordham University Press, 1950.

Padelford, Norman J. "Collective Security in the Pacific: Nine Years of the ANZUS Pact." *U.S. Naval Institute Proceedings,* September 1960, pp. 38-47.

Paige, Glenn D. *The Korean Decision: June 24-30, 1950.* Introduction by Richard C. Snyder. New York: Free Press, 1968. 394 pp.

Poats, Rutherford M. *Decision in Korea.* New York: McBride, 1954.

Rees, David. *Korea: The Limited War.* New York: St. Martin's Press, 1964. 511 pp.

Ridgway, Gen. Matthew B. *The Korean War.* Garden City, N.Y.: Doubleday, 1967. 291 pp.

_____. *Soldier: The Memoirs of Matthew B. Ridgway,* as told to H. H. Martin. New York: Harper & Bros., 1956.

Sarafan, B. D. "Military Government: Korea." *Far Eastern Survey,* 20 November 1946, pp. 349-52.

Sleeper, Col. Raymond S. "Korean Targets for Medium Bombardment." *Air University Quarterly Review,* Spring 1951, pp. 18-31.

Snyder, Richard C., and Paige, Glenn D. "The United States Decision to Resist Aggression in Korea: The

Application of an Analytical Scheme." *Administrative Science Quarterly* 3 (1958):341-78.

Starke, J. G. *The ANZUS Treaty Alliance.* Melbourne: Melbourne University Press, 1965.

Stevenson, Adlai. "Korea in Perspective." *Foreign Affairs* 30 (1952):349-60.

Stone, I. F. *The Hidden History of the Korean War.* New York: Monthly Review Press, 1952.

Stratton, Samuel S. "Korea: Acid Test of Containment." *U.S. Naval Institute Proceedings,* March 1952, pp. 237-49.

Thomas, Robert C. W. *The War in Korea, 1950-1953: A Military Study.* London: Gale & Polden, 1954.

Traverso, Edmund. *Korea and the Limits of Limited War.* Menlo Park, Calif.: Addison-Wesley, 1970. 81 pp.

Truman, Harry S. *Memoirs.* 2 vols. New York: Doubleday, 1955-56.

U.S. Congress, Senate Committee on Armed Services and Committee on Foreign Relations. 82d Cong., 1st Sess. *Military Situation in the Far East.* 5 vols. Washington, D.C.: Government Printing Office, 1951.

U.S. Congress, Senate Committee on the Judiciary, Subcommittee to Investigate the Administration of the Internal Security Act. 84th Cong., 1st Sess. *Korean War and Related Matters.* Washington, D.C.: Government Printing Office, 1955.

U.S. Congressional Record. *The United States and the Korean Problem, Documents, 1943-1953.* Senate Doc., no. 74. Washington, D.C.: Government Printing Office, 1953.

U.S. Department of State. *Events Prior to the Attack on June 25, 1950: The Conflict in Korea.* Washington, D.C.: Government Printing Office, 1951.

U.S. Department of the Army. *POW--The Fight Continues after the Battle.* Washington, D.C., 1955.

U.S. Department of the Army, Office of the Chief of Military History. *Combat Actions in Korea.* Prepared by Russell A. Gugeler. Washington, D.C.: Government Printing Office, 1970. 252 pp.

_____. *Korea--1950.* Prepared by J. Miller, O. J. Carroll, and M. E. Tackley. Washington, D.C.: Government Printing Office, 1952.

_____. *Korea, 1951-1953.* Prepared by J. Miller, O. J. Carroll, and M. E. Tackley. Washington, D.C.: Government Printing Office, 1956.

_____. *Military Advisors in Korea: KMAG in Peace and War.* Prepared by Maj. Robert K. Sawyer. Washington, D.C.: Government Printing Office, 1962. 216 pp.

Vatcher, William H., Jr. *Panmunjon: The Story of the Korean Military Armistice Negotiations.* Foreword by Adm. C. Turner Joy. New York: Frederick A. Praeger, 1958. 352 pp.

Warner, Albert L. "How the Korean Decision Was Made." *Harper's,* June 1951, pp. 99-106.

Wayland, Gen. O. P. "The Air Campaign in Korea." *Air University Quarterly Review,* Fall 1953, pp. 3-28.

Weinstein, Martin E. *Japan's Postwar Defense Policy, 1947-1968.* New York: Columbia University Press, 1971. 160 pp.

Westover, Capt. John G. *Combat Support in Korea.*

Washington, D.C.: Combat Forces Press, 1955. 254 pp.

Whiteley, Group Capt. E. A. "Allied Defense Co-operation in the Far East." *Journal of the Royal United Service Institution* 100 (1955):532-49.

Wilkinson, Allen B. *Up Front Korea.* New York: Viking, 1968. 440 pp.

Wint, Guy. *What Happened in Korea?* London: Batchworth, 1954.

"World Strategic Picture: Formosa and Pacific Strategy." *An Cosantoir: The Irish Defense Journal* 13 (1953):166-71.

7. Latin America and Caribbean

Ball, M. Margaret. *The OAS in Transition.* Durham, N.C.: Duke University Press, 1969. 721 pp.

Draper, Theodore. *The Dominican Revolt: A Case Study in American Policy.* New York: Commentary, 1968.

Einaudi, L. R. *Peruvian Military Relations with the United States.* RAND Paper 4389. Santa Monica, Calif.: RAND Corporation, 1970.

Kemp, Geoffrey. "Rearmament in Latin America." *World Today,* September 1967, pp. 375-84.

_____. *Some Relationships Between U.S. Military Training Programs in Latin America and the Weapons Acquisition Patterns of Recipients.* M.I.T. Publication, no. C/70-6. Cambridge, Mass.: M.I.T. Press, 1970.

Knorr, Klaus. "Failure in National Intelligence Estimates: The Case of the Cuban Missiles." *World Politics* 16 (1964):455-67.

Loftus, Joseph E. *Latin American Defense Expenditures, 1938-1965.* RAND Memorandum RM-5310-PR/ISA. Santa Monica, Calif.: RAND Corporation, 1968.

Mecham, J. Lloyd. *The U.S. and Inter-American Security, 1889-1960.* Austin: University of Texas Press, 1961.

Plank, John N. "The Caribbean: Intervention, When and How." *Foreign Affairs* 43 (1965):37-48.

Rockefeller, Nelson. *The Rockefeller Report on the Americas. The Official Report of a United States Presidential Mission for the Western Hemisphere.* Chicago: Quadrangle Books, 1969.

Slater, Jerome. *Intervention and Negotiation: The United States and the Dominican Revolution.* New York: Harper & Row, 1970. 254 pp.

U.S. Congress, Senate Committee on the Judiciary, Subcommittee to Investigate the Administration of Internal Security Act and Other Laws. 87th Cong., 1st Sess. *Communist Threat to the U.S. Through the Caribbean. Hearings.* Washington, D.C.: Government Printing Office, 1961.

U.S. Department of the Air Force, Air University, Aerospace Studies Institute, Documentary Research Division. *United States Military Aid to Latin America.* Prepared by Raymond Estep. Maxwell Air Force Base, Ala., 1966.

"U.S. Military Commitments in Latin America." *Current History,* June 1969, entire issue.

Vandevanter, E., Jr. *A Further Inquiry into the Nature of Alliances: NATO and OAS.* RAND Paper P-3832. Santa Monica, Calif.: RAND Corporation, 1968. 77 pp.

Whitaker, A. P. "The Organization of American
    States." *World Affairs* 13 (1959):115-30.

    8. Africa

Bell, M. J. V. *Military Assistance to Independent Af-
    rican States*. Adelphi Papers, no. 15. London:
    Institute for Strategic Studies, 1964.

VI

The Domestic Effects of Defense Policy

A. General Economic, Social, and Political
    Impact of U.S. Defense Policy
B. The Opportunity Costs of Arms Control
    and Disarmament

Section VI is subdivided into only two parts. Most of the literature in this area cuts across so many theoretical borders that it would be confusing to classify further. Part VI A contains works on the economic, social, and political consequences of defense policy. Part VI B is more specialized, containing works on the economic costs of arms control and disarmament.

Users of this section should consult also section IV E.

A. GENERAL ECONOMIC, SOCIAL, AND POLITICAL IMPACT
   OF U.S. DEFENSE POLICY

Ackley, Gardiner. "Economic Considerations in National Security." *Naval War College Review,* October 1965, pp. 1-18.

Barnet, Richard J. *The Economy of Death.* New York: Atheneum, 1969. 201 pp.

Benoit, Emile, ed. *Disarmament and World Economic In-terdependence*. New York: Columbia University Press, 1967. 260 pp.

_____. "Monetary and Real Costs of National De-fense." *American Economic Review* 58 (1968):410–12.

Benson, Robert S. *The Cost of Security: National De-fense and Military Assistance Requirements for the '70's*. Washington, D.C.: National Urban Coali-tion, 1971. 127 pp.

Bingham, Jonathan B. "Can Military Spending Be Con-trolled?" *Foreign Affairs* 48 (1969):51–66.

Blackman, J. A.; Basch, S. Fabricant; Gainsbrugh, M.; and Stein, E. *War and Defense Economics*. New York: Rinehart, 1952.

Blacksby, F. T., and Paige, D. C. "Defense Expenditures--Burden or Stimulus?" *Survival*, November–December 1960, pp. 242–46.

Bolton, Roger E. *Defense Purchase and Regional Growth*. Washington, D.C.: Brookings Institution, 1966. 189 pp.

Bowen, William. "The Vietnam War: A Cost Account-ing." *Fortune*, April 1966, pp. 119–23, 254, 259.

Brownlee, James F. *The Defense We Can Afford*. New York: Committee for Economic Development, 1960.

Burck, Gilbert. "The Guns, Butter, and Then Some Economy." *Fortune*, October 1965, pp. 118–21.

Cameron, Juan. "The Armed Forces' Reluctant Retrench-ment." *Fortune*, November 1970, pp. 68–73, 166, 173–74.

_____. "The Case for Cutting Defense Spending." *Fortune*, August 1969, pp. 68–73ff.

Caridi, Ronald J. *The Korean War and American Politics: The Republican Party as a Case Study.* Philadelphia: University of Pennsylvania Press, 1969. 319 pp.

Chamber of Commerce of the United States. *After Vietnam: A Report of the Ad Hoc Committee on Economic Impact of Peace after Vietnam.* Washington, D.C., 1968.

Chamber of Commerce of the United States, Committee on Economic Policy. *The Economics of Defense Spending.* Washington, D.C., 1965.

Chitwood, Stephen R., ed. *Economic Policies for National Strength: The Quest for Sustained Growth and Stability.* Washington, D.C.: Industrial College of the Armed Forces, 1968.

Christman, Henry M. *Peace and Arms: Report from the People.* New York: Sheed & Ward, 1964.

Clark, John J. *The New Economics of National Defense.* New York: Random House, 1966.

Clayton, James L. "Defense Spending: Key to California's Growth." *Western Political Quarterly* 15 (1962):280-92.

_____, ed. *The Economic Impact of the Cold War: Sources and Readings.* New York: Harcourt, Brace & World, 1970. 287 pp.

Coffin, Tristram. *The Armed Society: Militarism in Modern America.* Baltimore: Penguin Books, 1964.

_____. *The Passion of the Hawks: Militarism in Modern America.* New York: Macmillan, 1964.

Colm, Gerhard. *Can We Afford Additional Programs for National Security?* Planning Pamphlet, no. 84.

Washington, D.C.: National Planning Association, 1953.

Committee for Economic Development. *The National Economy and the Vietnam War: A Statement by the Research and Policy Committee, April 1968.* New York, 1969. 82 pp.

_____. *The Problems of National Security: Some Economic and Administrative Aspects.* Washington, D.C., 1958.

Cook, Fred J. *The Warfare State.* New York: Macmillan, 1962. 376 pp.

Cottrell, Leonard S., Jr., ed. *Public Reaction to the Atomic Bomb and World Affairs.* 2 pts. Ithaca, N.Y.: Cornell University Press, 1947.

Director, Aaron, ed. *Defense, Controls, and Inflation.* Chicago: University of Chicago Press, 1952.

Donovan, Col. James A. *Militarism USA.* New York: Charles Scribner's Sons, 1970. 265 pp.

Duscha, Julius. "Economics and National Security." *American Economic Review* 51 (1961):455-85.

Elliott, William Y. "Economic Potential of the United States for War." *Naval War College Review,* October 1948, pp. 17-28; April 1949, pp. 17-42.

Erskine, Hazel G. "The Polls, Atomic Weapons and Nuclear Energy." *Public Opinion Quarterly,* Summer 1963, pp. 155-90.

Falk, Stanley L. *The Environment of National Security.* Washington, D.C.: Industrial College of the Armed Forces, 1968.

_____. *Human Resources for National Strength.*

Washington, D.C.:   Industrial College of the Armed
Forces, 1960.

Fox, Bertrand.   "Economic Elements of U.S. War Potential."   *Naval War College Review,* May 1950, pp. 37-
52.

Georgetown University Center for Strategic Studies.
Economic Impact of the Vietnam War.   Special Report
Series, no. 5.   New York: Renaissance Editions,
1967.   86 pp.

Gilmore, John S.; Ryan, John J.; and Gould, William S.
*Defense Systems Resources in the Civil Sector: An
Evolving Approach, an Uncertain Market.*   Washing-
ton, D.C.:   Government Printing Office, 1967.

Gilpatric, Roswell L.   "Defense: How Much Will It
Cost?"   *California Management Review,* Winter 1962,
pp. 53-58.

Gilpin, Robert.   *American Scientists and Nuclear Weapons Policy.*   Princeton, N.J.:   Princeton University
Press, 1962.   352 pp.

Glick, Edward B.   *Soldiers, Scholars, and Society:
The Social Impact of the American Military.*   Pacific Palisades, Calif.:   Goodyear, 1971.   144 pp.

Gordon, Robert J.   "$45 Billion of U.S. Private In-
vestment Has Been Mislaid."   *American Economic Review* 59 (1969):221-38.

Grant, Carl E.   "A Comparison of the War Potential of
the U.S. and the U.S.S.R."   *Naval War College Review,* May 1952, pp. 1-61.

Greenberg, E.   "Employment Impacts of Defense Expenditures and Obligations."   *Review of Economics and
Statistics* 49 (1967):186-98.

_____.   "Some Aspects of the State Distribution of

Military Prime Contract Awards." *Review of Economics and Statistics* 48 (1966):205-10.

Hammond, Paul Y. *Resource Limits, Political and Military Risk-taking and the Generation of Military Requirements.* RAND Paper P-3421-1. Santa Monica, Calif.: RAND Corporation, 1966. 46 pp.

Herzog, Arthur. *The War-Peace Establishment.* New York: Harper & Row, 1963.

Hickman, Bert G. *The Korean War and United States Economic Activity, 1950-1952.* Washington, D.C.: National Bureau of Economic Research, 1955.

Hildebrand, George H., and Brecknor, Norman. "The Impacts of National Security Expenditure upon the Stability and Growth of the American Economy." In U.S. Congress, Joint Economic Committee, 85th Cong., 1st Sess., *Federal Expenditure Policy for Economic Growth and Stability.* Washington, D.C.: Government Printing Office, 1957.

Janeway, Eliot. *The Economics of Crisis: War, Politics, and the Dollar.* New York: Weybright & Talley, 1968. 317 pp.

Janis, Irving. *Air War and Emotional Stress.* New York: McGraw-Hill, 1951.

Janowitz, Morris. "American Democracy and Military Service." *Trans-Action,* March 1967, pp. 5-11, 57-59.

Javits, Jacob K.; Hitch, Charles J.; and Burns, Arthur F. *The Defense Sector and the American Economy.* New York: New York University Press, 1968. 110 pp.

Kaplan, Morton A. *Dissent and the State in Peace and War: An Essai on the Grounds of Public Morality.* New York: Dunellen, 1970.

Kaufman, Richard F. *The War Profiteers*. Indianapolis: Bobbs-Merrill, 1970.

Klare, Michael. *The University-Military Complex: A Directory and Related Documents*. New York: North American Congress on Latin America, 1969.

Klassen, Albert D., Jr. *Military Service in American Life since World War II: An Overview*. Report no. 117. Chicago: University of Chicago National Opinion Research Center, 1966.

Knoll, Erwin, and McFadden, Judith N., eds. *American Militarism 1970*. New York: Viking Press, 1969. 150 pp.

Knorr, Klaus. "The Concept of Economic Potential for War." *World Politics* 9 (1957):49-62.

_____. *The War Potential of Nations*. Princeton, N.J.: Princeton University Press, 1955.

Lasswell, Harold D. *National Security and Individual Freedom*. New York: McGraw-Hill, 1950.

Lederman, Leonard L., and Windus, Margaret L. *An Analysis of the Allocation of Federal Budget Resources as an Indicator of National Goals and Priorities*. Report BMI-NLVP-TR-69-1. 2 pts. Washington, D.C.: Government Printing Office, 1969.

Lincoln, George A., et al. *Economics of National Security*. Englewood Cliffs, N.J.: Prentice-Hall, 1950.

_____. *Economics of National Security: Managing America's Resources for Defense*. 2d ed. Englewood Cliffs, N.J.: Prentice-Hall, 1954.

McDonald, Col. W. C., and Larsen, Capt. L. J. *National Security Policy: Some Observations on Its Place in the American University*. Mimeographed. United

States Air Force Academy, Colo., n.d.

Mason, Edward S. "The Influence of Economic Considerations in the Formulations of National Strategy."
Naval War College Review, May 1954, pp. 1-24.

Melman, Seymour, ed. *The Defense Economy*. New York:
Frederick A. Praeger, 1970.

_____. *Pentagon Capitalism: The Management of the
New Imperialism*. New York: McGraw-Hill, 1970.
290 pp.

_____, ed. *The War Economy of the United States:
Readings in Military Industry and Economy*. New
York: St. Martin's Press, 1971. 247 pp.

Members of Congress for Peace through Law. *Report on
Military Spending*. Washington, D.C., July 1970.

Michael, Donald. "Civilian Behavior under Atomic Bombardment." *Bulletin of the Atomic Scientists* 11
(1955):173-77.

Millett, John D. "National Security in American Public Affairs." *American Political Science Review*
43 (1949):524-34.

Millis, Walter. *Arms and the State*. New York: Twentieth Century Fund, 1958.

_____. *The Constitution and the Common Defense*. New
York: Fund for the Republic, 1959. 48 pp.

_____. *Individual Freedom and the Common Defense*.
New York: Fund for the Republic, 1957. 80 pp.

Murphy, Charles J. V. "The Desperate Drive to Cut Defense Spending." *Fortune*, January 1964, pp. 95-97,
188-94.

Novick, David, and Springer, J. Y. *Economics of*

Defense Procurement and Small Business. RAND Paper
P-1462. Santa Monica, Calif.: RAND Corporation,
1958.

O'Connell, Donald. "Economic Factors Affecting Strategy." *Naval War College Review*, January 1955, pp.
23-49.

Okun, Arthur M. "The Challenges of Defense and High
Employment." In *Political Economy of Prosperity*,
pp. 62-99. New York: W. W. Norton, 1970.

Oliver, Richard P. "The Employment Effect of Defense
Expenditures." *Monthly Labor Review*, September
1967, pp. 9-19.

_____. "Increase in Defense-Related Employment Dur-
ing Viet Nam Buildup." *Monthly Labor Review*, February 1970, pp. 3-10.

Perlo, Victor. *Militarism and Industry*. New York:
International Publishers, 1963.

Peterson, Richard S., and Tiebout, Charles M. "Measuring the Impact of Regional Defense-Space Expenditures." *Review of Economics and Statistics* 46
(1964):421-28.

Purcell, W. R., Jr., ed. *Commercial Profits from
Defense-Space Technology*. Boston: Schur, 1965.

Pyle, Christopher. "CONUS Intelligence: The Army
Watches Civilian Politics." *Washington Monthly*,
January 1970.

Randell, Darrell; Fulbright, J. W.; and Benoit, Emile.
"The Impact of the Military on American Life." *Social Action*, February 1962, pp. 3-30.

Riefler, Roger, and Downing, Paul. "Regional Effect
of Defense Effort on Employment." *Monthly Labor
Review*, July 1968, p. 509.

Rosenberg, Milton J.; Verba, Sidney; and Converse, Philip E. *Vietnam and the Silent Majority*. New York: Harper & Row, 1970. 162 pp.

Rowan, Henry S. *National Security and the American Economy in 1960's: Joint Economic Committee Study Paper*. Washington, D.C.: Government Printing Office, 1960.

Rowan, Sir Leslie. *Arms and Economics: The Changing Challenge*. Cambridge: University Press, 1960. 63 pp.

Rukeyser, William S. "Where the Military Contracts Go." *Fortune*, 1 August 1969, pp. 74-75.

Russett, Bruce. *What Price Vigilance?* New Haven, Conn.: Yale University Press, 1970. 261 pp.

_____. "Who Pays for Defense?" *American Political Science Review* 63 (1969):412-26.

Sasaki, Kyohei. "Military Expenditures and the Employment Multiplier in Hawaii." *Review of Economics and Statistics* 45 (1963):298-304.

Schelling, Thomas C. "Strategic Analysis and Social Problems." *Social Problems* 12 (1965):367-79.

Schlesinger, James R. "Economic Growth and National Security." *Orbis* 6 (1962):465-69.

_____. *The Political Economy of National Security: A Study of the Economic Aspects of the Contemporary Power Struggle*. New York: Frederick A. Praeger, 1960. 292 pp.

_____. "Will the Defense Burden Be Lighter?" *Challenge*, June 1961, pp. 29-32.

Scitovsky, Tibor; Shaw, Edward S.; and Tarshis, Lorie.

Mobilizing Resources for War. New York: McGraw-
Hill, 1951.

Silberman, Charles E., and Parker, Sanford S. "The
Economic Impact of Defense." *Fortune,* June 1958,
pp. 102-5, 215-16, 218.

Smith, Louis. *American Democracy and Military Power.*
Chicago: University of Chicago Press, 1951.

Smithies, Arthur. "Fiscal Aspects of Preparedness for
War." *American Economic Review: Papers and Proceedings* 39 (1949):356-65.

Striner, Herbert E. "The Economics of Defense."
Army, January 1960, pp. 13-17.

Striner, Herbert E., *et al. Defense Spending and the
U.S. Economy.* 2 vols. Washington, D.C.: Johns
Hopkins University Operations Research Office,
1958.

Tiebout, C. "The Regional Impact of Defense Expenditures: Its Measurement and Problems of Adjustment." In U.S. Congress, Joint Economic Committee,
Nation's Manpower Revolution. Washington, D.C.:
Government Printing Office, 1963.

Tobin, James, and Davenport, John. "The Eisenhower
Economy and National Security: Two Views." *Yale
Review* 47 (1958):321-46.

United Nations Secretary General's Consultative Group.
*Effects of the Possible Use of Nuclear Weapons and
the Security and Economic Implications for States
of the Acquisition and Further Development of These
Weapons.* Report no. A/6858. New York, 1969.

U.S. Advisory Committee on the Study of Higher Education. *Effect of War Activities upon Colleges and
Universities.* Graham A. Barden Report. Washington, D.C.: Government Printing Office, 1945.

U.S. Congress, Joint Economic Committee. 86th Cong.,
    2d Sess. *National Security and the American Econo-
    my in the 1960's.* Prepared by Harry H. Ransom.
    Study Paper, no. 18. Washington, D.C.: Government
    Printing Office, 1960.

_____. 90th Cong., 1st Sess. *Economic Effect of
    Vietnam Spending . . . Hearings.* 2 vols. Washing-
    ton, D.C.: Government Printing Office, 1967.

_____. 90th Cong., 1st Sess. *Economic Effect of
    Vietnam Spending, Report.* Washington, D.C.: Gov-
    ernment Printing Office, 1967.

U.S. Congress, Senate Committee on Foreign Relations.
    91st Cong., 2d Sess. *Impact of the War in South-
    east Asia on the U.S. Economy. Hearings . . . .*
    Washington, D.C.: Government Printing Office,
    1970.

U.S. Department of Commerce, Economic Development Ad-
    ministration. *Report of the Independent Study
    Board on the Regional Effects of Government Pro-
    curement and Related Policies.* Washington, D.C.:
    Government Printing Office, 1967.

U.S. Department of Defense, Office of Director of De-
    fense Research and Engineering. *Project THEMIS: A
    Program to Strengthen the Nation's Academic Insti-
    tutions.* Washington, D.C.: Government Printing
    Office, 1967.

U.S. Department of Defense, Office of the Secretary of
    Defense. *Prime Contract Awards by State, 1967-
    1968.* Washington, D.C.: Government Printing Of-
    fice, 1967.

Vagts, Alfred. *A History of Militarism: Civilian and
    Military.* Rev. ed. New York: Meridian Books,
    1959. 542 pp.

Velvel, Lawrence R. *Undeclared War and Civil*

Disobedience: The American System in Crisis. New
York: Dunellen, 1970.

"The War and Its Impact on the Economy." *Review of
Radical Political Economics,* August 1970, pp. 1-72.

Welles, John G., *et al. The Commercial Application of
Missile Space Technology.* Denver, Colo.: University of Denver, 1963.

Yarmolinsky, Adam. *The Military Establishment: Its
Impact on American Society.* New York: Harper &
Row, 1971.

B. THE OPPORTUNITY COSTS OF ARMS CONTROL AND DIS-
ARMAMENT

Ackley, Gardner. *Report of the President's Committee
on the Economic Impact of Defense and Disarmament.*
Washington, D.C.: Government Printing Office,
1965.

Barber, Arthur. "Some Industrial Aspects of Arms Control." *Journal of Conflict Resolution* 7 (1963):
491-94.

Benoit, Emile. "Affording Disarmament: An Analysis,
a Model, Some Proposals." *Columbia University Forum,* Winter 1962, pp. 4-10.

_____. "Economic Adjustments to Arms Control."
Journal of Arms Control, April 1963, pp. 105-11.

_____. *Economic Adjustments to Disarmament.* New
York: Institute for International Order, 1961.   24
pp.

_____. "Economics of Disarmament." *Marquette Busi-
ness Review,* Winter 1962, pp. 16-21.

Benoit, Emile. "The Economics of Disarmament--Would Adjustment Be Difficult?" *Challenge*, June 1962, pp. 91-93.

_____. "Would Disarmament Mean a Depression?" *New York Times Magazine*, 28 April 1963, pp. 16, 44-50.

Benoit, Emile, and Boulding, Kenneth S., eds. *Disarmament and the Economy*. New York: Harper & Row, 1963. 310 pp.

Bolton, Roger E., ed. *Defense and Disarmament: The Economics of National Security*. Englewood Cliffs, N.J.: Prentice-Hall, 1966.

Cambern, John R. "Skill Transfers: Can Defense Workers Adapt to Civilian Occupations?" *Monthly Labor Review*, June 1969, pp. 21-25.

Cheney, Marshall G. *Disarmament Without Dislocation of U.S.A. Economy: A Study of Subsidization*. Berkeley, Calif.: by the author, 1960. 23 pp.

Christodoulou, Aris P. *Conversion of Nuclear Facilities from Military to Civilian Uses*. New York: Frederick A. Praeger, 1970. 118 pp.

Colm, Gerhard. "Economic Implications of Disarmament." *Illinois Business Review*, July 1957, pp. 6-8.

Daicoff, Darwin, *et al*. *Economic Impact of Military Base Closing*. 2 vols. Lawrence: University of Kansas, 1970.

"Economic Hazards of Arms Reduction: What We Must Pay for a Normal Economy in a Stable World." *Nation*, 28 March 1959. Special Issue.

"Economic Impact of Arms Control." *Bulletin of the Atomic Scientists*, December 1962, pp. 37-38.

Economist Intelligence Unit. *The Economic Effects of Disarmament.* Toronto: University of Toronto Press, 1963. 224 pp.

Fisherman, Leo, and Fisherman, Betty. "Disarmament: How Will the Economy Respond?" *Quarterly Review of Economics and Business,* August 1962, pp. 15-23.

Fishman, Leslie. "Economic Plan for Disarmament." *Bulletin of the Atomic Scientists,* March 1962, pp. 37-38.

Fishman, Leslie, *et al. Re-employment Experiences of Defense Workers: A Statistical Analysis of the Boeing, Martin and Republic Lay-Offs.* Washington, D.C.: Government Printing Office, 1968.

Harris, Seymour. "Can We Prosper Without Arms?" *New York Times Magazine,* 8 November 1959, pp. 20-24.

Hoeber, Francis P. "The Economic Impacts of Disarmament." *Orbis* 7 (1963):631-47.

Inkle, Doris M. *How Arms Controls Would Affect the National Security Budget.* RAND Paper P-2255. Santa Monica, Calif.: RAND Corporation, 1961.

Knorr, Klaus. "We Can Afford Disarmament—If We Make the Right Political Decisions." *Challenge,* January 1960, pp. 62-65.

Kokat, Robert G. "Some Implications of the Economic Impact of Disarmament on the Structure of American Industry." *Kyklos* 19 (1966):481-502.

Leontief, Wassily, *et al.* "The Economic Impact—Industrial and Regional—of an Arms Cut." *Review of Economics and Statistics* 47 (1965):217-41.

Leontief, Wassily, and Hoffenberg, Marvin. "The Economic Effects of Disarmament." *Scientific American,* April 1961, pp. 47-55.

Lynch, John E. *Local Economic Development after Military Base Closures.* New York: Frederick A. Praeger, 1970.

Mack-Forlist, Daniel M., and Newman, Arthur. *The Conversion of Shipbuilding from Military to Civilian
Markets.* New York: Frederick A. Praeger, 1970.

Melman, Seymour, ed. *The Defense Economy: Conversion
of Industries and Occupations to Civilian Needs.*
New York: Frederick A. Praeger, 1970. 558 pp.

_____. "Economic Alternatives to Arms Prosperity."
Annals of the American Academy 351 (1964):121-31.

Mosbaek, E. J. "Information on the Impact of Reduc-
tions in Defense Expenditures on the Economy."
Quarterly Review of Economics and Business, Fall
1965, pp. 47-67.

Mottur, Ellis R. *Conversion of Scientific and Technical Resources: Economic Challenge--Social Opportunity.* Washington, D.C.: George Washington University Program on Policy Studies in Science and Technology, 1971. 203 pp.

Nathan, Otto. "The Economics of Permanent Peace."
Bulletin of the Atomic Scientists, June 1963, pp.
21-34.

Nelson, R. R. "The Impact of Arms Reduction on Research and Development." *American Economic Review*
53 (1963):435-46.

Schelling, Thomas C. "Arms Control Will Not Cut Defense Costs." *Harvard Business Review,* March-April
1961, pp. 6-14.

Seligman, Ben B. "Disarmament and the Economy." *Commentary,* May 1963, pp. 369-77.

Silard, John, *et al.* "The Economics and Politics of

Arms Reduction." *Bulletin of the Atomic Scientists*, April 1964, pp. 6-23.

Ullmann, John E., ed. *Potential Civilian Markets for the Military-Electronics Industry: Strategies for Conversion*. New York: Frederick A. Praeger, 1970. 368 pp.

United Nations Department of Economics and Social Affairs. *Community Readjustment to Reduced Defense Spending: Case Studies of Potential Impact on Seattle-Tacoma, Baltimore, and New London-Groton-Norwich*. Prepared by the National Planning Association. ACDA/E-57. Washington, D.C.: Government Printing Office, 1965. 427 pp.

_____. *Economics and Social Consequences of Disarmament*. 2 vols. New York, 1962.

U.S. Arms Control and Disarmament Agency. *Adjustment of the U.S. Economy to the Reduction in Military Spending*. Edited by Bernard Ubis. Washington, D.C.: Government Printing Office, 1970.

_____. *Defense Industry Diversification: An Analysis with 12 Case Studies*. Prepared by John S. Gilmore and assisted by John G. Welles and Theodore D. Browne. Washington, D.C., 1966. 334 pp.

_____. *Dyna-Soar Contract Cancellation: A Case Study of the Effects of Dyna-Soar Contract Cancellation upon Employees of Boeing Company in Seattle, Washington*. Washington, D.C.: Government Printing Office, 1965. 303 pp.

_____. *The Economic and Social Consequences of Disarmament*. Washington, D.C.: Government Printing Office, 1964.

_____. *The Economic and Social Consequences of Disarmament: U.S. Reply to the Inquiry of the Secretary General of the United Nations*. Pt. 2.

Washington, D.C.:   Government Printing Office, 1962.   47 pp.

U.S. Arms Control and Disarmament Agency. *Economic Impacts of Disarmament: Report to the U.S. Arms Control and Disarmament Agency.*   Washington, D.C.: Government Printing Office, 1962.

_____. *The Implications of Reduced Defense Demand for the Electronics Industry.*   Prepared by Charles S. Peet, *et al.* Battelle Memorial Institute. Washington, D.C.:   Government Printing Office, 1965.

_____. *Re-employment Experiences of Martin Company Workers Released at Denver, Colorado, 1963-1964, Effects of Defense Employment Readjustment.*   Publication no. 36.   Washington, D.C.:   Government Printing Office, 1967.

"U.S. Arms Industry Could Shift to Peacetime Production."   *War/Peace Report,* November 1962, pp. 4-6.

U.S. Committee on the Economic Impact of Defense and Disarmament. *Report.*   Washington, D.C.:   Government Printing Office, July 1965.   92 pp.

U.S. Congress, Senate Committee on Labor and Public Welfare, Subcommittee on Employment and Manpower. 88th Cong., 2d Sess. *Convertibility of Space and Defense Resources to Civilian Needs: A Search for New Employment Potentials.*   Washington, D.C.:   Government Printing Office, 1964.

Wadsworth, James J. *The Price of Peace.*   New York: Frederick A. Praeger, 1962.

Warburg, James P. *Disengagement and the Economics of Disarmament.*   New York: Current Affairs Press, 1961.   16 pp.

Weidenbaum, Murray L. "Adjusting to a Defense Cutback: Public Policy Toward Business." *Quarterly*

Review of Economics and Business, Spring 1964, pp. 7-14.

Weidenbaum, Murray L. "Economic Adjustments to Disarmament." *University of Washington Business Review,* February 1963, pp. 3-11.

_____. "The Economic Impact of an Arms Cut: Comments." *Review of Economics and Statistics* 49 (1967):612-13.

VII

Periodicals That Regularly Include Articles on American Defense Policy

Most of the periodicals found in the following list do not cover defense policy exclusively--at least not defense policy as the term is used in this bibliography. The service-related journals tend to be devoted primarily to professional military matters, whereas the academic-associated journals tend to cover a broad range of policy issues, touching on defense problems only occasionally. The researcher must pick and choose carefully.

The journals in this section, however, can be expected to deal with defense policy or defense-related issues as a substantial part of their content on a fairly regular basis. Many of them have indices on an annual or other basis, and these should be checked to find particular articles on defense policy.

No attempt has been made to classify the journals into substantive categories.

Academy of Political Science, Proceedings. New York: Academy of Political Science, 1910-. Quarterly.

Adelphi Papers. London: International Institute for Strategic Studies, 1963-. Approximately 10 issues per year.

Administrative Science Quarterly. Ithaca, N.Y.: Graduate School of Business and Public Administration, Cornell University, 1955-. Quarterly.

Aerospace. Washington, D.C.: Aerospace Industries Association of America, 1963-.

Aerospace Historian. Formerly *Airpower Historian.* Manhattan, Kan.: Kansas State University Department of History, 1954-. Quarterly.

AFSC Newsreview. Formerly *ARDC News Review.* Washington, D.C.: Air Force Systems Command, United States Air Force, Andrews Air Force Base, 1957-. Monthly.

AIAA Bulletin. New York: American Institute of Aeronautics and Astronautics. 1964-. Monthly.

Airborne Quarterly. Fort Bragg, N.C.: Airborne Association, Inc., 1955-. Quarterly.

Air Force and Space Digest. Washington, D.C.: Air Force Association, 1946-71. Now *Air Force Magazine* from February 1971-. Monthly.

Air Force Comptroller. Washington, D.C.: Government Printing Office, 1967-. Quarterly.

Air Force Policy Letter for Commanders. Washington, D.C.: Department of the Air Force, Department of Information, 1952-. Semi-monthly.

Air Force Research Resumes. Arlington, Va.: U.S. Air Force Office of Aerospace Research. 1955-.

Air Reservist Magazine. Washington, D.C.: Headquarters USAF, 1954-. 10 issues per year.

Air University Review. Formerly *Air University Quarterly Review.* Maxwell Air Force Base, Ala.: Air University, 1948-. Quarterly.

All Hands. Washington, D.C.: Department of the Navy, 1914-. Monthly.

American Academy of Political and Social Science Annals. Philadelphia: American Academy of Political and Social Science, 1890-. Bi-monthly.

American Aviation Historical Society Journal. Redondo Beach, Calif., 1956-. Quarterly.

American Economic Review. Princeton: American Economic Association, 1911-. Quarterly.

American Historical Review. New York: American Historical Association, 1895-. Quarterly.

American Journal of Sociology. Chicago: University of Chicago Department of Sociology, 1895-. Bimonthly.

American Legion Magazine. Indianapolis: American Legion, 1919-. Monthly.

American Political Science Review. Washington, D.C.: American Political Science Association, 1906-. Quarterly.

American Security Council Washington Report. Chicago: American Security Council. Weekly.

American Sociological Review. Washington, D.C.: American Sociological Association, 1936-. Bimonthly.

Aradcom Argus. Colorado Springs: Headquarters, U.S. Army Air Defense Command, 1958-. Monthly.

Armed Forces Comptroller. Alexandria, Va.: American Society of Military Comptrollers, 1956-. Quarterly.

Armed Forces Journal. Washington, 1863-. Weekly. Formerly *Journal of Armed Forces,* to Vol. 105.

Armed Forces Management. Washington, D.C.: American

Aviation Publication, 1954-. Monthly.

Armor, The Magazine of Mobile Warfare. Washington,
    D.C.: U.S. Armor Association, 1888-. Bi-monthly.

Army. Washington, D.C.: Association of the United
    States Army, 1950-. Monthly.

Army Aviation Digest. Washington, D.C.: Department
    of the Army, Commandant of the Army Aviation
    School, 1955-. Monthly.

Army Aviation Magazine. Westport, Conn.: Army Avia-
    tion Publications, 1953-. Monthly.

Army Digest. Formerly *Army Information Digest.* Wash-
    ington, D.C.: Department of the Army, 1946-.
    Monthly.

Army Finance Journal. Alexandria, Va.: Army Finance
    Association, 1953-. Bi-monthly.

Army Research and Development Newsmagazine. Washing-
    ton, D.C.: Army Research Office, Office of the
    Chief of Research and Development, Department of
    the Army, 1960-. Monthly.

Army Reserve Magazine. Formerly *Army Reservist.*
    Washington, D.C.: Department of the Army, Office
    of Chief of Army Reserve, 1954-. 10 issues per
    year.

Army ROTC Newsletter. Fort Monroe, Va.: U.S. Conti-
    nental Army Command, 1967-. Bi-monthly.

Arrowhead: Combat Developments Command. Fort Bel-
    voir, Va., 1969-. Monthly.

*Astronautics and Aeronautics: Chronology on Science,
    Technology and Policy.* Washington, D.C.: Scien-
    tific and Technical Information Division, National

Aeronautics and Space Administration, 1915–60. Monthly.

Atlantic Community Quarterly. Washington, D.C.: Atlantic Council of the United States, 1963–. Quarterly.

Atlantic Studies: Etudes Atlantiques. Boulogne-sur-Seine, France: Atlantic Institute. 1963–.

Aviation Week & Space Technology. New York: McGraw-Hill, 1916–. Weekly.

Boeing Magazine. Seattle: Boeing Company, 1930–. Monthly.

Bulletin of the Atomic Scientists: A Journal of Science and Public Policy. Chicago: Education Foundation for Nuclear Science, 1945–. Monthly, September–June.

Bureau of Government Research Bulletin. Amherst, Mass.: Bureau of Government Research, 1967–. Quarterly.

Bureau of Ships Journal. Washington, D.C.: Department of the Navy. Monthly.

Combat Crew. Offutt Air Force Base, Nebr.: Directorate of Operations, Strategic Air Command, 1950–. Monthly.

Common Defense. Washington, D.C.: American Ordnance, 1945–. Monthly.

Congressional Digest. Washington, D.C., 1921–. 10 issues per year.

Congressional Quarterly Service Weekly Report. Washington, D.C., 1945–. Weekly.

Defense Indicators. Washington, D.C.: Department of Defense. Monthly.

Defense Industry Bulletin. Washington, D.C.: Office of the Assistant Secretary of Defense Public Affairs, Department of Defense, 1965–. Monthly.

Defense Management Journal. Formerly *Department of Defense Cost Reduction Journal.* Washington, D.C.: Office of the Assistant Secretary of Defense, Directorate for Cost Reduction and Management Improvement Programs, 1965–.

Editorial Research Reports. Washington, D.C., 1923–. 4 issues per month.

Esso Air World. Formerly *Esso Aviation Marketing Affiliates.* New York: Esso International, 1947–. Bi-monthly.

FAR Horizons Newsletter. Washington, D.C.: Foreign Area Research Coordination Group, Department of State. Bi-monthly.

Foreign Affairs: An American Quarterly Review. New York: Council on Foreign Relations, 1922–. Quarterly.

Foreign Policy. New York: National Affairs, Inc., 1971–. Quarterly.

Foreign Policy Briefs. Washington, D.C.: Department of State, 1950–. Bi-weekly.

Fortune. New York: Time, Inc., 1930–. Monthly.

Government Executive. Washington, D.C.: Reinhold, 1969–. Monthly.

Harvard Business Review. Cambridge, Mass.: Graduate School of Business Administration, Harvard University, 1922–.

Headline Series. New York: Foreign Policy Association. 1935-. Irregularly.

Infantry: The Professional Magazine for Infantrymen.
Fort Benning, Ga.: U.S. Army Infantry School,
1922-. Bi-monthly.

Interavia: Aviation, Astronautics, Electronics. Formerly *Interavia World Review of Aviation and Astronautics.* Geneva, 1946-. Monthly.

Interceptor. Ent Air Force Base, Colo.: Headquarters, Air Defense Command, 1959-. Monthly.

Intercom. New York: Center for War-Peace Studies,
1959-. Bi-monthly.

International Conciliation. New York: Carnegie Endowment for International Peace, 1907-.

International Defense Review. Geneva: Interavia,
1968-. Quarterly.

International Organization. Boston: Peace Foundation, 1947-. Quarterly.

International Studies Quarterly. Formerly *Background.*
International Studies Association, 1956-. Quarterly.

*Journal of Conflict Resolution: For Research Related
to War and Peace.* Formerly *Conflict Resolution.*
Ann Arbor: Center for Research on Conflict Resolution, University of Michigan, 1957-. Quarterly.

Journal of International Affairs. Montpelier, Vt.:
Capital City Press, 1947-. Semi-annually.

Journal of Politics. Austin: University of Texas
Southern Political Science Association, 1939-.
Quarterly.

Journal of the Armed Forces. Washington, D.C., 1963–.
   Weekly.

Leatherneck: Magazine of the Marines. Washington,
   D.C.: Leatherneck Association, 1917–. Monthly.

*Lockheed Reports: News of Lockheed Developments in
   Science and Industry.* Burbank, Calif.: Lockheed-
   California, 1948–. Monthly.

Logistics Review. Formerly *Logistics Review and Military Logistics Journal.* Berkeley, Calif.: Technical Economics, 1965–. 5 issues per year.

Logistics Spectrum. Long Beach, Calif.: Society of
   Logistics Engineers, 1967–. Quarterly.

M A C Flyer/Military Airlift Command. Washington,
   D.C.: Government Printing Office. Monthly.

*Marine Corps Gazette: The Professional Magazine for
   United States Marines.* Quantico, Va.: Marine
   Corps Association, 1916–. Monthly.

*Military Affairs: Devoted to American and World Mili-
   tary, Naval and Air History.* Manhattan: Kansas
   State University Department of History for the
   American Military Institute, 1937–. Quarterly.

Military Engineer. Washington, D.C.: Society of
   American Military Engineers, 1920–. Bi-monthly.

Military Government Journal & Newsletter. Falls
   Church, Va.: Military Government Association,
   1949–. Monthly.

Military Police Journal. Augusta, Ga.: Military Police Association, 1952–. Monthly.

Military Review. Fort Leavenworth, Ks.: U.S. Army
   Command and General Staff College, 1922–. Monthly.

*Monthly Catalog of United States Government Publica-
tions.* Washington, D.C.: Government Printing Office, Superintendent of Documents, 1895-.

National Defense Transportation Journal. Washington,
D.C.: National Defense Transportation Association,
1945-. Bi-monthly.

National Guardsman. Washington, D.C.: National Guard
Association of the U.S., 1947-. Monthly.

National Journal. Washington, D.C.: Center for Political Research, 1969-. Weekly.

National War College Forum. Washington, D.C.: National War College, 1965-. Semi-annually.

NATO's Fifteen Nations. Formerly *Fifteen Nations.*
Amsterdam: Jules Perel's, 1956-. Bi-monthly.

NATO Space Letter. Brussels: NATO, 1953-. Monthly.

*Naval Affairs: In the Interest of the U.S. Navy and
for the Personnel of the Navy and Marine Corps, Active Fleet Reserve and Retired.* Washington, D.C.:
Fleet Reserve Association, 1922-. Monthly.

Naval Aviation News. Washington, D.C.: Department of
the Navy, Chief of Naval Operations, Bureau of
Aeronautics, 1947-. Monthly.

Naval Engineers Journal. Washington, D.C.: American
Society of Naval Engineers, 1889-. Bi-monthly.

Naval Research Logistics Quarterly. Washington, D.C.:
Department of the Navy, Office of Naval Research,
1954-. Quarterly.

Naval Research Reviews. Washington, D.C.: Office of
Naval Research, 1954-. Monthly.

Naval Training Bulletin. Washington, D.C.:

Department of the Navy, Bureau of Naval Personnel, 1947-. Quarterly.

Naval War College Review. Newport, R.I.: U.S. Naval War College, 1947-. 10 issues per year.

Navigator. Washington, D.C.: Department of the Air Force, 1953-. Quarterly.

Navy: The Magazine of Sea Power. Washington, D.C.: Navy League of the United States, 1958-. Monthly.

Navy Management Review: Devoted to Better Management in the Navy and the Marine Corps. Washington, D.C.: Government Printing Office, 1956-. Monthly.

OAR Research Review. Arlington, Va.: Department of Air Force, Office of Aerospace Research, 1962-. Bi-monthly.

Officer. Washington, D.C.: Reserve Officers Association, 1924-. Monthly.

Operations Research. Baltimore: Operations Research Society of America, 1952-. Bi-monthly.

Orbis: A Quarterly Journal of World Affairs. Philadelphia: Foreign Policy Research Institute, University of Pennsylvania, 1957-. Quarterly.

Ordnance: Land-Sea-Air-Space. Washington, D.C.: American Ordnance Association, 1920-. Bi-monthly.

Our Navy. Brooklyn: Our Navy, Inc., 1892-. Monthly.

Parameters: The Journal of the Army War College. Carlisle Barracks, Pa.: U.S. Army War College, 1970-. Triennially.

Peace Research Abstracts. Oakville, Ontario: Canadian Peace Research Institute, 1964-. Monthly.

Peace Research Reviews. Dundas, Ontario: Canadian
Peace Research Institute, 1967-. Bi-monthly.

Perspectives in Military History. Carlisle Barracks,
Pa.: U.S. Army Military History Research Collection, 1970-.

Political Science Quarterly. New York: Academy of
Political Science, 1886-. Quarterly.

Politics. New York: Business-Industry Political Action Committee, 1964-. Bi-monthly.

Public Administration. Cambridge, Mass.: Harvard
University Press, 1940-.

Public Administration Review. Washington, D.C.:
American Society for Public Administration, 1940-.
Bi-monthly.

*Public Finance; International Journal Devoted to the
Study of Fiscal Policy and Related Problems.* The
Hague: Foundation Periodical for Public Finance,
1946-. Quarterly.

Public Opinion Quarterly. New York: Columbia University, 1937-. Quarterly.

Public Policy. Cambridge, Mass.: Harvard University
Press, 1940-68, annually; 1968-, quarterly. Publication suspended, 1943-52.

*Pugwash Conferences on Science and World Affairs:
Proceedings.* London: Pugwash, Ltd., 1958-.
Monthly.

Reserve Marine. Formerly *Reserve Bulletin.* Washington, D.C.: U.S. Marine Corps Headquarters, 1948-.
Monthly.

Retired Officer Magazine. Washington, D.C.: Retired
Officers Association, 1945-. Monthly.

Review of Politics. Notre Dame, Ind.: University of Notre Dame, 1939-. Quarterly.

Royal United Service Institution Journal. London: Royal United Service Institution, 1857-. Quarterly.

SAIS Review. Washington, D.C.: School of Advanced International Studies, Johns Hopkins University, 1956-. Quarterly.

Science Policy Bulletin. Columbus, Ohio: Battelle Memorial Institute, 1967-. Monthly.

Scientific American. New York: Scientific American, Inc., 1845-. Monthly.

Sealift Magazine. Formerly *MSTS.* Washington, D.C.: Department of the Navy, Military Sea Transportation Service, 1951-. Monthly.

SEATO Record. Bangkok, Thailand: SEATO Public Information Office, 1967-. 6 issues per year.

Selected Rand Abstracts: To Provide a Timely and Comprehensive Index-Guide to the Rand Corporation Unclassified Publications. Santa Monica, Calif.: RAND Corporation, 1963-. Quarterly.

Signal: Communications, Electronics, Photography. Washington, D.C.: Armed Forces Communications and Electronics Association, 1946-. Monthly.

South East Asia Treaty Organization Economic Bulletin. Bangkok, Thailand: SEATO Cultural and Economic Affairs Office, 1963-. Quarterly.

SRI Journal. Menlo Park, Calif.: Stanford Research Institute, 1957-63. Quarterly.

Survival. London: Institute for Strategic Studies, 1959-71, monthly; 1972-, bi-monthly.

Trans-Action: Social Science and Modern Society. St. Louis: Community Leadership Project of Washington University, 1963-. Bi-monthly.

U.S. Department of State Bulletin. Washington, D.C.: Department of State, 1939-. Weekly.

United States Department of State Newsletter. Washington, D.C.: Department of State, 1961-. Monthly.

U.S. Naval Institute Proceedings. Annapolis, Md.: U.S. Naval Institute, 1874-. Monthly.

V.F.W. Magazine. Kansas City, Mo.: Veterans of Foreign Wars, 1912-. Monthly.

War/Peace Report. New York: War/Peace Report, Inc., 1961-. Monthly.

What HUMRRO Is Doing. Washington, D.C.: Human Resources Research Office, George Washington University, 1963-. Bi-monthly.

World Affairs. Washington, D.C.: American Peace Society, 1837-. Quarterly.

World Politics: A Quarterly Journal of International Relations. Princeton, N.J.: Center of International Studies, Princeton University, 1948-. Quarterly.

american defense policy since 1945

A PRELIMINARY BIBLIOGRAPHY

This bibliography focuses on American defense policy in the post-World War II era, including topical areas that are connected to United States military programs and military security.

The material is arranged under six major subdivisions:
Bibliography of Bibliographies
The Factual Context: Data and Descriptive Material
Strategic Thought and Military Doctrine in the Nuclear Age
The Defense Policy Making Process
Defense Policy Output, Weapons Systems, and Military Programs
The Domestic Effects of Defense Policy

Containing approximately three thousand items, this tightly organized research tool will be of use to students, teachers, and other researchers trying to cope with the abundance of material available in the defense policy field.

Published for the National Security Education Program by

the University Press of Kansas

Lawrence/Manhattan/Wichita